THE
BAY AREA
DOG LOVER'S
COMPANION

By Maria Goodavage

Foghorn
Press
BOOKS BUILDING COMMUNITY™

1-57354-039-0

51795

9 781573 540391

Library of Congress ISSN Data:
June 1998
The Bay Area Dog Lover's Companion:
The Inside Scoop on Where to Take Your Dog
Third Edition
ISSN: 1078-8921

THE
BAY AREA
DOG LOVER'S
COMPANION

By Maria Goodavage

BOOKS BUILDING COMMUNITY™

The Bay Area Dog Lover's Companion

*The Inside Scoop on Where to Take Your Dog
in the Bay Area & Beyond*

CONTENTS

BAY AREA REFERENCE MAP

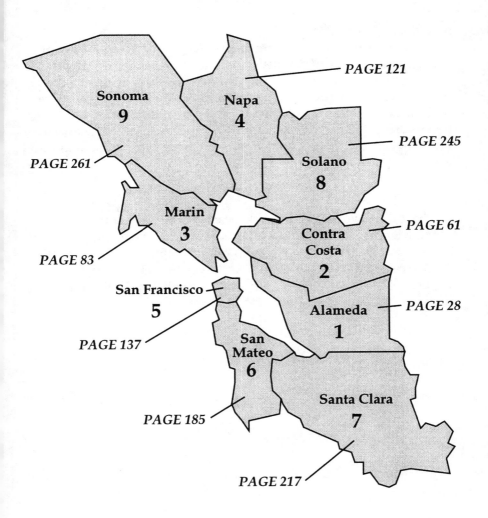

PAGE 121

Sonoma
9

Napa
4

PAGE 245

PAGE 261

Solano
8

Marin
3

Contra
Costa
2

PAGE 61

PAGE 83

San Francisco
5

Alameda
1

PAGE 28

PAGE 137

San
Mateo
6

Santa Clara
7

PAGE 185

PAGE 217

Note to all dog lovers:

While our information is as current as possible, changes to fees, regulations, parks, roads, and trails sometimes are made after we go to press. Businesses can close, change their ownership, or change their rules. Earthquakes, fires, rainstorms, and other natural phenomena can radically change the condition of parks, hiking trails, and wilderness areas. Before you and your dog begin your travels, please be certain to call the phone numbers for each listing for updated information.

Attention dogs of California:

If we've missed your favorite park, beach, outdoor restaurant, hotel, or dog-friendly activity, please let us know. You'll be helping countless other dogs get more enjoyment out of life in the Bay Area. We always welcome your comments and suggestions about *The Bay Area Dog Lover's Companion*. Please write to the Publisher, Foghorn Press, 340 Bodega Avenue, Petaluma, CA 94952.

For Mom, Dad, and Muttley, who made growing up
as much fun as walking in a lush redwood forest
with a dog who heeds every word you utter.

————————— 🐾 —————————

INTRODUCTION

INTRODUCTION

In dog heaven, all doors can be shoved open with a nose. Scratching is permitted and barking encouraged. Digging is okay, too. Cats, chickens, prize-sized rats, children, and strange people are available for the chase. Sofas are never covered with plastic.

On Sunday afternoons, dogs gather around meadows and lakes to socialize. The paunchy middle-aged ones tell dirty jokes. Puppies brag about the fine leather shoes they've consumed. And older dogs exchange tales of the 1950s—the good ol' days when Lassie and Rin Tin Tin were stars, and humans were smart enough to follow them.

But no matter what the age, breed, or social class of these Elysian dogs, the conversation always comes back to how grateful they are that they no longer have to hear those three words that haunted them during their lives on Earth. They were cruel words—abominable, loathsome, stinging syllables uttered by their idols day after day: "You can't go."

On Earth, dogs have many ways of coping with this news. Joe, my nine-year-old Airedale terrier, runs to the front window and stares until everyone is well out of sight and feeling plenty of guilt. Then, according to neighbors, he trots out the doggy door and drools over the cats next door until someone comes home—when he mysteriously appears at the front window again as if he hadn't budged for hours.

Other dogs take revenge. I've known those who, left home alone, have torn apart entire mattresses. A San Jose dog who asked not to be identified routinely lifts his leg on every plant in the house. Some dogs howl, others don't eat, others eat everything. A sharp-toothed mutt who frequents San Francisco's Alta Plaza Park once opened every can of Dinty Moore beef stew in the pantry.

After centuries of being told "You can't go," dogs are still complaining. Joe has persuaded me to take him along on more and more outings. He lives to hear the jingle of keys, the turn of a doorknob, the roar of an engine. Though we don't let him chase chickens or cats, we've discovered that the Bay Area is dog heaven on Earth, if you know where to go.

That's why we wrote this book. With it, you get the benefit of the exploring skills of Joe, who, together with his former co-researcher Dabney, has sniffed out the best places to take a dog—

not just the usual beaches and parks, but restaurants that serve you outside, drive-in movies, street fairs, cable cars, ferries, surries, special dog hikes, flea markets, and some incredible lodgings that welcome dogs.

Since the last edition of this book, there have been some noteworthy changes: First my wonderful, clever co-author, Lyle York, has decided to explore dog haunts on a non-professional basis. In other words, she's moved on to other things. Much of her research and writing remains in this edition, so although she may be gone, she's still with us. Part of her decision came when her dear Dabney Dog passed away in 1997 at 15 years old. She got another dog, a sprightly, energetic big black poodle named Calvin, but she said doing research without ol' Dabs just wouldn't have been the same. We'll miss both of you, Lyle and Dabney.

Time has also taken another beloved companion, Nisha, the most deliriously happy, on-the-go dog I've ever met. She was part of my husband's life for 15 years, part of my life for six. She remains with us in countless ways, including the fact that her spirit seems to have been re-incarnated in our daughter, Laura, who at press time is 17 months old and barks and pants just like Nisha, and has the same energy and enthusiasm for life as that tireless soul. Like Nisha, she also tries to nudge Joe Dog from his bowl so she can eat his food.

The third edition of this book also has some significant, exciting changes. I've found dozens more parks, hotels, and fun things to do with your pooch. If you thought the Bay Area was dog heavenly before, you should see it now. Dogs can shop in the ritziest stores, eat at restaurants that put the "wow" in bow-wow, visit more leash-free parks than ever, stay at some of the dearest inns imaginable, and even attend a San Francisco Giants game. (Sorry, Oakland A's fans, but your team hasn't gone to the dogs yet.) I've also added a new category called "Doggy Days." It's for festivals and fun events revolving around dogs.

Joe Dog thinks this book is the best yet. He obviously has very good taste. We hope you agree with him.

THE PAWS SCALE

At some point, we've got to face the facts: Humans and dogs have different tastes. We like eating oranges and smelling lilacs and covering our bodies with soft clothes. They like eating roadkill and smelling each other's unmentionables and covering their bodies with horse manure.

The parks, beaches, and recreation areas in this book are rated with a dog in mind. Maybe your favorite park has lush gardens, a duck pond, a few acres of perfectly manicured lawns, and sweeping views of a nearby skyline. But unless your dog can run leash-free, swim in the pond, and roll in the grass, that park doesn't deserve a very high rating.

The very lowest rating you'll come across in this book is the fire hydrant symbol (🛠). When you see it, that means the park is merely "worth a squat." Visit one of these parks only if your dog just can't hold it any longer. These parks have virtually no other redeeming qualities for canines.

Beyond that, the paws scale starts at one paw (🐾) and goes up to four paws (🐾🐾🐾🐾), with increments of half a paw in between (such as 🐾🐾½). A one-paw park isn't a dog's idea of a great time. Maybe it's a tiny park with few trees and too many kids running around. Or perhaps it's a magnificent-for-people national park that bans dogs from every inch of land except paved roads and a few campsites.

Four-paw parks, on the other hand, are places your dog will drag you to visit. Some of these areas come as close to dog heaven as you can get on this planet. Many have water for swimming or zillions of acres for hiking. Some are small, fenced-in areas where leash-free dogs can tear around without danger of running into the road. Many four-paw parks give you the option of letting your dog off leash (although most have restrictions, which I detail in the descriptions).

This book is not a comprehensive guide to all of the parks in the Bay Area. If a book included all the parks, it would break your back to lug it around. I tried to find the best, largest, and most convenient parks. Some counties have so many wonderful parks that I had to make some tough choices in deciding which to include and which to leave out. Other counties had such a limited supply of parks that, for the sake of dogs living and visiting there, I ended up listing parks that might not otherwise be worth mentioning.

I've given very specific directions to the major parks and to parks located near highways. Other parks are listed by their cross streets. I highly recommend picking up detailed street maps from the California Automobile Association (they're free to members) before you and your dog set out on your adventures.

Note: I'll no longer be using the foot symbol (◄●), which in previous editions indicated places humans would find interesting. I found this was such a subjective rating that it wasn't worth it. Some people think just about any park is wonderful, others need trees, others prefer perfectly manicured places, others long for historic parks, others only want to rough it on long trails, and on and on. So from now on, the only feet you'll see here are dog feet.

TO LEASH OR NOT TO LEASH

That is not a question that plagues dogs' minds. Ask just about any normal, red-blooded American dog if she'd prefer to visit a park and be on leash or off, and she'll say "Arf!" No question about it, most dogs would give their canine teeth to be able to frolic about without a cumbersome leash.

When you see the running dog symbol in this book (🐕), you'll know that under certain circumstances, your dog can run around in leash-free bliss. The rest of the parks demand leashes. I wish I could write about the parks where dogs get away with being scofflaws. Unfortunately, those would be the first parks the animal control patrols would hit. I don't advocate breaking the law, but if you're going to, please follow your conscience and use common sense.

The Bay Area is probably the best urban area in the United States for leash-free dogs. Thanks to entities like the East Bay Regional Park District, the Marin Open Space District, and the Golden Gate National Recreation Area, dogs who hunger for their freedom can have it here.

THERE'S NO BUSINESS LIKE DOG BUSINESS

There's nothing appealing about bending down with a plastic bag or a piece of newspaper on a chilly morning and grabbing the steaming remnants of what your dog ate for dinner the night before. It's disgusting. Worse yet, you have to hang on to it until you can find a trash can. And how about when the newspaper doesn't endure before you can dispose of it? Yuk! It's enough to make you wish your dog could wear diapers.

But as gross as it can be to scoop the poop, it's worse to step in it. It's really bad if a child falls in it, or—gasp!—starts eating it. And have you ever walked into a park where few people clean up after their dog? The stench could make a hog want to hibernate.

Unscooped poop is one of a dog's worst enemies. Public policies banning dogs from parks are enacted because of it. At present, a few wonderful Bay Area parks and beaches that permit dogs are in danger of closing their gates to all canines because of the negligent behavior of a few owners. A worst-case scenario is already in place in a few local communities—dogs are banned from all parks. Their only exercise is a leashed sidewalk stroll. That's no way to live.

Just be responsible and clean up after your dog everywhere you go. Stuff plastic bags in your jackets, your purse, your car, your pants pockets—anywhere you might be able to pull one out when needed. Or if plastic isn't your bag, newspapers do the trick. If it makes it more palatable, bring along a paper bag, too, and put the used newspaper or plastic bag in it. That way you don't have to walk around with dripping paper or a plastic bag whose contents are visible to the world.

If you don't enjoy the squishy sensation, try one of those cardboard or plastic bag pooper-scoopers sold at pet stores. If you don't feel like bending down, buy a long-handled scooper. There's a scooper for every taste.

This is the only real lecture you'll get on scooping in this entire book. To help keep parks alive, I should harp on it in every park description, but that would take another 100 pages, and you'd start to ignore it anyway. And if I mentioned it in some parks and not others, it might convey that you don't have to clean up after your dog in the descriptions where it's not mentioned.

A final note: Don't pretend not to see your dog while he's doing his bit. And don't pretend to look for it without success. And don't fake scooping it up when you're really just covering it with sand. I know these tricks because I've been guilty of them myself—but no more. I've seen the light. I've been saved. I've been delivered from the depths of dog-doo depravity.

ETIQUETTE REX:
THE WELL-MANNERED MUTT

While cleaning up after your dog is your responsibility, a dog in a public place has his own responsibilities. Of course, it really boils down to your responsibility again, but the burden of action is on your dog.

Etiquette for restaurants and hotels is covered in other sections of the introduction. What follows is some very basic dog etiquette. I'll go through it quickly, but if your dog's a slow reader, he can go over it again:

No vicious dogs; no jumping on people; no incessant barking; dogs should come when they're called; dogs should stay on command; no leg lifts on surfboards, backpacks, human legs, or any other personal objects you'll find hanging around beaches and parks.

Joe Dog has managed to violate all but the first of these rules. Do your best to remedy any problems. It takes patience and it's not always easy. For instance, there was a time during Joe's youth when he seemed to think that human legs were tree trunks. Rather than pretending I didn't know the beast, I strongly reprimanded him, apologized to the victim from the depths of my heart, and offered money for dry cleaning. Joe learned his lesson—$25 later.

SAFETY FIRST

A few essentials will keep your traveling dog happy and healthy.

•*Heat:* If you must leave your dog alone in the car for a few minutes, do so only if it's cool out, and if you can park in the shade. Never, ever, ever leave a dog in a car with the windows rolled up all the way. Even if it seems cool, the sun's heat passing through the window can kill a dog in a matter of minutes. Roll down the window enough so your dog gets air, but so that there's no danger of your dog getting out or someone breaking in. Make sure your dog has plenty of water.

You also have to watch out for heat exposure when your car is in motion. Certain cars, like hatchbacks, can make a dog in the backseat extra hot, even while you feel okay in the driver's seat.

Try to take your vacation so you don't visit a place when it's extremely warm. Dogs and heat don't get along, especially if the dog isn't used to heat. The opposite is also true. If a dog lives in a hot climate and you take him to a freezing place, it may not be a healthy shift. Check with your vet if you have any doubts. Spring and fall are usually the best times to travel.

• *Water:* Water your dog frequently. Dogs on the road may drink even more than they do at home. Take regular water breaks, or bring a heavy bowl (the thick clay ones do nicely) and set it on the floor so your dog always has access to water. I use a non-spill bowl, which comes in really handy on curvy roads. When hiking, be sure to carry enough for you and a thirsty dog.

• *Rest stops:* Stop and unwater your dog. There's nothing more miserable than being stuck in a car when you can't find a rest stop. No matter how tightly you cross your legs and try to think of the desert, you're certain you'll burst within the next minute. But think of how a dog feels when the urge strikes and he can't tell you the problem.

How frequently you stop depends on your dog's bladder. If your dog is constantly running out the doggy door at home to relieve himself, you may want to stop every hour. Others can go significantly longer without being uncomfortable. Watch for any signs of restlessness and gauge it for yourself.

• *Car safety:* Even the experts differ about how a dog should travel in a car. Some suggest doggy safety belts, available at pet supply stores. Others firmly believe in keeping a dog kenneled. They say it's safer for the dog if there's an accident, and it's safer for the driver because there's no dog underfoot. Still others say you should just let your dog hang out without straps and boxes. They believe that if there's an accident, at least the dog isn't trapped in a cage. They say that dogs enjoy this more anyway.

I'm a follower of the last school of thought. Joe loves sticking his snout out of the windows to smell the world go by. The danger is that if the car kicks up a pebble or ires a bee, his nose and eyes could be injured. So far he's okay, but I have seen dogs who needed to be treated for bee stings to the nose because of this practice. If in doubt, try opening the window just enough so your dog can't stick out much snout.

Whatever way you choose, your pet will be more comfortable if he has his own blanket with him. A veterinarian acquaintance uses a faux-sheepskin blanket for his dogs. At night in the hotel, the sheepskin doubles as the dog's bed.

• *Planes:* Air travel is even more controversial. Personally, unless my dogs could fly with me in the passenger section (which very tiny dogs are sometimes allowed to do), I'd rather find a way to drive the distance or leave them at home with a friend. I've heard too many horror stories of dogs suffocating in what was supposed to be a pressurized cargo section, and of dogs dying of heat exposure, and of dogs going to Miami while their people end up in Seattle. There's just something unappealing about the idea of a dog flying in the cargo hold, like he's nothing more than a piece of luggage. Of course, many dogs survive just fine, but I'm not willing to take the chance.

But if you need to transport your dog by plane, try to fly nonstop, and make sure you schedule takeoff and arrival times when the temperature is below 80 degrees (or not bitterly cold in winter). You'll want to consult the airline about their regulations and required certificates. And check with your vet to make sure your pooch is healthy enough for the trip.

The question of tranquilizing a dog for a plane journey is very controversial. Some vets think it's insane to give a dog a sedative before flying. They say a dog will be calmer and less fearful without taking a disorienting drug. Others think it's crazy not to afford your dog the little relaxation he might not otherwise get without a tranquilizer. Discuss the issue with your vet, who will take the trip's length and your dog's personality into account.

Many Web sites deal with air-bound pooches, as do some books on dog health. Check them out for further info on air travel with your dog.

THE ULTIMATE DOGGY BAG

Your dog can't pack his own bags, and even if he could, he'd probably fill them with dog biscuits and chew toys. It's important to stash some of those in your dog's vacation kit, but here are some other items to bring along: bowls, bedding, a brush, towels (for those muddy days), a first-aid kit, pooper-scoopers, water, food, prescription drugs, tags (see below), treats, toys, and, of course, this book.

Be sure your dog wears his license, identification tag, and rabies tag. On a long trip, you may even want to bring along your dog's rabies certificate. Some parks and campgrounds require rabies and licensing information. You never know how picky they'll be.

It's a good idea to snap one of those barrel-type IDs on your dog's collar, too, showing the name, address, and phone number of where you'll be vacationing, or of a friend who will be home to field calls. That way, if your dog should get lost, at least the finder won't be calling your empty house. My friend Gina Spadafori has a great suggestion in her wonderful book, *Dogs for Dummies:* If you're going to be stopping at a few different locations during your travels, buy a pack of those paper key chains at the hardware store. (They're very inexpensive, and usually come in little bags of 100.) Each day, you can use a new tag and write down the current info on where you'll be staying, even if it's just a campground site number. That way, if your dog finds herself missing, there will be an easy way to get in touch with you locally. You'd be surprised at how many people don't want to make a long-distance phone call.

Some people think dogs should drink only water brought from home, so their bodies don't have to get used to too many new things. I've never had a problem feeding my dogs tap water from other parts of the state, nor has anyone else I know. Most vets think your dog will be fine drinking tap water in most other U.S. cities.

"Think of it this way," says Pete Beeman, a longtime San Francisco veterinarian. "Your dog's probably going to eat poop if he can get hold of some, and even that's probably not going to harm him. I really don't think that water that's okay for people is going to be bad for dogs."

DINING WITH DOG

In Europe, dogs enter restaurants and dine alongside their folks as if they were people, too. (Or at least they sit and watch and drool while their people dine.) Not so in America. Rightly or wrongly, dogs are considered a health threat. But health inspectors I've spoken with say they see no reason why clean, well-behaved dogs shouldn't be permitted inside a restaurant. "Aesthetically, it may not appeal to Americans," an environmental specialist with the state Department of Health told me. "But the truth is, there's no harm in this practice."

Ernest Hemingway made an expatriate of his dog, Black Dog (aka Blackie), partly because of America's restrictive views on dogs in dining establishments. In "The Christmas Gift," a story published in *Look* magazine in 1954, he describes how he made the decision to take Black Dog to Cuba, rather than leave him behind in Ketchum, Idaho.

"This was a town where a man was once not regarded as respectable unless he was accompanied by his dog. But a reform movement had set in, led by several local religionists, and gambling had been abolished and there was even a movement on foot to forbid a dog from entering a public eating place with his master. Blackie had always tugged me by the trouser leg as we passed a combination gambling and eating place called the Alpine where they served the finest sizzling steak in the West. Blackie wanted me to order the giant sizzling steak and it was difficult to pass the Alpine.... We decided to make a command decision and take Blackie to Cuba."

Fortunately, you don't have to take your dog to a foreign country in order to eat together at a restaurant. The Bay Area is full of restaurants with outdoor tables, and hundreds of them welcome dogs to join their people for an alfresco experience. The law on patio-dining dogs is somewhat vague, and each county has differing versions of it. But in general, as long as your dog doesn't go inside a restaurant (even to get to outdoor tables in the back) and isn't near the food preparation areas, it's probably legal. The decision is then up to the restaurant proprietor.

The restaurants listed in this book have given us permission to tout them as dog-friendly eateries. But keep in mind that rules can change and restaurants can close, so I highly recommend phoning before you get your stomach set on a particular kind of cuisine.

Since some of the restaurants close during colder months, phoning ahead is a doubly wise thing to do. (Of course, just assume that where there's snow or ultracold temperatures, the outdoor tables are indoors for a while.) If you can't call first, be sure to ask the manager of the restaurant for permission before you sit down with your sidekick. Remember, it's the restaurant owner, not you, who will be in trouble if someone complains.

Some basic restaurant etiquette: Dogs shouldn't beg other diners, no matter how delicious their steak looks. They should not attempt to get their snouts (or their entire bodies) up on the table. They should be clean, quiet, and as unobtrusive as possible. If your dog leaves a good impression with the management and other customers, it will help pave the way for all the other dogs who want to dine alongside their best friends in the future.

A ROOM AT THE INN

Good dogs make great hotel guests. They don't steal towels, and they don't get drunk and keep the neighbors up all night.

The Bay Area is full of lodgings whose owners welcome dogs. This book lists dog-friendly accommodations of all types, from motels to bed-and-breakfast inns to elegant hotels. But the basic dog etiquette rules are the same.

Dogs should never be left alone in your room. Leaving a dog alone in a strange place is inviting serious trouble. Scared, nervous dogs can tear apart drapes, carpeting, and furniture. They can even injure themselves. They can also bark nonstop and scare the daylights out of the housekeeper. Just don't do it.

Only bring a house-trained dog to a lodging. How would you like a houseguest to go to the bathroom in the middle of your bedroom? It helps if you bring your dog's bed or his blanket. Your dog will feel more at home and won't be tempted to jump on the bed. If your dog sleeps on the bed with you at home, bring a sheet and put it on top of the bed so the hotel's bedspread won't get furry or dirty.

After a few days in a hotel, some dogs come to think of it as home. They get territorial. When another hotel guest walks by, it's "Bark! Bark!" When the housekeeper knocks, it's "Bark! Snarl! Bark! Gnash!" Keep your dog quiet or you'll both find yourselves looking for a new home away from home.

For some strange reason, many lodgings prefer small dogs as guests. All I can say is, "Yip! Yap!" It's really ridiculous. Large dogs are often much calmer and quieter than their tiny, high-energy cousins. If you're in a location where you can't find a hotel that will accept you and your big brute, it's time to try a sell job. Let the manager know how good and quiet your dog is (if he is). Promise he won't eat the bathtub or run around and shake the hotel. Offer a deposit or sign a waiver, even if they're not required for small dogs. It helps if your sweet, soppy-eyed dog is at your side to convince the decision-maker.

I've sneaked dogs into hotels, but I don't recommend doing it. The lodging might have a good reason for its rules. Besides, you always feel as if you're going to be caught and thrown out on your petard. You race in and out of your room with your dog as if ducking sniper fire. It's better to avoid feeling like a criminal and move on to a more dog-friendly location.

The lodgings described in this book are for dogs who obey all the rules. I list the range of a lodging's rates, for the lodging's least expensive room during low season to the lodging's priciest room during high season. Most of the rooms are doubles, so there's not usually a huge variation. But when you see a room get into the thousands of dollars, you know we're looking at royal suites here. Joe can only drool.

Some lodgings charge extra for your dog. If you see "Dogs are $5 (or whatever the amount is) extra," that means $5 extra *per night*. Some charge a fee for the length of a dog's stay, and others ask for a deposit. Those are also noted in the lodging's description. Many still ask for nothing more than your dog's promise that you'll be on your best behavior. So if no extra charge is mentioned in a listing, it means your dog can stay with you for free.

RUFFING IT TOGETHER

Whenever we go camping, Joe insists on sleeping in the tent. He sprawls out and won't budge. At the first hint of dawn, he tiptoes outside (sometimes right through the bug screen) as if he'd been standing vigil all night. He tries not to look shamefaced, but under all that curly hair lurks an embarrassed grin.

Actually, Joe might have the right idea. Some outdoor experts say it's dangerous to leave even a tethered dog outside your tent at night. The dog can escape or can become bait for some creature hungry for a late dinner.

All state parks require dogs to be in a tent or vehicle at night. Some county parks follow suit. Other policies are more lenient. Use good judgment.

If you're camping with your dog, chances are that you're also hiking with him. Even if you're not hiking for long, you have to watch out for your dog's paws, especially the paws of those who are fair of foot. Rough terrain can cause a dog's pads to become raw and painful, making it almost impossible to walk. Several types of dog boots are available for such feet. It's easier to carry the booties than to carry your dog home.

Be sure to bring plenty of water for you and your pooch. Stop frequently to wet your whistles. Some veterinarians recommend against letting your dog drink out of a stream, because of the chance of ingesting giardia and other internal parasites, but it's not always easy to stop a thirsty dog.

On any but the most strenuous hikes, most dogs can muscle a little of the load themselves, if given the right attire. Dog backpacks are becoming more widely available these days in pet stores and catalogs, as well as outdoor stores. They enable a pooch to carry dog food, maps, bowls, or just about any other essentials that aren't too heavy. They're also convenient if you bring your dog fishing. What dog wouldn't want to help you carry a bunch of worms?

If you can't find a backpack in your neck of the woods, call Dog Togs at (800) DOG-TOGS. They've got some terrific backpacks, including one that comes with ethylene foam inserts that quickly convert the backpack into a buoyancy vest. Joe, who can't swim, finds he's a little more at ease around water with his "backpack" on. (And he doesn't have to tell his friends it's really a life jacket.)

NATURAL TROUBLES

Chances are that your adventuring will go without a hitch, but you should always be prepared to deal with trouble. Make sure you know the basics of animal first aid before you embark on a long journey with your dog.

The more common woes—ticks, foxtails, poison oak, and skunks—can make life with a traveling dog a somewhat trying experience.

Ticks are hard to avoid in Northern California. They can carry Lyme disease, so you should always check yourself and your dog all over after a day in tick country. Don't forget to check ears and between the toes. If you see one, just pull it straight out with tweezers, not your bare hands.

The tiny deer ticks that carry Lyme disease are difficult to find. Consult your veterinarian if your dog is lethargic for a few days, has a fever, loses her appetite, or becomes lame. These symptoms could indicate Lyme disease. Some vets recommend a new vaccine that is supposed to prevent the onset of the disease.

Foxtails—those arrow-shaped pieces of dry grass (see the illustration on page 23) that attach to your socks, your sweater, and your dog—are an everyday annoyance. But in certain cases, they can be lethal. They can stick in your dog's eyes, nose, ears, or mouth and work their way in. Check every nook and cranny of your dog after a walk if you've been anywhere near dry grass. Despite my constant effort to find these things in Joe's curly fur, I've missed a few and they've beaten a path through his foot and into his leg. Be vigilant.

Poison oak (see the illustration below) is also a common California menace. Get familiar with it through a friend who knows nature or through a guided nature walk.

In the Emergencies chapter (page 307), there are some remedies for poison oak, tick, skunk, and snake encounters, simple first-aid instructions, and a list of 24-hour emergency animal hospitals.

HE, SHE, IT

In this book, whether neutered, spayed, or *au naturel*, dogs are never referred to as "it." They are either "he" or "she." I alternate pronouns so no dog reading this book will feel left out.

BEYOND THE BORDERS

There may be times when you and your dog actually find yourselves leaving the Bay Area. Because *The Bay Area Dog Lover's Companion* has been so well received, Foghorn Press has launched a Dog Lover's series of books for different parts of the country. *The California Dog Lover's Companion*, written by me and Joe Dog, is probably of most interest to Bay Area folks, but other titles in the series include Seattle, Boston, Atlanta, Washington, D.C., Florida, and Texas. All of the authors are experts in their areas and have

Foxtail   Poison Oak

adventurous dogs who help them explore and rate various attractions. If you can't find them in local bookstores, call Foghorn Press at 1-800-FOGHORN (364-4676) to order yours.

Another fun way to keep up with dog travel news around the country is through a subscription to a doggone fine newsletter called *DogGone*. As its masthead states, *DogGone* is "about fun places to go and cool stuff to do with your dog." A subscription to this attractive, informative 12-page publication is $24 per year (six issues). For more information, or to subscribe, write to: DogGone, P.O. Box 651155, Vero Beach, FL 32965. You can also e-mail *DogGone* at doggonenl@aol.com.

Freedom-loving dogs now have a fun, informative Web site devoted to cool off-leash places to take a dog nationally. At press time, the Freedog site was just starting to branch out beyond the Bay Area, but it's growing fast and shows great promise. The writing is wry, funny, and clever. Your dog will laugh out loud. You'll find the site at www.freedog.com.

A DOG IN NEED

If you don't currently have a dog but could provide a good home for one, I'd like to make a plea on behalf of all the unwanted dogs who will be euthanized tomorrow and the day after that and the day after that. Animal shelters and humane organizations are overflowing with dogs who would devote their lives to being your best buddy, your faithful traveling companion, and a dedicated listener to all your tales of bliss and woe.

Need a nudge? Remember the oft-quoted words of Samuel Butler: "The great pleasure of a dog is that you may make a fool of yourself with him and not only will he not scold you, but he will make a fool of himself, too."

KEEP IN TOUCH!

Our readers mean everything to us. We explore the Bay Area so you and your dogs can spend true quality time together. Your input to this book is very important. In the last few years, we've heard from many wonderful dogs and their people about new dog-friendly places, or old dog-friendly places we didn't know about. We check out the tip and if it turns out to be a good one, we include it in the next edition, giving a thank-you to the dog and/ or person who sent in the tip.

Now we're making it easier than ever to get in touch with us. You can call the new California Dog Lover's Companion Hotline at (707) 773-4264 and leave your tip. When you call, be sure to leave your name, city, and your dog's name so we can give you credit in the book. It's our way of paying homage to you and your best friend. You can also write to Joe Dog and me at 340 Bodega Avenue, Petaluma, CA 94952. And you can e-mail us at foghorn@well.com.

INTRODUCTION

BAY AREA
COUNTY LISTINGS

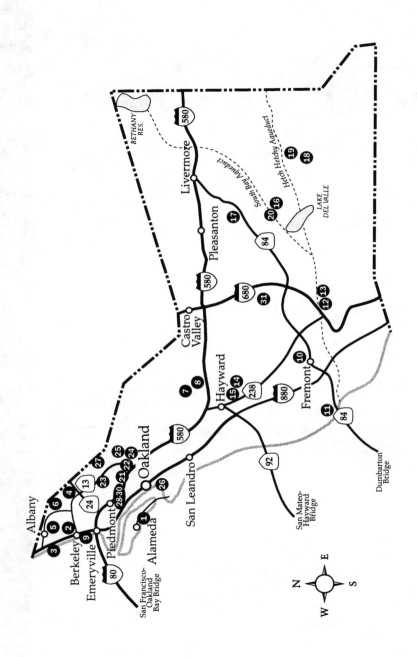

ALAMEDA COUNTY

1
ALAMEDA COUNTY

From the hallowed hippie havens of Berkeley's Telegraph Avenue to the pleasing suburban pleasantries of Pleasanton, Alameda County is like California in miniature: It has nearly every level of population density and type, and nearly every temperate natural environment. Somehow, it all works.

Dogs dig it here, whether they're rasta dogs or shaved shih tzus. The county is like the creek it's named after—it's been lined with concrete, filled with trash, and dammed into oblivion, yet it still manages to gush joyfully onward. Some of the wildest country in the Bay Area is located in this county, full of hidden gems of nature. So many of these parks are off-leash havens that your dog may think he's dreaming.

The 12-mile Alameda Creek Regional Trail (see page 42) is a favorite among dogs. They can run off leash on most of the trail, but where signs say leashes are required, heed the message.

An even more invigorating trail is the East Bay Skyline National Recreation Trail. Well-behaved, leash-free dogs are welcome on the entire 31-mile length of this trail. Wowza wowza and howlelujah! The trail stretches from the northern end of Wildcat Canyon Regional Park in Contra Costa County (see page 77) to the southern end of Anthony Chabot Regional Park (see page 40). Plenty of horses also use this trail, so if your dog is a hoof chaser, keep him leashed.

As if all this wasn't enough good news, your dog's hair will stand on end when he learns that unless he's a pit bull, he's allowed to run leashless on thousands of acres of parkland within the East Bay Regional Parks District. Some 50 parks and recreation areas and 20 regional trails—75,000 acres in all—fall under the district's jurisdiction. Pooper-scooper dispensers are installed at the most heavily used areas, such as Point Isabel Regional Shoreline (see page 75).

The only places where dogs must be leashed within the district's parks are in developed areas, parking lots, picnic sites, lawns, and in posted Nature Areas. They aren't permitted on beaches (Point Isabel Regional Shoreline is a major exception), wetlands, marshes, or in the Tilden Nature Area. In addition, at press time, the district was deciding whether dogs have to be leashed along Redwood Regional Park's Stream Trail (see page 53). Call (510) 635-0138 for more information on the East Bay Regional Park system.

A couple of bits of good news: The city of Oakland now has its very own pooch park. It opened in 1997, and at press time it wasn't a very good one, but it's headed for improvement. (Please see Hardy Dog Park, page 50.) Plus it seems to have inspired talk of other locations for pooch parks in the city. In addition, the Friends of Cesar Chavez Park, in Berkeley, has taken over what can seem like impossible fight to convert 15 acres of this bayside park to an off-leash poochy paradise. It's a high-energy, dog-lovin', tail waggin' group that needs your help if you can lend a paw. See the introduction to Berkeley on page 33 for more on this group and its efforts.

Dogs who enjoy the great outdoors are truly in pooch heaven here, because this is the home base for the San Francisco Bay chapter of the Sierra Club. The club holds dozens of fun hikes for dogs each year, via its Canine Hike unit, and most of the hikes are in the East Bay. Dogs get to hike and play off leash, as long as they're well-behaved and under voice control. Hikes are of varying difficulties and lengths. Some involve easy swimming (I hear the water dogs drooling), some involve camping, some even involve meeting the love of your life (when Sierra Singles and their dogs come out to play). Get yourself an activities schedule at the chapter bookstore, or call and order one. They're $3.50 in person, $4.50 by mail. The schedule includes all the hikes, doggy and non-doggy, for the quarter. Schedules are available at the chapter bookstore, at 6014 College Avenue, Oakland, CA 94618. Call before you send a check, if ordering by mail, in case the price has changed; (510) 658-7470. You can call and order by credit card, too. This is money very well spent. The folks who participate in the canine hikes are almost as friendly and fun-loving as their dogs.

ALAMEDA

PARKS, BEACHES, AND RECREATION AREAS

• **Washington Park** 🐾🐾 *See ❶ on page 28.*

Washington Park, next to Robert Crown Memorial State Beach (sorry, pooches, no can go), is Alameda's largest park. It has lots of great amenities for people, and leashed dogs enjoy the wide green expanses, the bike path, and the edge of the marsh here. Unfortunately for hungry dogs, pooches aren't permitted at the picnic areas.

From downtown, take Central Avenue toward Webster Street. The park is at the corner of Central and Eighth Street. For the beach, continue on Eighth Street. Call (510) 635-0135 for beach information or (510) 748-4565 for park information.

RESTAURANTS

The Good & Plenty Cafe & Deli: This wonderful cafe is a veritable Noah's Ark. Animals of all kinds come to the outdoor tables here with their people. It's not uncommon to see cats on laps and birds on shoulders. But dogs are by far the best—er, most common—critters who visit while their people dine on delicious deli food. Kira, a 100-pound malamute who moved here from Arizona to live on a boat, convinced her "dad" to write and tell us that the food servers "welcome pets with open arms and have been known to get suckered out of a snack or two by the appropriate big, brown-eyed doggy look . . . Kira gives this place a four-paw rating with no hesitation." The cafe is located near the Ballena Isle Marina, at 1132 Ballena Boulevard; (510) 769-2132.

DIVERSIONS

Seize the Bay: Water-loving dogs just about swoon when they learn they're allowed on the Blue & Gold Fleet's ferries that run between Oakland, Alameda, and San Francisco. Please turn to page 181 in the San Francisco chapter for more details.

ALBANY

RESTAURANTS

For a pleasant street with dog-friendly people and at least a couple of restaurants with outdoor tables, try Albany's Solano Avenue.

Barney's Gourmet Hamburgers: While its street address is in Berkeley, it's just over the border from Albany. Dogs drool while watching you eat gourmet burgers at the outdoor tables. 1591 Solano Avenue, Berkeley; (510) 526-8185.

Marco Polo's Deli Cafe: Dogs enjoy watching you eat tasty sandwiches at the outdoor tables here. 1158 Solano Avenue; (510) 524-5667.

BERKELEY

Berkeley, well known for its tolerance of eccentricity, is equally eccentric when it comes to dogs. Like most of Alameda County, it features strict leash laws: You break the law, you pay the price—which can be above $100 for the second offense.

But there is a unique loophole. If your dog is obedience-trained, Berkeley doesn't require him to be leashed. If an animal control officer sees you with your unleashed dog, you'll be asked to demonstrate that your dog is under absolute voice control. If the officer is not persuaded, you'll be cited and asked to appear in court with your dog, where you'll have another chance to prove it. (I can just picture Joe sitting, lying down, and rolling over in court. Well, maybe if a treat were involved. Nahhh.)

Whether they're all under absolute voice control or not, you'll see a lot more unleashed dogs in Berkeley than in any other Bay Area city. The University of California at Berkeley also has a leash law, but the campus is swarming with loose dogs, too. The only leashed animal you'll see is a local pet pig whose owner walks him there. Go figure.

Berkeley created the country's first official dog park, Ohlone Dog Park (see page 35). Still, it's been slow in approving a plan to allow dogs to run free on 15 of the 40 undeveloped acres of Cesar Chavez Park in the marina. A citizens' group that calls itself AARF (Area for Animals to Run Free) worked valiantly for five years to convert the space, but its efforts got swallowed by a bureaucratic sinkhole in 1993. A new, highly energetic group has emerged to continue the fight. They're called the Friends of Cesar Chavez Park—"The Friends" for short. At press time, they were still battling park naysayers who want this former landfill to remain as undoggy as possible. Foes include the Sierra Club and a blind woman. (Fortunately, the Girl Scouts and the Pope are staying out of this one.) Obviously The Friends needs as much help as it can get. It's a wonderful group, with terrific, responsible, environmentally concerned people, and the best regional dog newsletter—*The Berkeley Bark*—I've ever seen. For info on the group, its newsletter, or upcoming relevant city meetings, contact Claudia Kawczynska at Friends of Cesar Chavez Park, 2810 Eighth Street, Berkeley, CA 94710; (510) 704-0827.

PARKS, BEACHES, AND RECREATION AREAS

• **Aquatic Park** 🐾🐾½ *See* ❷ *on page 28.*

Take advantage of this city park for a quick stroll by the water. Conveniently located off Interstate 80, it's fairly tranquil, even with the lagoon's powerboats and water-skiers whizzing by. The lagoon's banks are planted with a mixture of grass, willows, cypress, and eucalyptus. Boy dogs have lifted many a leg in homage here.

Thanks to its greenery, birds are plentiful. Dogs like to bird-watch from the paved paths and the parcourse. Leashed dogs enjoy splashing around the shallow, calm lagoon water.

From Interstate 80, take the Ashby exit and turn north on Bay Street. There's a small parking lot. If you come from the north side of the park, you can park at a couple of areas on Bolivar Drive, along the park's east side. (510) 644-6530.

• **Cesar Chavez Park** 🐾🐾🐾 *See* ❸ *on page 28.*

Someday, 15 of the 40 undeveloped acres of this 90-acre bayside park may become an off-leash pooch paradise. (Please see the introduction to Berkeley on page 33 for more on a group called Friends of Cesar Chavez Park and its efforts toward this commendable canine cause.) Meanwhile, you and your leashed dog can enjoy the grassy hills surrounded by the beautiful San Francisco Bay. Trails meander up and down the rolling hills and wind through a couple of quiet meadows.

The views of San Francisco, the Golden Gate Bridge, and the Bay Bridge are some of the best around. The park is equipped with plenty of pooper-scooper stations crammed with "Mutt Mitts." Use them. Impress those who could make this a leash-free mutt mecca. In fact, pick up an occasional "orphan" poop while you're at it, and the cards just may become stacked in favor of off-leash pooches. For more on how to help the park, contact Claudia Kawczynska at Friends of Cesar Chavez Park, 2810 Eighth Street, Berkeley, CA 94710; (510) 704-0827.

This is also a great place to fly a kite, and there are plenty of instructions posted on how to do it safely around here.

Take University Avenue west past the Interstate 80 interchange and follow the signs to the Berkeley marina and Cesar Chavez. (510) 644-6371.

• **Claremont Canyon Regional Preserve** 🐾🐾🐾🐾 🐕
See ❹ on page 28.

This large park is full of steep hillside trails that lead to crests with stunning views of the university and the surrounding hills and valleys. If your dog likes eucalyptus trees and doesn't like leashes, take him here. It's one of those tree-filled, leashes-optional parks.

From Highway 13 (Ashby Avenue), drive north on College Avenue. Turn right on Derby Street, past the Clark Kerr Campus. The trailhead is at the southeast corner of the school grounds, near the beginning of Stonewall Road. (510) 635-0135.

• **Ohlone Dog Park** 🐾🐾🐾 🐕 *See ❺ on page 28.*

Since 1979, when it opened as the first leash-free dog park in America, Ohlone has provided a model for other cities willing to experiment with the concept. Dogs across America revere Ohlone. It's kind of like the Mecca of mutts.

The park can get pretty beat up during winter, with mud overtaking everything, including the mulch and woodchips used to cover the mud. But even after years of unflagging popularity, the park is still in relatively good shape. This can be credited in large part to a conscientious park upkeep committee that keeps an eye on facilities and provides plastic bags for cleaning up after your dog. You'll find a water faucet, complete with a dog bowl set in concrete, and two picnic tables for owners who want to relax while their dogs socialize. The grass isn't always green here, but it's definitely better than what's on the other side of the fence.

The park is at Martin Luther King Jr. Way and Hearst Street. (510) 644-6530.

• **Tilden Regional Park** 🐾🐾🐾🐾 🐕 *See ❻ on page 28.*

Humans and dogs alike give Tilden a big thumbs-up (dewclaws-up). Leash-free dogs find the scents from its western ridge delectable and humans find the ridge's breathtaking views of the entire San Francisco Bay equally enticing.

Escapes from civilization are everywhere in this 2,078-acre park. Try the trails leading east from South Park Drive. They connect with the East Bay Skyline National Recreation Trail.

You can pick up the Arroyo Trail at the Big Springs sign and take it all the way to the ridgetop. There's a great stream at the trailhead that you can follow through laurel, pine, toyon, and scrub on your low-grade ascent. Your dog may want to take a dip in the stream for refreshment.

After the trail veers from the stream, it steepens and leads into cypress-studded meadows and eucalyptus groves. Eventually it feeds into the Skyline National Recreation Trail, also known as the Sea View Trail, offering vistas over the bay along the way.

Dogs aren't allowed in the large nature area at the northern end or in the Lake Anza swimming area. Leashes are required in all the developed areas, including picnic grounds and ball fields. Remember to watch your step in the areas frequented by dogs, as some owners neglect to clean up after their furry friends. There's nothing like stepping in a steaming pile of dog dung to put a damper on a day of exploring nature.

Speaking of steaming, be sure to check out Tilden's miniature steam train for a riveting good time. (See Diversions, page 38.)

From Highway 24, take the Fish Ranch Road exit north (at the eastern end of the Caldecott Tunnel). At the intersection of Fish Ranch, Grizzly Peak Boulevard, and Claremont Avenue, take a right on Grizzly Peak and continue north to South Park Drive. One more mile north brings you to Big Springs Trail. During peak season, continue on Grizzly Peak to the Shasta Gate. (510) 635-0135.

RESTAURANTS

Just north of University Avenue, a three-block stretch of Shattuck Avenue is home to several restaurants with outdoor seating. Here are a few:

Fontina Caffe Italiana: Dogs like dining with their people at the two umbrella-topped tables here. The food is snout-licking good. But what they like even better is that Fontina is right next door to the Shattuck Cat Clinic. Poor Joe Dog will never know the pleasures of Fontina, because he knows too well the pleasures of cats. 1730 Shattuck Avenue; (510) 649-8090.

The French Hotel Cafe: Someone sneaked Joe a saucer of espresso and he barked at feet for the rest of the day. It's the real stuff—good and strong. Sip it at the outside tables, but let your dog stick with water. 1540 Shattuck Avenue; (510) 548-9930.

Istanbul Grill: Mmm good! The food here is a delectable combination of Turkish, Mediterranean, and California cuisine. Dine with your dog at the outdoor tables. 1686 Shattuck Avenue; (510) 549-2316.

Elsewhere in Berkeley, you'll find many other outdoor options, including these:

Bongo Burger: There's only one regular ol' hamburger here. Other burgers include the Persian burger (marinated ground lamb) and the shish kebab burger (marinated chunks of beef). Joe and I highly recommend the Mediterranean plate, which involves things like falafel and hummus. There are three of these yummy places around Berkeley, but Joe's favorite for the flavor of the neighborhood is the one at 2154 Center Street; (510) 540-9014.

College Avenue Delicatessen: Dogs enjoy watching you eat standard deli fare at the outdoor tables here. 3185 College Avenue; (510) 655-8584.

La Mediterranée: This delicious and inexpensive Middle Eastern restaurant has built up quite a following; there's usually a line on weekends when Cal is mid-semester. The folks here will let your dog sit quietly at your feet at the outdoor tables, which have the added benefit of an outdoor heater on cool nights. You might want to tie your dog up on the sidewalk outside the fence separating the tables if it's especially crowded. 2836 College Avenue; (510) 540-7773.

NeFeli: The light Greek cuisine at NeFeli really hits the spot. Try the Athenian panini if you like your Greek sans meat. It's a real treat. Dogs get to join you at tables under the awning in front. 1854 Euclid Avenue; (510) 841-6374.

Noah's New York Bagels: Noah's has benches on the sidewalk, though no tables—but it's still a must-visit for you and your dog, if bagels and cream cheese are your yen. It's very popular on Sunday mornings. 3170 College Avenue; (510) 654-0944.

Peet's Coffee: Not only Peet's but the Bread Garden Bakery and various other cafes and shops encircle a sunny patio with benches. Nearly every morning, crowds of hungry bicyclists and amblers congregate to sit in the sun, argue (this is Berkeley), eat pastries, and sip Peet's coffee, which many call the best in the Bay Area. Dogs' noses don't stop quivering and they can often meet other frustrated dogs. 2816 Domingo Avenue off Ashby. Peet's: (510) 843-1434. Bread Garden: (510) 548-3122.

Rick & Ann's Restaurant: Dogs feel really at home here, because Rick and Ann and their staff love dogs. This is also a popular place among people. The food is delicious and unique. It may take you a while to choose something from the imaginative menu, but just about anything you select will be great. The restaurant is located next to Peet's (see page 37), at 2822 Domingo Avenue; (510) 486-8119.

Sea Breeze Market and Deli: Smack in the middle of the Interstate 80 interchange, you won't even notice the traffic as you and your dog bask at sunny picnic tables, where crab claws crunch underfoot and begging is outstanding. Dogs are perfectly welcome so long as they don't wander into the store itself. You can buy groceries, beer, wine, classy ice cream, or a meal from the deli: fresh fish-and-chips, calamari, prawns, scallops, chicken, and quiche. The deli serves croissants and coffee early; if you live in the East Bay, you can zip in for a quick croissant and a dog walk at Cesar Chavez Park (see page 34) before work. It's located at the foot of University Avenue, past the Interstate 80 entrance. 598 University Avenue; (510) 486-8119.

PLACES TO STAY

Golden Bear Motel: Rates are $45 to $65. Small dogs only, please, and they require a onetime $5 fee. 1620 San Pablo Avenue, Berkeley, CA 94702; (510) 525-6770.

DIVERSIONS

Ride a dog-sized train: If your dog's not an escape artist or the nervous type, he's welcome to ride with you on Tilden Regional Park's miniature train. The open-car train takes you for a 12-minute ride through woods and past stunning views of the surrounding area. Adventurous dogs like it when the train toots its whistle as it rumbles past a miniature water tower, a car barn, and other such train accessories. When Joe Dog appeared on *Bay Area Backroads* riding the train, he was fine until we hit the little tunnel—then he decided he wanted to go home. He's relieved that part ended up on the cutting-room floor.

The Redwood Valley Railway Company runs trains between 11 A.M. and 6 P.M. weekends and holidays only, except during spring and summer school vacations, when it runs weekdays, noon to 5 P.M. and weekends until 6 P.M. Tickets are $1.50; kids under two and dogs ride free. You must keep the dog on a tight leash and make sure he doesn't jump out. It's in the southeast corner of Tilden Regional Park. From the intersection of Grizzly Peak Boulevard and Lomas Cantadas, follow the signs. (510) 548-6100.

Flea to the Market: If your dog has the itch to shop, and promises not to do leg lifts on furniture even when it's outdoors, you can have a relaxed time at the Ashby Flea Market. Crowds will be tolerant, but keep him on a short leash and watch out for chicken bones and abandoned cotton candy. Joe's friend Dabney, for instance, is a dog who knows how to shop for scraps, nose to the ground for hours. He's been to his last flea market.

Good dogs love the easy camaraderie they'll find here. If it's hot, though, keep it short. This market is held every Saturday and Sunday at the Ashby BART station parking lot.

From Interstate 80, take the Ashby exit and drive about 1.5 miles east to the intersection of Adeline Street.

Go shopping in 1967: You and your dog can shop in the autumn of love when you stroll through the sidewalks of Telegraph Avenue near the UC Berkeley campus. Street vendors sell tie-dyed clothes, crystals, pottery, and T-shirts airbrushed with clouds. Street performers sing, juggle, beg for money, or do whatever else comes naturally. Incense and other herbaceous odors waft through the air, but dogs prefer the scents of all the non-deodorized humans.

Dogs who reminisce about the 1960s really dig it here. They're perceived as totally cool dudes and given major amounts of love from people who like to hug dogs hard. A palm reader made friends with Joe on a recent visit, but since Joe isn't a believer in soothsaying, he steadfastly refused to give her his paw. (Actually, he only gives a paw for food, not friendship. He's a very pragmatic Airedale.)

Some dogs—and humans—may find the weekend crowds a sensory overload. If your schedule allows, try a cool afternoon. From Interstate 80, take the Ashby exit, go about two miles east to Telegraph, and turn left (north). The street-merchant part begins around the intersection of Dwight Way. On weekends, parking is challenging.

Sniff out a good book: Dogs love Avenue Books, because the people at this bookstore love dogs. If they're not too busy, they'll make sure your dog gets a special doggy treat to munch on while you peruse the great selection of books. Joe thinks the pet section here is tops. "Dogs also like the nature section, but we try to be careful about that," joked one store manager. The store is in the Elmwood shopping district, at 2804 College Avenue, near the corner of Ashby Avenue; (510) 549-3532.

CASTRO VALLEY

PARKS, BEACHES, AND RECREATION AREAS

•**Anthony Chabot Regional Park** 🐾🐾🐾🐾 🐕
*See **7** on page 28.*

You and your leash-free dog can throw your urban cares to the wind when you visit this 4,684-acre park filled with magnificent trails and enchanting woodlands. Except for the occasional sounds of gunfire, you'll scarcely believe you're in the hills east of metropolitan Oakland. But fear not—the guns you'll hear are merely being used for target practice at the park's marksmanship range.

The trails here are so secluded that if no one is firing a gun, the only sounds you may hear are those of your panting dog and the singing birds. Adventure-loving dogs like to take the Goldenrod Trail, starting at the southern terminus of Skyline Boulevard and Grass Valley Road. It connects with the East Bay Skyline National Recreation Trail, which winds through Grass Valley and climbs through eucalyptus forests. Lucky dogs can be off leash everywhere but in developed areas.

Campsites are $15 to $20. Dogs are $1 extra. Reserve by phoning (925) 373-0144. No reservations are taken between October 1 and March 31, when the 23 sites are first come, first served.

From the intersection of Redwood Road and Castro Valley Boulevard in Castro Valley, go north on Redwood about 4.5 miles to Marciel Gate. (The campground is about two miles inside the gate.) From Oakland at the intersection of Redwood Road and Skyline Boulevard, go about 6.5 miles east on Redwood to Marciel Gate. For general park info, call (510) 635-0135.

•**Cull Canyon Regional Recreation Area** 🐾🐾🐾½ 🐕
*See **8** on page 28.*

Dogs may be off leash up on the grassy slopes laced with eucalyptus stands, but they have to wear their leashes in the areas designed for human fun. It's not such a bad fate, considering that there are plenty of grassy slopes away from developed areas.

In summer, fishing and swimming are popular here. But pooches may not go near the swimming complex, which includes an attractive pavilion and sandy beach. Leashed dogs may visit picnic areas, the Cull Creek area, and the willow-lined reservoir that sports a wooden bridge and a handful of ducks and coots.

From Interstate 580, take the Center Street/Crow Canyon Road exit. Go left on Center Street and take a right on Castro Valley Boulevard. Follow it to Crow Canyon Road and take a left. Take another left on Cull Canyon Road. It's a half mile to the park entrance. (510) 635-0135.

PLACES TO STAY
Anthony Chabot Regional Park: See Anthony Chabot Regional Park on page 40 for camping information.

EMERYVILLE

PARKS, BEACHES, AND RECREATION AREAS
• **Emeryville Marina Park** 🐾 🐾 *See ❾ on page 28.*
If you're a human, this is a fine park. If you're a leashed dog, it's just so-so. A concrete path follows the riprap shoreline past cypress trees and through manicured grass. A quick and scenic stroll down the north side will give you a fine view of the marina and a miniature bird refuge where egrets, sandpipers, blackbirds, and doves inhabit a tiny marsh. Dogs who like to bird-watch think it's cool here.

Dogs who like to fish don't have it so easy. Pooches aren't allowed on the fishing pier. But if you console them with an offer to picnic at tables with grand views of the Bay Bridge, they usually snap out of their funk.

From Interstate 80, take the Powell Street exit at Emeryville and go west on Powell to the end of the marina. There's lots of free parking. (510) 596-4340.

DIVERSIONS
Take your dog to daycare: Hey, dogs! If your person works and leaves you at home to chew up the shoes and stare at the walls, casually leave the book open to this page and your life might soon change. Most pooches who visit Every Dog Has Its Day Care have so much fun that they're drooling to come back day after day.

Dogs get lots of room to run and play and hang out with others of their ilk all day. Just like kiddy day care, dogs also get quiet time if they need a snooze, and lots of toys to sink their teeth into. Unlike kiddy day care, they get individual laptime, which includes brushing, petting, and scratching by a dog-lovin' staffer. These activities might be frowned upon in kiddy day-care circles, but they're great for pooches.

The rate is $25 daily, or $450 per month (four free days). At least it's cheaper than kiddy day care, and you don't have to deal with nasty runny noses or chicken pox. 1306 65th Street, Emeryville, CA 94608; (510) 655-7821. The Web site is www.everydog.com.

FREMONT

PARKS, BEACHES, AND RECREATION AREAS

• **Alameda Creek Regional Trail** 🐾🐾🐾 🐕

See ⑩ on page 28.

This 12.4-mile trail runs from the bayshore to the East Bay hills, and dogs can actually be off leash in many sections. But they may be disappointed when they discover that it's not as pristine a trail as the name might imply. First of all, the trail is paved. Second of all, the creek is paved. (You'll see what I mean.) But more important, the trail doesn't just pass through farmland and greenbelt areas. It also runs alongside railyards, industrial lots, and quarries. Junkyard dogs like it. Wilderness dogs just shrug their hairy shoulders. A scenic stretch of this paved trail is at the Niles Canyon end. Dogs find it especially interesting in winter after a storm, when there's actually water in the concrete-lined creek and ducks and coots splash around.

You may enter this trail at many points between the creek's mouth—in the salt flats of the bay by Coyote Hills Regional Park. The trail officially begins in Fremont's Niles district, at the intersection of Mission Boulevard (Highway 238) and Niles Canyon Road (Highway 84).

Although the East Bay Regional Parks District's usual liberal leash rules apply here, it has posted a good many areas with "leash up" symbols. If you see one, do so. On this trail, as on any you share with other hikers, horses, and bicycles, just use common sense. (510) 635-0135.

• **Coyote Hills Regional Park** 🐾🐾🐾 *See* ⑪ *on page 28.*

This park is a paradox. It's a working research project on Ohlone Indian history, a teeming wildlife sanctuary, and a family picnic and bicycling mecca—all rolled into 966 acres.

Dogs used to be able to run leashless in the small hills that give the park its name, but leashes are now the law. We understand. (Waaah.) Wildlife is abundant here. You'll see red-tailed hawks, vultures, and white-tailed kites that swoop down on unsuspecting squirrels. Joe hasn't ever seen one of these kite-gets-squirrel incidents, but since he's never even come close to capturing a squirrel, he'd give his canine teeth to witness such a spectacle.

The beautiful Bayview Trail climbs quickly up behind the visitors center. From the crest of Red Hill—green even in the dry season because its ground cover is drought-tolerant—you look down on varied colors of marsh grasses, waterfowl, and wading birds, and the shallow salt ponds in the bay. Most of the park is a fragile sanctuary, and dogs must stay on the little hills or at the picnic area by the visitors center.

Special doggy alert: We just got word that the park is offering guided dog walks once a month! Call the park for dates and times.

From Interstate 880, take the Decoto Road/Highway 84 exit in Fremont. Go west on Highway 84 to the Thornton Avenue/Paseo Padre Parkway exit. Go north on Paseo Padre about one mile to Patterson Ranch Road/Commerce. A left on Patterson Ranch Road brings you to the entrance. When the kiosk is staffed, the parking fee is $3. The dog fee is $1. For information on tours and activities, call (510) 795-9385. For general information, call (510) 635-0135.

• **Mission Peak Regional Preserve** 🐾🐾🐾🐾 🐕
See ⑫ *on page 28.*

Smart Fremont dwellers take their dogs to this 2,596-acre park. It's a huge expanse of grass, dotted with occasional oak groves and scrub. Unfortunately for humans who get short of breath, the foot trails head straight up. Trails to the top rise 2,500 feet in three miles. (Pant, pant.)

Leash-free dogs love this place. The entrance at Stanford Avenue offers a gentler climb than the entrance from the Ohlone College campus. You'll pass Caliente Creek if you take the Peak Meadow Trail, but in hot weather, there won't be much relief from the sun. Be sure to carry water for yourself and your dog. The main point of puffing up Mission Peak is the renowned view stretching from Mount Tamalpais to Mount Hamilton. (On very clear days, you can see to the Sierra's snowy crest.) Your dog may not care much for the scenery, but she'll probably appreciate the complete freedom of the expanse of pasture here.

From Interstate 680, take the southern Mission Boulevard exit in Fremont (there are two; the one you want is in the Warm Springs district). Go east on Mission to Stanford Avenue, turn right (east), and in less than a mile, you'll be at the entrance. (510) 635-0135.

• **Sunol Regional Wilderness** 🐾🐾🐾🐾 🐕
See ⑬ on page 28.

You and your leash-free dog will howl for joy when you visit this large and deserted wilderness treasure. It's like going to a national park without having to leave your poor pooch behind.

One of the best treats for canines and their companions is a hike along the Camp Ohlone Trail, which you reach via the main park entrance, on Geary Road. The trail takes you to an area called Little Yosemite. Like its namesake, Little Yosemite is magnificent. It's a steep-sided gorge with a creek at the bottom, lofty crags, and outcrops of greenstone and basalt that reveal a turbulent geological history. Its huge boulders throw Alameda Creek into gurgling eddies and falls. There's no swimming allowed here, much to Joe's relief.

You can return via the higher Canyon View Trail or head for several other destinations: wooded canyons, grassy slopes, peaks with peeks of Calaveras Reservoir or Mount Diablo. The park brochure offers useful descriptions of each trail. Dogs may run leashless on trails except for on the Backpack Loop.

Dogs are allowed only at the Family Campground site at headquarters and not at the backpacking campsites farther in. Sites are $11. The dog fee is $1. Dogs must be leashed in the campground or confined to your tent. (Anyone whose dog has ever chased off after a wild boar in the middle of the night understands the reason for this rule, and this park has plenty of boars.) Call (510) 636-1684 to reserve. Reserved sites are held until 5 P.M.

From Interstate 680, take the Calaveras Road exit, then go left (east) on Geary Road to the park entrance. The park may be closed or restricted during fire season, from June to October. (925) 862-2244.

PLACES TO STAY

Best Western Thunderbird Inn: Rates are $109 to $128. Dogs must pay a $50 fee per stay. 5400 Mowry Avenue, Fremont, CA 94538; (510) 792-4300.

Sunol Regional Wilderness: See the Sunol Regional Wilderness on page 44 for camping information.

HAYWARD

PARKS, BEACHES, AND RECREATION AREAS

Leashed pooches are permitted at five parks run by the Hayward Area Recreation and Park District: San Lorenzo Community Center and Park, San Felipe, East Avenue, Tennyson, and the Eden Greenway, which runs parallel to the BART tracks between Hesperian Boulevard and Whitman Street.

• **Garin Regional Park and Dry Creek Regional Park**
🐾 🐾 🐾 🐾 🐕

See ⑭ on page 28.

Garin Regional Park is about one mile and one century away from one of the busiest streets in Hayward. It's a fascinating place for you and your dog to learn about Alameda County farming and ranching. The parking lot next to Garin Barn—an actual barn, blacksmith's shop, and tool shed that is also Garin's visitors center—is strewn with antique farm machinery.

A total of 20 miles of trails, looping among the sweeps of grassy hills, beckon you and your dog. Off-leash dogs are fine on the trails once you've left the visitors center. Dogs seem to like to think they're on their own farm here, looking for all the world like they're strutting down their very own property and watching out for evil feline intruders.

Dry Creek, which runs near the visitors center, was a delightful small torrent one day when we were there after a March storm. There isn't much shade on hot days, though. That's when you might want to try cooling your paws at tiny Jordan Pond. It's stocked with catfish, should your dog care to join you on his kind of fishing excursion.

From Highway 238 (Mission Boulevard), Tamarack Drive takes you quickly up the hill to Dry Creek Regional Park. Garin Avenue takes you to Garin, or you can enter Garin from the California

State University, Hayward campus. The parking fee is $3 on weekends and holidays. Dogs are $1 extra. (510) 635-0135.

• **Hayward Memorial Park Hiking and Riding Trails** 🐾 🐾 🐾
   See ⑮ on page 28.

For humans, Memorial Park offers all kinds of amenities, including an indoor pool, tennis courts, kids' swings and slides, picnic tables, a band shell, and even a slightly funky cage full of doves. But really, if you're a dog, the big question is "Who cares?"

The fun for dogs begins when you get on the Wally Wickander (poor guy) Memorial Trail and enter the greenbelt portion of the park, laced with dirt fire trails designed for hikers and horses. Dogs must remain leashed, but the trail is so beautiful that it doesn't seem to matter. It follows a steep-sided creek lined with a thick tangle of oak, laurel, maple, and lots of noisy birds. The trash pickup is a little lax, but if you're looking for solitude in a city park, you'll find it here.

You can enter through Hayward Memorial Park, at Mission Boulevard (Highway 238) just south of the intersection of Highway 92. You can also enter at the parking lots on East Avenue through East Avenue Park on the north end, or on Highland Boulevard through Old Highland Park on the south end. (510) 881-6715.

PLACES TO STAY

Motel 6: Rates are $32 for the first adult, $6 for the second. Small dogs only, please, and only one per room. 30155 Industrial Parkway Southwest, Hayward, CA 94544; (510) 489-8333.

Vagabond Inn: Rates are $65 to $75. Dogs are $5 extra. 20455 Hesperian Boulevard, Hayward, CA 94541; (510) 785-5480.

LIVERMORE

PARKS, BEACHES, AND RECREATION AREAS

• **Del Valle Regional Park** 🐾 🐾 🐾 🐾 🐕   *See ⑯ on page 28.*

This popular reservoir is best known for swimming, boating, fishing, and camping. Like Anthony Chabot Regional Park (see page 40), it's primarily a manicured and popular human recreation area, with neat lawns and picnic tables (where dogs must be leashed).

But, glory be to dog, the park sports several unspoiled trails for leash-free hiking in the surrounding hills. And, unlike at Lake Chabot, here you're permitted to take a dog on a rented boat. Every dog can have his day here.

From this recreation area, you can enter the Ohlone Wilderness Trail—28 miles of gorgeous trail through four regional parks. (See Ohlone Regional Wilderness, below.)

The 150 sites at Family Camp allow dogs, but only on leash or confined to your tent. Sites are $15 to $18. Reserve by calling (925) 373-0144.

From Interstate 580, take North Livermore Avenue from downtown Livermore. It will become South Livermore Avenue, then Tesla Road. Take a right (south) on Mines Road, then turn right on Del Valle Road. The parking fee is $4, and $5 from March through October. The dog fee is $1. (510) 635-0135.

• **Livermore Canine Park** 🐾🐾🐾🐾 🐕 *See* ⓱ *on page 28.*

If it weren't for the efforts of local vet Martin Plone, Livermore wouldn't have this slice of dog paradise in Max Baer Park. After seeing leash-free dog parks in Marin, Dr. Plone asked himself, "Why don't we have one in Livermore?" Then he asked the city. In the spring of 1993, Livermore agreed to try it on a six-month trial basis, provided that the park be privately funded. Dr. Plone raised the needed cash from other local veterinarians, and it's been a smashing success ever since.

The half-acre, fenced-in park is level and grassy, with lots of shady trees. Inside the run are disposable scoopers, a water fountain and bowls, and chairs where people can hang out while their dogs romp. On summer evenings, as many as 25 to 30 dogs enjoy the park. "Everybody loves it," Plone says. "It's become a meeting place for people. While their dogs are playing, people form friendships." Jerry Ingledue, the city's parks superintendent, is just as pleased with response to the dog park. He has received more than 20 enthusiastic thank-you notes—more than a few co-signed with paw prints.

From Interstate 580 east, take the Portola exit. Go south on Murietta Boulevard. Turn right on Stanley Boulevard and follow it to Murdell Lane. Turn left on Murdell and go about two miles to the park. To get to the dog park area, park at the far end of the lot and follow the concrete path. (925) 373-5700.

• **Ohlone Regional Wilderness** 🐾🐾🐾🐾 🐕
See ⓲ *on page 28.*

The centerpiece of this magnificent parkland is the 3,817-foot

Rose Peak—only 32 feet lower than Mount Diablo. Leash-free dogs are in heaven on earth as they explore the surrounding 6,758 acres of grassy ridges. Wildlife is abundant, so if your dog isn't obedient, it's best to keep her leashed. The tule elk appreciate it, and your dog will appreciate it, too, should you run into a mountain lion.

The regional parks system shares the wilderness with the San Francisco Water District, which wants to limit the human presence here. Dogs may not stay overnight in the campgrounds.

To enter this wild and breathtaking area east of Sunol Regional Wilderness, you must pick up a permit (which includes a detailed trail map and camping information) for $2 at East Bay Regional Parks headquarters or at the Del Valle, Coyote Hills, or Sunol kiosks. (510) 635-0135.

•**Ohlone Wilderness Trail** 🐾 🐾 🐾 🐾 🐕 *See* **19** *on page 28.*

Some of the area's most remote and peaceful wilderness areas are accessible only by way of this 28-mile trail. The trail stretches from Mission Peak, east of Fremont, through Sunol Regional Wilderness and Ohlone Regional Wilderness to Del Valle Regional Park, south of Livermore. You and your occasionally leash-free dog (signs tell you when it's allowed) will hike through oak and bay woods and grassy uplands that are carpeted with wildflowers in spring.

You'll also see abundant wildlife—if you're quiet and lucky, you might even see an endangered bald eagle. If your dog can't take the pressure of merely watching as tule elk and deer pass by, you should keep him leashed.

A permit is required. Because of some restrictions, you won't be able to do all 28 miles at once with your dog. That's okay. In fact, that's probably just fine with your dog. (510) 635-0135.

•**Sycamore Grove Regional Park** 🐾 🐾 🐾 *See* **20** *on page 28.*

Sycamore Grove is an unusual and attractive streamside park. In rainy times, it can look semi-swampy, as most of the Central Valley used to look. In fact, it is Lake Del Valle's floodplain, and federal flood controllers occasionally send runoff into this park's stream, Arroyo Del Valle, when Lake Del Valle rises too high.

With its low hills, tall grass, and loud sounds of birds and squirrels, it's almost an African savanna. Blackbirds and swallows swoop over the stream and marshy spots, grabbing insects. Poppies are plentiful in spring. Kids, dogs, miniature horses, potbel-lied pigs, and llamas live in harmony here, mostly because every-one obeys the leash law. Water dogs and their kin love wading in the stream pools near the picnic tables. Follow the paths far enough and the place becomes satisfyingly wild.

The park is quite flat, perfect for dogs who don't do well in low gear. Take Interstate 580 to Livermore; exit to Portola Avenue. Go east to North Livermore Avenue and turn right. After 2.5 miles, North Livermore turns into Arroyo Road. Turn right on Wetmore Road. There's a $2 fee. (925) 373-5700.

PLACES TO STAY

Del Valle Regional Park: See Del Valle Regional Park on page 46 for camping information.

Residence Inn by Marriott: These are convenient little apart-ments/suites if you need more than just a room. Rates are $89 to $128, and there's a $75 fee per doggy visit, so you might want to stay a while. Dogs also have to pay $6 extra daily. 1000 Airway Boulevard, Livermore, CA 94550; (925) 373-1800.

OAKLAND

Oakland, the most urban city in the East Bay, is also blessed with a collection of generous and tolerant city parks. Unfortu-nately, what we call the "white gloves" part of Oakland—the parklands ringing Lake Merritt and the Oakland Museum—is off-limits to dogs. But read on. The city now has its very own leash-free dog park. See Hardy Dog Park, page 50.

PARKS, BEACHES, AND RECREATION AREAS

• **Dimond Park** 🐾 🐾 🐾 *See ㉑ on page 28.*

Dimond Park is a small jewel of a canyon, dense and wild in the midst of the city. Your leashed dog's eyes will sparkle when she sees this lush place. The Dimond Canyon Hiking Trail begins to the east of El Centro Avenue. There's a small parking lot at El Centro where it bisects the park. A short foot trail goes off west of El Centro, ending quickly at the Dimond Recreation Center and an attractive jungle gym for children.

The main trail is wide and of smooth dirt. It starts on the east side and follows Sausal Creek about a quarter of a mile up the canyon. At that point, the trail becomes the creek bed, so you can continue only in dry season. But what a quarter mile! The deciduous tangle of trees and ivy makes the canyon into a hushed, cool bower, and the creek is wide and accessible to dogs longing for a splash. When the water level is high enough, there are falls and, except in the driest months, there's enough for a dog pool or two. After the trail goes into the creek bed, the going is a little rougher, but you can follow it all the way to the ridge at the eastern end.

From Interstate 580, take the Fruitvale Avenue exit north to the corner of Fruitvale and Lyman Road, the eastern entrance. Or, to park at the trailhead, take the Park Boulevard exit from Highway 13 and turn left (south) on El Centro Avenue. (510) 482-7831.

• Hardy Dog Park 🐾🐾½ 🐕 *See* 🄬 *on page 28.*

This fenced, quarter-acre patch of packed dirt is the city's first leash-free dog park. We applaud Oakland for taking this step. (A city parks person tells me that this park has been such a success that it could pave the way for other such parks in Oakland.) Hardy Dog Park is not a great park, but at least it's a dog park. And from what I hear, it's going to get bigger and better in the not-too-distant future.

On the plus side, the park has easy freeway access and plenty of shade. On the minus side, the park is right under the freeway, which is what creates the shade. When no other dog people are here, it doesn't feel very safe. Signs at the entrance ask users not to talk loudly. I find that amusing, being that the din of Highway 24 and BART (which also runs overhead) can already create an aural overload.

The fence is very tall, foiling escape artists. There's water for doggy drinking, and a couple of plastic chairs for human sitting. I want to thank Fulton Dog, Mattie Dog, Chelsea Dog, and Isaac Dog for giving us the heads-up about this park. They like it because it's close to the Rockridge Market Center, where they can grab a baked good and a sandwich with their people.

To get to the park from Highway 24, take the Claremont exit and follow Claremont Avenue back under the freeway. The park is under the freeway, at Claremont and Hudson Street. (510) 238-3791.

• Joaquin Miller Park 🐾 🐾🐾 *See* 🄬 *on page 28.*

This large, beautiful city park is nestled at the western edge of the huge Redwood Regional Park (see page 53). If it weren't for the Oakland city parks' rule that dogs must always be leashed,

Joaquin Miller would be dog heaven.

Dogs can't enter some of the landscaped areas, such as around Woodminster Amphitheater. On the deliciously cool and damp creek trails below, however, you and your dog will feel like you own the place.

The West Ridge Trail, reachable from Skyline Boulevard, is popular with mountain bikers. It's waterless, but it's still a good run. The best trails can be entered from the ranger station off Joaquin Miller Road. The Sunset Trail descends about one-eighth of a mile to a cool, ferny stream winding through second- and third-growth redwoods, pines, oak, and laurel. It then ascends to a ridge overlooking cities and the bay. In spring, the ridge is peppered with wildflowers. Plenty of picnic tables and water fountains are scattered throughout the park.

From Highway 13 in Oakland, take the Joaquin Miller Road exit and go one-half mile east to the ranger station. (510) 238-7275.

• **Leona Heights Park** 🐾 🐾 🐾 1/2 *See* **24** *on page 28.*

This park is a miniature version of the incomparable Redwood Regional Park (see page 53), which is most dogs' idea of nirvana. Leona Heights would be among the best parks in the city, if not for Oakland's leash law. Few bikes can negotiate the trails here and few people know about the secluded areas of the park. You're likely to find yourselves on your own in this lush setting.

Park at the entrance on Mountain Boulevard. There are plenty of paths on both sides, but we recommend walking east on Oakleaf Street, past Leona Lodge. The street is actually the York Trail, which follows boulder-lined Horseshoe Creek, with falls and plentiful dog pools. The dirt path is passable for about a quarter mile, over wooden bridges and through glades of eucalyptus, ferns, oak, pines, redwoods, bay, and French broom. When you reach the stream crossing that's lacking a bridge, don't continue unless you're prepared to clamber, slide, and grab trees the rest of the way. Unfortunately, there's a distinct lack of trail maintenance here. Several spots on the York Trail are downright dangerous, and the lack of railings next to steep creek banks and slippery boulders rules out bringing any young kids along.

Take the Redwood Road exit from Highway 13 and go south on Mountain Boulevard. Park when you see the sign for Leona Lodge. There is also a fire trail starting behind Merritt College's recycling center—at the first parking lot on the right on Campus Drive (off Redwood Road). A new hiking trail leading down into the park from this lot will soon be open. (510) 238-6888.

• **Leona Heights Regional Open Space** 🐾🐾🐾 🐕
  See ㉕ on page 28.

Unmarked on most maps, this open space stretches from Merritt College south to Oak Knoll, and from Interstate 580 east to Anthony Chabot Regional Park. Since it's part of the East Bay Regional Parks system, your dog need not be on leash. A bumpy fire trail goes from Merritt College downhill to the southern entrance, just north of Oak Knoll.

The best way to enter is to park at a lot off Canyon Oaks Drive, next to a condominium parking lot. Right at this entrance is a pond, but you won't see any more water as you ascend. It's a dry hike in warm weather.

The fire trail leads gently uphill all the way to Merritt, through coyote brush and oak woodland. In spring, it's full of wildflowers and abuzz with the loud hum of bees. Watch out for poison oak.

From Interstate 580, exit at Keller Avenue and drive east to Campus Drive. Take a left (north), then a left on Canyon Oaks Drive. (510) 635-0135.

• **Martin Luther King Jr. Regional Shoreline (formerly San Leandro Bay Regional Shoreline)** 🐾🐾½
  See ㉖ on page 28.

The Oakland shoreline doesn't have much to offer a dog besides this park, which is well maintained by the East Bay Regional Parks system. And it has a major flaw: The parks system classifies the whole thing as a developed area, so you must leash. The kind of fun a dog most wants—running full-out across grass or swimming in the bay—is illegal.

But you can have a genteel good time on a sunny day that's not too windy, ambling together along the extensive paved bayside trails. Amenities for people are plentiful: picnic tables, a few trees, fountains, a parcourse, a tiny beach, and a huge playing field.

There's a wooden walkway over some mudflats for watching shorebirds and terns fishing. For bird-watching, go at low tide. Keep your dog firmly leashed and held close to you and hike along the San Leandro Creek Channel to Arrowhead Marsh. If you enter from Doolittle Drive, walk along the Doolittle Trail. There's a small sandy beach here, but dogs aren't allowed to swim. (The usual East Bay Regional Parks rules apply: No dogs allowed on beaches.)

From Interstate 880, exit at Hegenberger Road in Oakland. Go west on Hegenberger and turn on Edgewater Drive, Pardee Drive, or Doolittle Drive. Parking is free at each of these entry points. (510) 635-0135.

• **Redwood Regional Park** 🐾 🐾 🐾 🐾 🐕 *See* ㉗ *on page 28.*

Although it's just a few miles over the ridge from downtown Oakland, Redwood Regional Park is about as far as you can get from urbanity while still within the scope of the Bay Area. Dogs who love nature at its best, and love it even more off leash, adore the 1,836-acre park. People who need to get far from the madding crowd also go gaga over the place.

The park is delectable year-round, but it's a particularly wonderful spot to visit when you need to cool off from hot summer weather. Much of the park is a majestic forest of 150-foot coast redwoods (known to those with scientific tongues as *Sequoia sempervirens*). The redwoods provide drippy cool shade most of the time, which is a real boon for dogs with hefty coats. Back in the mid-1800s, this area was heavily logged for building supplies for San Francisco, and it wasn't a pretty sight. But fortunately, sometimes progress progresses backward, and the fallen trees have some splendid replacements.

There's something for every dog's tastes here. In addition to the redwoods, the park is also home to pine, eucalyptus, madrone, flowering fruit trees, chaparral, and grasslands. Wild critters like the park, too, so leash up immediately if there's any hint of a deer, rabbit, or other woodland creatures around. Many dogs, even "good" dogs, aren't able to withstand the temptation to chase.

Mud is inevitable if you follow the Stream Trail, so be sure to keep a towel in the car. Water dogs may try to dip their paws in Redwood Creek, which runs through the park. But please don't let them. This is a very sensitive area. Rainbow trout spawn here after migrating from a reservoir downstream, and it's not an easy trip for them. If you and your dog need to splash around somewhere, try the ocean, the bay, or your bathtub. At press time, the East Bay Regional Parks District was looking at making dogs leash up along the Stream Trail to prevent any "foe paws." Please keep your eyes peeled for signage, in case this goes through.

No parking fee is charged at Skyline Gate at the north end (in Contra Costa County—the park straddles Contra Costa and Alameda Counties). Entering here also lets you avoid the tempting smells of picnic tables at the south end. The Stream Trail leads steadily downhill, then takes a steep plunge to the canyon bottom. It's uphill all the way back, but it's worth it. From Highway 13, exit at Joaquin Miller Road and head east to Skyline Boulevard. Turn left on Skyline and go four miles to the Skyline Gate.

If you prefer to go to the main entrance on Redwood Road, exit Highway 13 at Carson/Redwood Road and drive east on Redwood Road. Once you pass Skyline Boulevard, continue two miles on Redwood. The park and parking will be on your left. The Redwood Road entrance charges a $3 parking fee and a $1 dog fee. (510) 635-0135.

RESTAURANTS

Oakland's College Avenue, in the Rockridge district, has a tolerant family atmosphere. Lawyers with briefcases buy flowers on the way home from the BART station, and students flirt over ice cream. I've never seen anyone in this neighborhood who didn't love dogs. Even so, you should leash for safety on this busy street.

The avenue is known to be a food lover's paradise, and among the attractions are a string of restaurants with outdoor tables.

Cafe Rustica: The pizza here is elegant. Eat it at the outdoor tables with your drooling dog. 5422 College Avenue; (510) 654-1601.

Oliveto Cafe: This cafe and Peaberry's, next door, share a building with the Market Hall, God's own food emporium. The food's the best, but for a dog, the atmosphere is congested. It's not for nervous dogs. Oliveto serves very classy pizza, tapas, bar food, desserts, coffees, and drinks, but alcohol is not allowed at the sidewalk tables. 5655 College Avenue, just south of Rockridge BART; (510) 547-5356.

Peaberry's: Enjoy coffees, pastries, and desserts at the outdoor tables here. This is a favorite with BART commuters. 5655 College Avenue; (510) 653-0450.

Royal Coffee: This is a cheery and popular place with very good coffee (in the bean or in the cup), tea, and supplies. On weekend mornings, it's dog central. 307 63rd Street at College Avenue; (510) 653-5458.

Salty Dog: Located at the end of the pier in Jack London Square, this sandwich shop has four outside tables where you and your dog can chow down. The Salty Dog crew will even give your thirsty dog a bowl of water.

When asked what the specialties are, the owner said, "We make 25 different sandwiches and they're all special." On Sundays in the summer, after strolling through the farmers market, you might enjoy the barbecued burgers and spareribs while watching the sailboats cut across the estuary. 53 Jack London Square; (510) 452-2563.

PLACES TO STAY

Clarion Suites Lake Merritt Hotel: Dogs dig the lovely digs here. Some suites with kitchenettes are available. Rates are $109 to $149. Be sure to stay a while if you bring your dog, because there's a $75-per-visit pet fee, in addition to a $75 deposit. 1800 Madison Avenue, Oakland, CA 94612; (510) 832-2300.

Oakland Airport Hilton: They prefer the tinier pooches here. In fact, you'll need a ruler because the rule is that dogs must be no more than 12 inches high. Rates are $144 to $164. Dogs are $10 extra, and there's a $200 deposit. 1 Hegenberger Road, Oakland, CA 94614; (510) 635-5000.

DOGGY DAYS

Give your paw: The Oakland SPCA boasts one of the oldest dog walks in the country, with activities that include a two-mile run, a one-mile walk, an alumni parade (bring a hanky, this one's sweet), and various contests. The paper-retrieving contest is a fun one to watch, and has proven inspirational to more than one couch-potato dog (or at least his person). At last count, about 1,000 walkers and their dogs attended the event, usually held the first Sunday of October at the San Leandro Marina Par Course. Call (510) 569-2591 for details.

DIVERSIONS

Rent a flick together: The Video Room videotape rental store is so doggone dog-friendly that not only can pooches come in and help you choose a movie, they get a big dog biscuit just for accompanying you. If you have a choice between renting a video here or at a big chain store, give this medium-sized shop a shot. Your dog will be glad you did. 4364 Piedmont Avenue; (510) 655-6844.

Don't Eat the Furniture!: It's an admonition that has a familiar ring to dogs with splinters in their gums. It's also the name of an eclectic furniture/arts/pet supply store that welcomes well-behaved dogs. Actually, Don't Eat the Furniture! is just the first half of the name. The second half: For Pets and the People They Own. Aww.

You and your pooch can shop for unique furniture, including pieces made in Indonesia from "recycled" mahogany. Owner Rose Nied and her faithful briard, Lulu, have also filled the small store with hundreds of other unusual, high-quality items, such as gargoyles, cards, books, jewelry, and an interesting assortment of pet goodies. It's the perfect place to shop for someone who has everything (including your dog). 4024 Piedmont Avenue; (510) 601-PETS.

Seize the Bay: Ahoy doggies! Pooches who enjoy the bay are thrilled to learn that they're allowed on the Blue & Gold Fleet's ferries that run between Oakland, Alameda, and San Francisco. Please turn to page 181 in the San Francisco chapter for more details on this salty adventure.

PIEDMONT

Piedmont, the incorporated town in the midst of Oakland, is almost entirely residential and very proper and clean. This means you won't be able to find a stray scrap of paper to scoop with, so be prepared. Its quiet streets are delightful for walking, offering views from the hills.

Piedmont has no official park curfews. "We don't have the kind of parks people would be in after dark," says a woman at the city's recreation department, and it's true.

PARKS, BEACHES, AND RECREATION AREAS

• **Beach Park** 🐾 🐾 🐕 *See ㉘ on page 28.*

It's not beachy here, and it's not parky either. But hey, it's off leash, so we have to give it a couple of paws. This is just a strip of pavement running down a narrow patch of grass about the length of one city block. There's some shade. The "park" is set along a hill, but it's too close to a couple of roads for true off-leash comfort—at least with a dog like Joe.

Beach Park is across from Beach School, at Linda and Lake Avenues. You'll see the little doggy signs. (510) 420-3070.

• Dracena Park 🐾🐾🐾🐾 🐕 *See ㉙ on page 28.*

Parts of this park are grassy, with tall shade trees here and there. But the part dogs long for is the off-leash section. It's a lovely area, with a paved path up and down a wooded, secluded hill. Tall firs and eucalyptus provide plenty of shade, and sometimes it's so quiet here you can hear several kinds of birds. The area isn't fenced, and at the top and bottom there's potential for escape artists to run into the road, so be careful and leash up at these points if you have any doggy doubts.

Pooper-scoopers are provided. Be sure to scoop the poop, because the fines are stiff—the equivalent of several 40-pound bags of dog food, or $200. The trail takes about 15 minutes round-trip, if you assume a very leisurely pace. We like to enter on Artuna Avenue at Ricardo Avenue, because it's safest from traffic and parking's plentiful on the park side of the street. But lots of folks enter at Blair and Dracena Avenues. (510) 420-3070.

• Piedmont Park 🐾🐾🐾🐾 🐕 *See ㉚ on page 28.*

The huge off-leash section of this beautiful park is one of the best examples of a leash-free dog area in the state. A few salmon-pink concrete pathways lead you and your happy dog alongside a gurgling stream and up and down the hills around the stream. It's absolutely gorgeous and serene back here. (On our last visit, a hummingbird greeted us at the entrance, and was back again when we left.) The park smells like heaven, with eucalyptus, redwood, acacia, pine, and deep, earthy scents wafting around everywhere. It reminds me of a serene Japanese garden, minus the Japanese plants.

The stream is fed year-round by a spring higher in the hills. This is pure bliss for dogs during the summer months. The trails for dogs and their people run on the cooler side anyway, with all the tall trees. Almost the entire leash-free section is set in a deep canyon, so it's very safe from traffic. A leisurely round-trip stroll will take you about an hour, if you want it to. Pooper-scoopers are supplied at a few strategically located stations along the paths. Use them. The fine for not scooping is about $200, and the police station flanks the park.

A hint if you want your walk to be as peaceful as possible: Don't come here during the school year around lunchtime or quittin' time for school. The high school at the top of a hill on the other side of the stream can spew forth some very loud students at those times. On one ill-timed visit, a couple of them were throwing glass bottles into the stream. Joe Dog almost got thwacked right in the ol' kisser.

Joe and I want to thank Lady Golden Rod and her person, Anna Castagnozzie Bush, for the tip that led us to this magnificent park. They thought this piece of dog heaven was too good to keep from other dogs.

To get to the leash-free section of this elegant park, come in through the main entrance at Highland and Magnolia Avenues. You'll see a willow tree just as you enter. Continue on the path past the willow tree and follow it down to the left side of the stream. You'll see signs for the dog area. Be sure to leash up in other parts of the park, should you explore beyond the stream area. (510) 420-3070.

PLEASANTON

PARKS, BEACHES, AND RECREATION AREAS

• **Pleasanton Ridge Regional Park** 🐾 🐾 🐾 🐾 🐕
  See ③ on page 28.

This fairly recent and beautiful addition to the East Bay Regional Parks system is an isolated treat. Dogs may run off leash on all the secluded trails here as soon as you leave the staging area.

You can access Pleasanton Ridge from either Foothill or Golden Eagle Roads. At the Foothill Staging Area, there are fine picnic sites at the trailhead. Climb up on the Oak Tree fire trail to the ridgeline, where a looping set of trails goes off to the right. The incline is gentle, through pasture (you share this park with cattle) dotted with oak and—careful—poison oak. Wildflowers riot in spring. It's a hot place in summer. At the bottom of the park, however, is a beautiful streamside stretch along Arroyo de la Laguna. There's no water above the entrance, so be sure to carry plenty.

From Interstate 680, take the Castlewood Drive exit and go left (west) on Foothill Road to the staging area. (510) 635-0135.

PLACES TO STAY

Crown Plaza: Rates are $60 to $135. Dogs require a $50 deposit. 11950 Dublin Canyon Road, Pleasanton, CA 94588; (925) 847-6000.

Doubletree Hotel: Rates are $60 to $100. Dogs are $15 extra. 5990 Stoneridge Mall Road, Pleasanton, CA 94588; (925) 463-3330.

SAN LEANDRO

DOGGY DAYS

Hustle your tail for a good cause: On the first Sunday of October, the Oakland Society for the Prevention of Cruelty to Animals holds a fund-raising dog run. You and your dog can do a two-mile run or a scenic one-mile walk, watch the World Canine Frisbee Champs perform, or enter contests—goofy pet tricks, tail-wagging, that sort of thing. It's held in the San Leandro Marina. For this year's date and info on fees, call the Oakland SPCA at (510) 569-0702.

CONTRA COSTA COUNTY

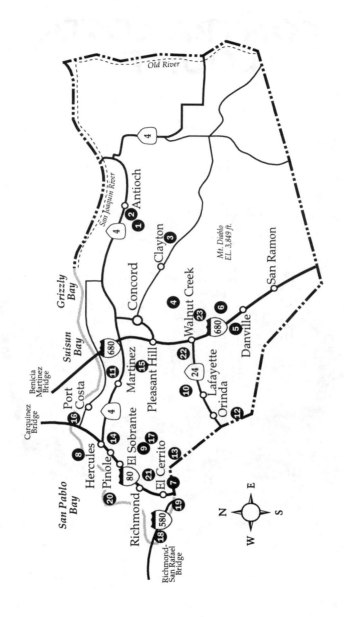

2
CONTRA COSTA COUNTY

Although much of Contra Costa County is considered a sleepy bedroom community for San Francisco, it's a rip-roaring frontierland of fun for dogs. From the renowned off-leash dog haven of Point Isabel Regional Shoreline (see page 75) to the leash-free inland nirvanas such as the Morgan Territory (see page 65), this county enables every dog to have her day, day after day.

For dogs who like long hikes through highly diverse lands, 10 long regional trails lace Lafayette, Walnut Creek, and the other urban areas of the Diablo Valley. There are 62 miles of trails in all, linking together a dozen towns and many beautiful parklands. Dogs must be leashed, but with all the horses and bikes that can visit here, it's a sensible rule.

The Briones to Diablo Regional Trail is one of the more popular trails. It's about 12 miles long and it snakes through some terrific parkland, including the off-leash wonderlands of the Acalanes Ridge Open Space Recreation Area (see page 79) and the Shell Ridge Open Space Recreation Area (see page 79). The trail, which is part paved/part dirt, starts at Briones Regional Park's Lafayette Ridge Staging Area, located on Pleasant Hill Road just north of Highway 24.

The Contra Costa Canal Regional Trail is a good one for dogs who like to look at water but not set foot in it. Joe loves this 12-mile trail that follows the off-limits canal. For information and a trail map of all 10 regional trails, call (510) 635-0135.

ANTIOCH

Antioch is pretty much a desert for dogs, but south of town are two charming spots of relief.

PARKS, BEACHES, AND RECREATION AREAS
• **Black Diamond Mines Regional Preserve** 🐾🐾🐾🐾 🐕
See ❶ on page 62.
Leash-free dogs, especially leash-free dogs of the male persua-

sion, think this park is an excellent place to visit. The coal miners who worked and lived here in the 1862s and 1870s planted a variety of drought-tolerant trees not usually found in the East Bay, including something called "trees of heaven." Dogs who sniff these trees seem to know why they're called trees of heaven. Their noses just can't get enough as they press them deep into the bark.

The hills of Black Diamond Mines are jumbled and ragged, looking a lot like the Sierra foothills. From the parking lot, it's a moderate climb to the Rose Hill Cemetery, where Protestant Welsh miners (the tombstones bear the names Davis, Evans, and Jenkins) buried victims of mine accidents and many of their children, who died of diphtheria, typhoid, and scarlet fever.

Plenty of tunnel openings and piles of tailings have been preserved by the park for walkers to examine. A brochure marks mine sites. You should be alert for rattlers during warm seasons, although any rattler not actually snoozing will probably get out of your way before you even know he's near.

You can walk into this East Bay regional preserve from the Contra Loma Regional Park just below it (see below). But from that direction, the trails are too hot and dry for a dog in summer. Instead, enter from the north by car via Somersville Road and park in the last lot, which has some shady trees.

From Highway 4 at Antioch, exit at Somersville Road and drive south to the park entrance. Keep driving for a bit more than one mile if you want to park in the lot farthest in. You'll pass wonderful old mining-era houses and barns, now used as park headquarters and offices. (510) 635-0135.

• **Contra Loma Regional Park** 🐾 🐾 *See ❷ on page 62.*

This 776-acre park is so well hidden amid barren hills north of Black Diamond Mines that you might not ever know it was here. A few attractive trails, including a trail leading into Black Diamond Mines Regional Preserve (see previous listing), rise into the surrounding hills for you and your leash-free dog to explore.

Unfortunately, as in all regional parks, your dog may not accompany you in the swimming area. Nor can he take an informal swim himself in the fishing areas, since the park managers want to protect his feet from stray fishhooks. It's probably better not to bring your dog here on a hot day. Instead, save the trip for winter or spring, when the wildflowers burst open.

From Highway 4, take the Lone Tree Way exit. Go south on Lone Tree for a little more than a half mile, then turn right onto Bluerock Drive. Follow Bluerock along the park's east side to the entrance. The fee for parking is $3 or $4, depending on the season. The dog fee is $1. (510) 635-0135.

CLAYTON

PARKS, BEACHES, AND RECREATION AREAS

• **Morgan Territory Regional Preserve** 🐾🐾🐾🐾 🐕

See ❸ on page 62.

Morgan Territory, named after a farmer who owned the land long before it became part of the East Bay Regional Parks system, is as far away from the Bay Area as you can get while still being in the Bay Area. From its heights, on a rim above the Central Valley, you see the San Joaquin River, the Delta, the valley, and, on a clear day, the peaks of the Sierra. Eagles and hawks soar above as you and your leash-free pooch explore ancient twisted giant oaks and lichen-covered sandstone outcrops below. Morgan Territory is close to the end of the earth and well worth the journey.

As the crow flies, Morgan Territory is equidistant from Clayton, Danville, San Ramon, Livermore, Byron, and Brentwood. And "distant" is the key word.

This 2,164-acre preserve has miles of hiking and riding trails. If you don't want to climb much but want great views of the Central Valley, try the Blue Oak Trail, which starts at the entrance. You'll even see the "backside" of Mount Diablo. It's an unusual vantage point for Bay Area folks.

Most of the creeks are dry in the summer, though your dog can splash into cattle ponds, if he's so inclined. Watch for wicked foxtails in these grasses. These are the sticky wickets that help make veterinarians a well-off breed.

The easiest access is from Livermore in Alameda County. From Interstate 580, take the North Livermore Avenue exit and drive north on North Livermore Avenue. Shortly after the road curves left (west), turn right, onto Morgan Territory Road, and follow it 10.7 miles to the entrance. From the Walnut Creek/Concord area, take Clayton Road to Marsh Creek Road, then turn right onto Morgan Territory Road. The entrance is 9.4 miles from Marsh Creek Road. (510) 635-0135.

RESTAURANTS

Skipolini's Pizza: The folks here serve New York–style pizza, as well as salads and sandwiches. They welcome dogs at their outdoor tables. It's at Main Street and Diablo Road; (925) 672-5555.

CONCORD

PARKS, BEACHES, AND RECREATION AREAS

Most of Concord's parks are run-of-the-mill on-leash parks. But for a real treat, try this one:

•**Lime Ridge Open Space Recreation Area** 🐾🐾🐾🐾 ➤
See ❹ on page 62.

This open space reserve is huge, sprawling across parts of both Walnut Creek and Concord. It's undeveloped and open to lucky leash-free dogs. You can sometimes find a creek, depending on the time of year and status of drought, and that's a real relief during the long, hot summers.

The only entry point from Concord is from the parking lot on Treat Boulevard west of Cowell Road. (925) 671-3270.

PLACES TO STAY

Holiday Inn Concord: Rates are $79 to $99. Dogs require a $50 deposit. 1050 Burnett Avenue, Concord, CA 94520; (925) 687-5500.

Sheraton Concord Hotel: "Smallish" dogs only at this attractive hotel, which features a 23,000-square-foot atrium (with a swimming pool . . . ahhhh . . . but not for dogs) and an exercise facility (also not for dogs, which is fine with Joe). Rates are $95 to $139. Dogs are $10 extra. 45 John Glenn Drive, Concord, CA 94520; (925) 825-7700.

DANVILLE

PARKS, BEACHES, AND RECREATION AREAS

•**Las Trampas Regional Wilderness** 🐾🐾🐾🐾 ➤
See ❺ on page 62.

This regional wilderness is remarkable for its sense of isolation from the rest of the Bay Area. You can experience utter silence at this 3,62-acre park, and the views from the ridge tops are breathtaking.

Rocky Ridge Trail (from the parking lot at the end of Bollinger

Canyon Road) takes you and your leash-free pooch on a fairly steep three-quarter-mile ascent to the top of the ridge, where you'll enter the East Bay Municipal Utility District watershed. Since dogs aren't allowed here and permits are even required for humans, it's better to head west on any of several trails climbing the sunny southern flanks of Las Trampas Ridge.

Creeks run low or dry during the summer, so bring plenty of water. Your dog should know how to behave around cattle, deer, and horses.

From Interstate 680 about six miles north of the intersection with Interstate 580, take the Bollinger Canyon Road exit and head north on Bollinger Canyon Road to the entrance. (Go past the entrance to Little Hills Ranch Recreation Area, where dogs aren't allowed.) (510) 635-0135.

•**Oak Hill Park** 🐾🐾🐾 *See* ❻ *on page 62.*

Here's a very clean, beautiful park run by the city of Danville. It's about as good as a park designed for people can get, offering picnic tables, a pond with ducks and geese and waterfalls, volleyball and tennis courts, and an unusually attractive children's play area with swings, a slide, and its own waterfall. The rest of the park is natural oak-studded hillside laced by an equestrian/hiking/exercise dirt trail, from which there is a fine view of Mount Diablo. Dogs will enjoy this path, but must remain on leash. No wading in the pond, either.

The park is at Stone Valley Road and Glenwood Court. (925) 820-6274.

PLACES TO STAY

Danville Inn: Rates are $62 to $90. 803 Camino Ramon, Danville, CA 94526; (925) 838-8080.

EL CERRITO

PARKS, BEACHES, AND RECREATION AREAS

•**Hillside Park** 🐾🐾🐾🐕 *See* ❼ *on page 62.*

El Cerrito dogs have something to bark about: Hillside Park, an official off-leash dog run. It's not the prettiest park around; the southern end is mostly an eroded hillside of scrubby grass with power lines. But off Schmidt Lane is the much more attractive El

Cerrito Foundation Memorial Grove. A bumpy dirt path leads up through coyote brush to eucalyptus groves at the hilltop, over-looking El Cerrito, the Golden Gate and Bay Bridges, and Mount Tamalpais. The trail doesn't go far into the open space.

Enter off Schmidt Lane, which runs north off San Pablo Avenue. (510) 215-4300.

EL SOBRANTE

PARKS, BEACHES, AND RECREATION AREAS

• **Sobrante Ridge Regional Preserve** 🐾 🐾 🐾 🐾 🐕
See ❽ on page 62.

Dogs love visiting this quiet preserve, but Sobrante Ridge hasn't always been a place where animals smile. In the 1970s, the property belonged to Cutter Laboratories, which raised horses and cattle and used their blood to produce various vaccines. That breeze you may feel while visiting is just an equine and bovine sigh of relief that Cutter is outta here.

These days, Sobrante is a happy place, full of deer, coyotes, sala-manders, and oodles of birds. Unless your dog is under perfect voice control, it's a good idea to use a leash here. From the Coach Way entrance, follow the dirt trail branching back to the left 100 feet from the entrance. This is the Sobrante Ridge Trail, which will take you through grass, dwarf manzanita, oaks, and coyote brush, up a half mile to views of both Mount Tam and the top of Mount Diablo. Branch off on the short loop, Broken Oaks Trail, for a pic-nic at one of the tables under cool oaks.

This 277-acre preserve is the habitat of the extremely rare Alameda manzanita. So that your dog knows what to watch out for, this manzanita is a gnarled, red-barked shrub that may have sprays of urn-shaped blossoms or clusters of red berries, depend-ing on the time of year. The manzanitas cling to the hillsides. Don't let your boy dog do anything the manzanitas wouldn't want him to do.

From Interstate 80 in Richmond, exit at San Pablo Dam Road and drive south to Castro Ranch Road. Turn left on Castro Ranch, then left at Conestoga Way, going into the Carriage Hills housing development. Take another left on Carriage Drive and a right on Coach Way. Park at the end of Coach and walk into the preserve. (510) 635-0135.

HERCULES

PARKS, BEACHES, AND RECREATION AREAS

• **San Pablo Bay Shoreline Park** 😊 😊 😊 ½ 🐕
See ⑨ on page 62.

This tiny, undeveloped East Bay Regional Park shoreline is just right if you happen to be in Hercules exploring the old Santa Fe Railroad yard. A paved trail runs about one-eighth of a mile along the tracks. New housing developments and interesting restored Victorian railroad workers' housing surround a small but pretty area of grass, swamp, and eucalyptus trees. Best of all, you and your dog can check it all out without a leash.

If you follow Railroad Avenue to its end, across the line into Pinole, there's a very small and beautifully landscaped city park behind the wastewater treatment plant (which smells fresh as a rose). You must keep your dog on leash here.

From Interstate 80, exit at Pinole Valley Road and travel north. Pinole Valley Road becomes Tennent Avenue, then Railroad Avenue. Park somewhere around the Civic Arts Facility, a cluster of Victorian buildings in a grove of palms and eucalyptuses. Call (510) 724-9004 or (510) 635-0135.

LAFAYETTE

PARKS, BEACHES, AND RECREATION AREAS

• **Briones Regional Park** 😊 😊 😊 😊 🐕 *See ⑩ on page 62.*

From both main entrances to this park, you can walk one-quarter of a mile and be lost in sunny, rolling hills or cool oak woodlands. Unless you stick to the stream areas, it's not a good park for hot summer days. But with a good supply of your own water, you and your dog, who may run blissfully leashless, can walk gentle ups and downs all day on fire roads or foot trails.

The north entrance requires an immediate uphill climb into the hills, but you're rewarded with a quick view of Mount Diablo and the piping of ground squirrels, all of whom are long gone safely into their burrows by the time your dog realizes they might be fun to chase (much to Joe's chagrin). If your dog is a self-starter, this end of the park is fine for you. The Alhambra Creek Trail, which follows Alhambra Creek, does offer water in the rainy season. Stay away from the John Muir Nature Area (shaded on your brochure map), where dogs aren't allowed.

When we're feeling lazy, we prefer the south entrance at Bear Creek, just east of the inaccessible (to dogs) Briones Reservoir. Here you have an immediate choice of open hills or woodsy canyons, and the land is level for a few miles. The Homestead Valley Trail leads gently up and down through cool, sharp-scented bay and oak woodlands.

Watch for deer, horses, and cattle. Some dogs near and dear to me (they shall remain nameless, Joe and Bill) love rolling in fresh cow patties—an additional hazard of the beasts existing in close proximity.

From Highway 24, take the Orinda exit; go north on Camino Pablo, then right on Bear Creek Road to Briones Road, to the park entrance. The parking fee is $3 and the dog fee is $1. (510) 635-0135.

RESTAURANTS

Geppetto's Cafe: Gourmet coffee, gelati, and pastries may be enjoyed at sidewalk tables. Dogs are welcome. It's a good spot for a cool drink after a hot summer hike in Briones. 3563 Mount Diablo Boulevard; (925) 284-1261.

MARTINEZ

Martinez has a charming historic district right off the entrance to its regional shoreline park, so spend some time walking with your dog around the Amtrak station and antique shops. You'll see plenty of fellow strollers taking a break from the train.

PARKS, BEACHES, AND RECREATION AREAS

• **City of Martinez Hidden Lakes Open Space** 🐾🐾🐾
See ⓫ on page 62.

Although the city park called Hidden Valley Park doesn't allow dogs, the open space to the south of it does. It's crossed by one of the East Bay Regional Parks' trails (the California Riding and Hiking Trail) on its way from the Carquinez Strait Regional Shoreline to where it connects with the Contra Costa Canal Trail. Call (510) 635-0135 to order a map of the Contra Costa Regional Trails.

One entrance to Hidden Lakes is off Morello Avenue, where it intersects with Chilpancingo Parkway. (925) 313-0930.

ORINDA
PARKS, BEACHES, AND RECREATION AREAS

• **Robert Sibley Volcanic Regional Preserve** 🐾🐾🐾🐾 🐕
See ⑫ *on page 62.*

We're not exactly talking Mount St. Helens here, but this 371-acre park has some pretty interesting volcanic history. Geologically inclined dogs can wander leashless as you explore volcanic dikes, mudflows, lava flows, and other evidence of extinct volcanoes.

The preserve is actually closer to Oakland than Orinda, but it lies in Contra Costa County. From the entrance on Skyline Boulevard, you can get on the East Bay Skyline National Recreation Trail and walk north to Tilden Regional Park (see page 35) or south to Redwood Regional Park (see page 53). Or, for a shorter stroll, take the road to Round Top, the highest peak in the Berkeley Hills, made of volcanic debris left over from a 10-million-year-old volcano.

More attractive and less steep is the road to the quarries. It's partly paved and smooth enough for a wheelchair or stroller, but it becomes smooth dirt about halfway to the quarries. Both trails are labeled for geological features. (Pick up a brochure at the visitors center.) At the quarry pits, there's a good view of Mount Diablo. This is a dry, scrubby, cattle-grazed area, but in the rainy season your dog may be lucky enough to find swimming in a pit near the quarries. In the spring, look for poppies and lupines.

From Highway 24 east of the Caldecott Tunnel, exit on Fish Ranch Road, drive north to Grizzly Peak Boulevard, then take a left. Go south on Grizzly Peak to the intersection with Skyline Boulevard. Go left on Skyline. The entrance is just to the east of the intersection. (510) 635-0135.

• **San Pablo Dam Reservoir** 🐾🐾🐾½ *See* ⑬ *on page 62.*

This reservoir is a top fishing spot in the Bay Area. It's stocked with more trout than any lake in California. That's great news for humans, but dogs could care less. They're not allowed to set paw in this magnificent body of water (and neither are people), so hanging out alongside a human angler is out of the question. You can't even take your pooch out on your own boat.

The paved and dirt trails around the reservoir are lovely and often empty once you and your leashed dog wind into the hills. The dirt trails get rougher as you leave the popular fishing areas. You'll have to ford some creek beds or streams, and there's too much poison oak for comfort if your dog doesn't step daintily right down the middle of the trail. The trails are wild and woodsy, though, and dogs recommend them highly.

The entrance fee is $5 for parking and $1 for dogs. You can buy a season ticket for $75 a car or $80 a boat. The lake itself is open from mid-February through mid-November.

From Interstate 80, exit at San Pablo Dam Road and drive east about six miles. From Highway 24, exit at Camino Pablo/San Pablo Dam Road and go north about 5.5 miles. (510) 223-1661.

RESTAURANTS

High Tech Burrito: The burritos and fajitas here are really, really good. The ingredients are fresh and combined in very interesting ways. Try the veggie burrito. It's *muy bien*. Dogs can dine with you (no spicy scraps, please!) at the many courtyard tables at Theatre Square. 2 Theatre Square; (925) 254-8884.

Pasta Cuisine: Of all the yummy pastas, soups, and salads served here, the one dish I've heard the most raves about is the special Caesar salad. It's made with smoked chicken and prawns. Joe drools just thinking about it. I get hives just thinking about it (allergic to shellfish). You can dine with doggy at the courtyard tables at Theatre Square. But beware: A server here tells us that patrons sometimes bring cats. If your dog thinks cats are entrées, keep your eyes peeled. 2 Theatre Square; (925) 254-5423.

PINOLE

PARKS, BEACHES, AND RECREATION AREAS

• **Pinole Valley Park** 🐾 🐾 🐾 *See* **⑭** *on page 62.*

This city park is fortunate enough to be contiguous with Sobrante Ridge Regional Preserve (see page 68). The paved bike path off to the right past the children's playground leads to Alhambra Creek—a good plunge for your dog, if he can negotiate the banks wearing a leash. The path then becomes a fire trail and ambles through brush, oaks, and nicely varied deciduous trees. This trail is quite wild and litter-free. It ends at an outlet on Alhambra Road.

The entrance is at Pinole Valley Road and Simas Avenue. (510) 724-9062.

PLACES TO STAY

Motel 6: Rates are $47 for the first adult and $6 for the second. This Motel 6, like most others, permits one small pooch per room. 1501 Fitzgerald Drive, Pinole, CA 94564; (510) 222-8174.

PLEASANT HILL

PARKS, BEACHES, AND RECREATION AREAS

• **Paso Nogal Park** 😺😺😺😺 🐕 *See* **15** *on page 62.*

This large park has smooth dirt trails along gentle oak-dotted slopes. Dogs must be on leash in the park, but locals use the lawn area as a leash-free dog run. Owners are expected to carry a leash, clean up after their dogs (there are no scoopers available), and cooperate with park rangers if there's a complaint. But "no complaint, no problem" is the operable phrase here.

The park is at Morello Avenue and Paso Nogal Road. (925) 682-0896.

PORT COSTA

Port Costa is a sleepy, picturesque town of Victorian cottages. In the nineteenth century, it was a booming wheat export dock. Of course, if your dog remembers Frank Norris' book *The Octopus*, he already knows this.

PARKS, BEACHES, AND RECREATION AREAS

• **Carquinez Strait Regional Shoreline** 😺😺😺😺 🐕
See **16** *on page 62.*

This regional shoreline, run by the East Bay Regional Parks, lies just east of Crockett. From the Bull Valley Staging Area, on Carquinez Scenic Drive, you can choose one of two leash-free hillside trails. The Carquinez Overlook Loop, to the right, gives better views of Port Costa, the Carquinez Bridge, and Benicia. We surprised a deer here sleeping in the shade of a clump of eucalyptus.

The eastern portion of the park, east of Port Costa, is contiguous with Martinez Regional Shoreline. But beware: You can't get there from here. (Carquinez Scenic Drive is closed at a spot between Port Costa and Martinez. You must turn south on twisty McEwen Road to Highway 4 instead.)

To get to the Carquinez Strait Regional Shoreline from Interstate 80, exit at Crockett and drive east on Pomona Street through town. Pomona turns into Carquinez Scenic Drive, from which you'll see the staging area. (510) 635-0135.

RICHMOND

Point Richmond, the Richmond neighborhood tucked between the Richmond–San Rafael Bridge and Miller-Knox Regional Shoreline, is a cheerful small-town hangout for you and your dog. Consider stopping by for a snack on your way to some of the magical, four-paw shoreline here.

Sit on a bench in the Point Richmond Triangle, the town center. You'll be surrounded by nicely preserved Victorian buildings, the Hotel Mac, and many delis and bakeries, some with outdoor tables. We were asked not to mention one by name because it welcomes cats as well as dogs. Grrrr. The Santa Fe Railroad rattles past periodically, blowing the first two notes of "Here Comes the Bride."

From Interstate 580, on the Richmond end of the Richmond–San Rafael Bridge, exit at Cutting Boulevard and drive west to town. Bear right on Richmond Avenue. The Triangle is at the intersection of Richmond and Washington Avenues and Park Place.

PARKS, BEACHES, AND RECREATION AREAS

• **Kennedy Grove Regional Recreation Area** 🐾 🐾 🐾
See **17** *on page 62.*

This is a large picnic and play area for folks who like softball, volleyball, and horseshoes. Dogs must be leashed. The best part of this park is that you can get to the Bay Area Ridge Trail from here from a gate to the right as you enter the park, or from a trailhead at the Senior Parking Area. You'll cross some East Bay Municipal Utility District land (no permits necessary in this section) and San Pablo Dam Road. The trail ascends and soon becomes the Eagle's Nest Trail. If you're really inspired and your pooch isn't pooped, you can then climb all the way to Inspiration Point in Tilden Regional Park (see page 35). Dogs like Joe firmly put their paw down when it comes to such rigorous tasks. He just sits there riveted to the ground like a fire hydrant. You can almost see him shaking his head "no way."

From Interstate 80, take the San Pablo Dam Road exit and go south; the entrance is a quarter-mile past the intersection of Castro

Ranch Road. There's a $3 parking fee and $1 dog fee from April through October. (510) 635-0135.

• **Miller-Knox Regional Shoreline** 🐾🐾🐾🐾 🐕
   See ⑱ on page 62.

Hooray! Wooooof! Yap! (The last utterance was from a dogette—the kind Joe likes to pretend is a cat.) Although your dog must be leashed in developed areas, she can run free on the hillside trails east of Dornan Drive in this 259-acre park.

West of Dornan is a generous expanse of grass, pine, and eucalyptus trees with picnic tables, a lagoon with egrets (so there's no swimming), and Keller Beach (dogs are prohibited). It's breezy here and prettier than most shoreline parks by virtue of its protecting gentle hills, whose trails offer terrific views of the Richmond–San Rafael Bridge, Mount Tamalpais, Angel Island, and San Francisco. Ground squirrels stand right by their holes and pipe their alarms. Although you can't bring your dog onto Keller Beach, there's a paved path above it along riprap shoreline, where your dog can reach the water if he's so inclined. In the picnic areas, watch for discarded chicken bones!

You can also tour the Richmond Yacht Harbor by continuing on Dornan Drive south to Brickyard Cove Road, a left turn past the railroad tracks. Or, from Garrard Boulevard, drive south till you see the Brickyard Cove housing development. The paved paths lining the harbor offer views of yachts, San Francisco, Oakland, and the Bay Bridge.

From either Interstate 80 or Interstate 580, exit at Cutting Boulevard and go west to Garrard Boulevard. Go left, pass through a tunnel, and park in one of two lots off Dornan Drive. (510) 635-0135.

• **Point Isabel Regional Shoreline** 🐾🐾🐾🐾 🐕
   See ⑲ on page 62.

One exception to the East Bay Regional Parks' rule that dogs must be on leash in "developed" areas is Point Isabel Regional Shoreline. This is a decidedly unwild but terrific shoreline park with plenty of grass and paw-friendly paved paths. It's swarming with dogs. In a recent census by the park district, 558,930 people and 784,370 pooches visited in one year. Fortunately, people here are generally very responsible, and the park looks pretty good, despite being accosted by more than four million feet and paws annually. (Note: Pit bulls must be on leash here. Unfortunately, all pit bulls must pay the price for a few bad owners and their pit bulls.)

The large lawn area is designed for fetching, Frisbee throwing, and obedience training. People are often seen lobbing tennis balls for their expert retrievers or hollering, "Hey! Run! Go!" at a dog like Joe who can't catch anything except an occasional cold. The dog owners police themselves and their dogs very effectively.

And owners, as in most parks frequented by dogs, love to socialize. Even the shyest person will feel brave enough to start a conversation with another dog owner. It's one of life's mysteries.

There are benches, picnic tables, rest rooms, a water fountain for people and dogs, and many racks full of bags for scooping. A bulletin board posts lost-and-found dog notices, news of AARF (Area for Animals to Run Free) and its campaign for more open dog-run space, and membership information for the Point Isabel Dog Owners' Association (PIDO), which keeps the scooper dispensers full and otherwise looks out for dogs' interests in the park.

Cinder paths run along the riprap waterfront, where you can watch windsurfers against a backdrop of the Golden Gate and Bay Bridges, San Francisco, the Marin Headlands, and Mount Tamalpais. On a brisk day, a little surf even splashes against the rocks.

After a wet and wonderful walk, you may want to take your pooch to Mudpuppy's Tub and Scrub, which is located right here, for a little cleaning up (see Diversions, page 78). From Interstate 80 in Richmond, exit at Central Avenue and go west to the park entrance, next to the U.S. Postal Service Bulk Mail Center. To reach the front parking lot, pass Costco and turn right. (510) 635-0135.

•**Point Pinole Regional Shoreline** 🐾 🐾 🐾 🐾 🐕
See ❷⓿ on page 62.

Of all the East Bay Regional Parks' shorelines, this is the farthest from civilization and its discontents, and thus the cleanest and least spoiled. It's also huge and a heavenly walk for dog or owner, with its views of Mount Tamalpais across San Pablo Bay, and its docks, salt marsh, beaches, eucalyptus groves, and expanses of wild grassland waving in the breeze. Some of the eucalyptus trees are so wind-carved they could be mistaken for cypresses.

The park has fine bike paths, and your dog should be leashed for safety on these, but he's free on the unpaved trails—even on the dirt paths through marshes, such as the Marsh Trail. Just make sure he stays on the trail and doesn't go into the marsh itself. Dogs may not go on the fishing pier or on the shuttle bus to the pier.

From Interstate 80, exit at Hilltop Drive, go west and take a right on San Pablo Avenue, then left on Atlas Road to the park entrance. There's a $3 parking fee and a $1 dog fee. (510) 635-0135.

• **Wildcat Canyon Regional Park** 🐾 🐾 🐾 🐾 🐕
   See ㉑ on page 62.

This is Tilden Regional Park's northern twin. Tilden (see page 35) has its attractive spots, but it's designed for people. Wildcat seems made for dogs, because not much goes on here. Dogs really dig this. Who needs all those human feet passing by anyway? (Unless, of course, they're tracking along *eau d' cow patty* or some other savory scent.) Best of all, you can leave your dog's leash tucked away in your pocket.

Large coast live oaks, madrones, bay laurels, and all kinds of chaparral thrive on the east side. And since the area was ranchland from the days of Spanish land grants and traces of house foundations remain, it isn't surprising that a lot of exotic plants flourish here alongside the expected ones. You'll find berries, nasturtiums, and cardoon thistle, which looks like an artichoke allowed to grow up. All kinds of grasses and wildflowers cover the western hillsides.

At the entrance parking lot is Wildcat Creek, which gets low but usually not entirely dry in summer. Then you can follow the Wildcat Creek Trail (actually an abandoned paved road); it travels gently uphill and then follows the southern ridge of the park. Or follow any of the nameless side trails, which are wonderfully wild and solitary. You can hear train whistles all the way up from Emeryville and the dull roar of civilization below, but somehow it doesn't bother you up here.

Other trails lead through groves of pines or follow Wildcat Creek. The park is roughly three miles long. If you come to the boundary with Tilden, remember that dogs aren't allowed in the nature area across the line. You can get on the East Bay Skyline National Recreation Trail (Nimitz Way), running along the park's north side. Don't branch off onto the Eagle's Nest Trail, however; it belongs to the East Bay Municipal Utility District, which requires a permit and frowns on dogs. But there's plenty of room here. You and your dog could spend several blissful days in Wildcat.

From Interstate 80, southbound, take the McBryde exit and turn left on McBryde Avenue to the park entrance. If you're northbound, take the Amador/Solano exit. Go three blocks north on Amador Street and turn right (east) on McBryde to the entrance. No fees are charged. (510) 635-0135.

DIVERSIONS

Drive your pooch to the pulpit: Want to take your dog to church? If you don't think he's ready to pray in a pew, you can bring him along to attend a service in the comfort of your car. Since 1975, the First Presbyterian Church of Richmond has offered a drive-in service in a shopping mall parking lot. Held at 8:30 A.M. every Sunday outside the Pinole Appian 80 shopping center, the ceremony attracts about 40 worshipers every week.

Reverend Don Mulford transmits the service over shortwave radio from a mobile pulpit, complete with a sermon and choral music. Church elders bring communion around to each car on a silver platter and parishioners honk and flash their headlights at the pastors to say "Amen." It's quite a scene—and afterward you can go shopping. Dogs are as welcome to attend as anyone. For more information, call (510) 234-0954.

Foof him up: Is your pooch starting to smell like a dog? If you go to Point Isabel (see page 75), you can give your dog both the walk of his life and a bath. Mudpuppy's Tub and Scrub, the park's very own dogwash, offers full- or self-service scrubbings in four elevated tubs—$15 for full service, $10 if you and your dog take charge of the tub. Not bad, considering it includes shampoo, drying, and someone else to clean the tub afterward. Owners Cynthia and Holly, and their mascot Hobie, provide a fun, clean atmosphere. Weekend reservations are a must. Mudpuppy's is next to the big parking lot at the front end of the park. (510) 559-8899.

SAN RAMON

PLACES TO STAY

San Ramon Marriott at Bishop Ranch: The folks who run this attractive hotel are very friendly to creatures of the doggy persuasion. Rates are $89 to $169. 2620 Bishop Drive, San Ramon, CA 94583; (925) 867-9200.

DIVERSIONS

Work up a lather: What kind of dog wags his tail about getting a bath? The kind of dog who visits ShamPooches. It's a dog-friendly environment, where you can wash your dirty dog for 45 minutes for $12. Special shampoos and dips are extra. 3151-1 Crow Canyon Place, at Crow Canyon Commons; (925) 806-0647.

WALNUT CREEK

Walnut Creek's big secret is its beautiful creeks and canals, former irrigation ditches that now adorn golf courses and housing developments. Walnut Creek, San Ramon Creek, the Contra Costa Canal, and the Ygnacio Canal all pass through town. Dogs must be leashed everywhere, except in the undeveloped areas of city-owned open spaces.

PARKS, BEACHES, AND RECREATION AREAS

• **Acalanes Ridge Open Space Recreation Area**
🐾🐾🐾🐾 🐕 *See ㉒ on page 62.*
In 1974, the city of Walnut Creek set aside a few open spaces for a limited-use "land bank." Dogs must be "under voice or sight command." (Translation: off leash if obedient.) Hoo boy! The trails are open to hikers, dogs, horses, and bicycles, however, so on a fine day, your dog may have some competition.

Acalanes Ridge, close to Briones Regional Park (see page 69), is crossed by the Briones to Diablo Regional Trail. Like the others, it lacks water.

A good entry point is from Camino Verde Circle, reached by driving south on Camino Verde from the intersection of Pleasant Hill and Geary Roads. For information on any of the open spaces, call (925) 943-5899.

• **Shell Ridge Open Space Recreation Area** 🐾🐾🐾🐾 🐕
See ㉓ on page 62.
Dogs may run off leash everywhere but in the developed areas (parking lots, picnic grounds), but "must be under positive voice and sight command." The people who write these rules must be retired military document writers or part-time computer-manual writers.

Within the Shell Ridge Open Space is the Old Borges Ranch, a demonstration farm staffed irregularly by rangers. The ranch house is sometimes open on Sundays from noon to 4 P.M. Call first to check. For information or to make a reservation to visit, call (510) 943-5862.

You can enter by the Sugarloaf–Shell Ridge Trail at the north edge. From Interstate 680, take the Ignacio Valley Road exit, go east on Ignacio Valley Road to Walnut Avenue (not Boulevard), turn right and right again on Castle Rock Road. Go past the high school, turn right, and follow the signs. (925) 943-5899.

RESTAURANTS

Walnut Creek's "downtown," your respite from mallsville, is Main Street. Here, you'll find several welcoming outdoor restaurants, benches for just sitting, and good weather. A couple of our favorites follow.

Original Hot Dog Place: Every kind of hot dog is served in this tiny shop with a neat hot dog mural on the wall and a wooden Indian outside next to the tables. 1420 Lincoln Avenue at Main Street; (925) 256-7302.

Pascal French Oven: You and your dog will drool over the baked goodies. Waitresses often bring buckets of water out to dogs. 1372 North Main Street; (925) 932-6969.

PLACES TO STAY

Embassy Suites: This attractive hotel is eight stories high, with an atrium in the middle. Suites consist of a bedroom, living room, and galley kitchen. Couch-potato pooches enjoy the fact that there are two TVs per suite, each with cable and remote. Joe Dog has been known to change channels with the remote in his mouth once in a while, but since it usually ends up on something like channel 823, I can only guess this is an accident. Rates are $129 to $179. Dogs have to pay a $50 cleaning fee per visit, so make your stay at this lovely hotel a long one so it's worth the cost. 1345 Treat Boulevard, Walnut Creek, CA 94596; (925) 934-2500.

Holiday Inn: A few months before writing this, I got a letter from Daniel Fevre, general manager of this hotel. "My first question (when I took this job) was—you guessed it—'Do we take pets?' The answer was 'No.' My reply was 'We do now!' To test the program, I stayed with my two dogs (and one cat) for several days until the movers arrived, and the staff was great." He went on to tell me about how the hotel was also considering holding pet adoptions or pet education community events. He sounded like just the kind of hotelier this book loves.

When we finally called to get more information, we were told he was no longer with the hotel. But they still had Fevre's legacy—the dog-friendly policy—intact. What's really special about this place is its proximity to a hiking trail. They'll tell you about it at the front desk. Rates are $98 to $109. 2730 North Main Street, Walnut Creek, CA 94598; (925) 932-3332.

Walnut Creek Motor Lodge: Very small dogs only, please (15 pounds or under). Rates are $55 to $80. 1962 North Main Street, Walnut Creek, CA 94596; (925) 932-2811.

MARIN COUNTY

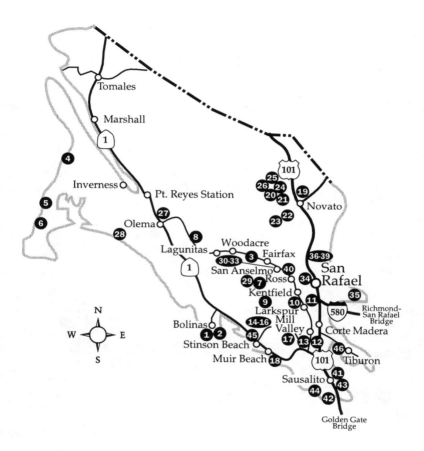

Tomales

Marshall

1

④

Inverness

⑤

⑥

101

㉕
㉖ ㉔
⑳ ㉑
⑲

Pt. Reyes Station

㉗

Novato

Olema

②⑦ ㉒

㉓

②⑧

⑧

Woodacre

Lagunitas

Fairfax

③

30-33

1

㊵

San Anselmo

36-39

San
Rafael

㉙ ⑦

Ross

㉞

Kentfield

⑨

⑩

⑪

35

Larkspur

580

Richmond-
San Rafael
Bridge

N

14-16

Mill
Valley

Corte Madera

Bolinas

W   E

①②

⑰

⑬⑫

45

S

⑱

46

Stinson Beach

Muir Beach

101

Tiburon

㊶

Sausalito

㊸

㊹

㊷

Golden Gate
Bridge

3
MARIN COUNTY

Long known as the home of hot tubs, back rubs, and ferny pubs, this comfortable, green county is also a heavenly place for the canines among us.

As you cross over the Golden Gate Bridge into this magical land, look to your left. See those hills overlooking the ocean and the bay? Dogs can explore many of the scenic trails here (see Marin Headlands Trails, page 113). Two magnificent beaches, run by the Golden Gate National Recreation Area, actually permit buck-naked (leashless) pooches. The GGNRA offers a helpful "Pet Trail Map." Phone (415) 556-0560.

In addition to those off-leash havens, Marin County operates 26 Open Space District lands. The landscapes include grassy expanses, wooded trails, redwood groves, marshes, and steep mountainsides. The idea is to set aside bits of land so that Marin never ends up looking like the Santa Clara Valley. The Open Space parks are free, completely undeveloped, and open 24 hours. Until 1995, dogs were permitted off leash just about everywhere on these lands. But now they can run leashless only on designated fire roads. They must be leashed on trails. It's still a pretty good deal, since most dogs don't mind the wide berth. For maps (they're $2 when ordered by mail), call (415) 499-6387.

Most dogs are surprised to discover that if they wear a leash, they're permitted to explore a bit of beautiful Mount Tamalpais (see Mount Tamalpais State Park, page 95, and Mount Tamalpais–Marin Municipal Water District Land, page 97).

Their mouths also tend to drop open when you mention they can visit parts of the 65,000-acre Point Reyes National Seashore. Because it's a delicate ecosystem and a national treasure, dogs are banned from campgrounds, most trails, and several beaches. Point Reyes National Seashore is home to 350 species of birds and 72 species of mammals (not including dogs). Where dogs are permitted, they must be on leash. It's a small price to pay to be able to peruse the place with the pooch at all. Kehoe Beach, Point Reyes Beach South, and Point Reyes Beach North (see page 89) are the seashore's most dog-friendly areas.

The Marin County ordinance doesn't specifically require dogs to be on leash. It states, "Dogs must be under the control of a responsible person at all times." But most towns—and even the parks within unincorporated areas—have their own leash laws that supersede this laid-back law. Bolinas is a refreshing exception (see below). If dogs could live in any town in Marin, this mellow hamlet would surely be their paws-down pick.

Dog-owning residents of Novato and San Rafael are about to make their communities even more dog-friendly than they are. At press time, each had just received word that their dream of a dog park was about to come true! See the introductions to these cities for more on their commendable efforts.

BOLINAS

Bolinas is famous for hiding from curious visitors—thereby drawing hordes of them. They keep coming, even though town citizens regularly take down the turnoff sign on Highway 1. So if you're coming from the east (San Francisco area), turn left at the unmarked road where Bolinas Lagoon ends. If you're coming from the west, turn right where the lagoon begins.

Sometimes it seems as if half the inhabitants of Bolinas are dogs, most of them black. They stand guard outside bars, curl at shop owners' feet, snooze in the middle of the road. There's no city hall in Bolinas, an unincorporated area, and no Chamber of Commerce. Dogs are always welcome here, but cars, horses, bicycles, and too many unleashed dogs compete for space. Be thoughtful and keep your pooch leashed in town.

PARKS, BEACHES, AND RECREATION AREAS

• **Agate Beach** 🐾🐾🐾🐾 🐕 *See ❶ on page 84.*

The county ordinance applies here: Dogs must be on leash or under voice control. There are lots of dogs on this narrow beach flanked by rock cliffs. Kelp bulbs pop satisfyingly underfoot. Watch that the high tide doesn't sneak up on you.

From the Olema-Bolinas Road (the Bolinas turnoff from Highway 1), turn west on Mesa Road, left on Overlook Drive, right on Elm Road, and drive all the way to the end. (415) 499-6387.

• **Bolinas Beach** 🐾🐾🐾½ 🐕 *See ❷ on page 84.*

At the end of the main street, Wharf Road, is a sand and pebble beach at the foot of a bluff. Dogs are free to run off leash. But watch for horses—with riders and without—thundering past without warning. It's animal anarchy here, and not the cleanest beach in Marin. We give it points for fun, though. (415) 499-6387.

RESTAURANTS

Bolinas Bay Bakery and Cafe: Eat pizza, salads, desserts, and baked goodies, and sip espresso on the outside benches with your dog. 20 Wharf Road; (415) 868-0211.

The Shop: This is a very dog-friendly spot for breakfast, lunch, and dinner, beer, wine, and ice cream. "Dogs are great," one enthusiastic waiter told Joe Dog. 46 Wharf Road; (415) 868-9984.

CORTE MADERA

Dogs are banned from all parks here. But mope not, pooches, because at least you get to munch on cafe cuisine.

RESTAURANTS

Book Passage Cafe: Whether your dog is illiterate or erudite, he's welcome to join you at the many shaded tables outside this incredible bookstore/cafe. You can dine on sandwiches, muffins, and a few assorted hot entrées, as well as tasty coffees and healthful smoothies. Dogs aren't allowed inside the bookstore, so if you want to peruse (and who wouldn't—the bookstore is one of the best we've seen), bring a friend and take turns dog-sitting. 51 Tamal Vista Boulevard; (415) 927-1503.

Twin Cities Market: Pick up a fresh deli sandwich (with your dog's favorite cold cuts, of course) and eat it with your pooch at the three tables outside. It's casual, but that's how most dogs like it. 118 Corte Madera Avenue; (415) 924-7372.

FAIRFAX

PARKS, BEACHES, AND RECREATION AREAS

•**Cascade Canyon Open Space Preserve** 🐾🐾🐾🐾 🐕
See ❸ on page 84.

As on all of Marin's open space lands, dogs can cavort about off leash on the fire roads. The fire road here is vehicle-free except for rangers. It's a pleasant walk that leads all the way into the Marin Municipal Water District lands of Mount Tamalpais. (Once you enter these, you must leash.)

These days, dogs must be leashed on all open space hiking trails.

But the trails are so enticing that they're actually worth trying despite the new leash law. The main trail sticks close to San Anselmo Creek, which is reduced to a dry creek bed in summer. A no-bicycles trail branches off to the right and disappears into the creek; the left branch fords the creek. When the water's high, you may be stopped right here. But in summer, you can walk a long way. Side trails lead you into shady glens of laurel and other deciduous trees, but there's lots of poison oak, too.

The park is at the end of Cascade Drive. There's a Town of Fairfax sign saying "Elliott Nature Preserve," but it's official open space. Please don't park at the end of Cascade. Spread out so the folks who live at the end of Cascade don't get so inundated with dogs. Pooches have been a problem for some residents, whose beautiful flowers and lawns have succumbed to dog feet and pooch poop. Be courteous, and think how you'd feel if the shoe were on the other paw. (415) 499-6387.

INVERNESS

PARKS, BEACHES, AND RECREATION AREAS

• **Kehoe Beach** 🐾 🐾 🐾 1/2 *See ❹ on page 84.*

This is our favorite of the Point Reyes National Seashore beaches that allow dogs, since it's both the most beautiful and the least accessible. The only parking is at roadside. You take a half-mile cinder path through wildflowers and thistles, with marsh on one side and hill on the other. In the morning, you may see some mule deer. Then, you come out on medium-brown sand that stretches forever. Since the water is shallow, the surf repeats its crests in multiple white rows, as in Hawaii. Behind you are limestone cliffs. Scattered rocks offer tidepools filled with mussels, crabs, anemones, barnacles, snails, and sea flora.

In such a paradise of shore life, the leash rule makes sense. The chief reasons for leashing dogs (or banning them altogether) at the Point Reyes National Seashore beaches are the harbor seals that haul out onto the beaches. They're in no position to get away fast from a charging dog. Snowy plovers, a threatened shorebird that nests on the ground, also appreciate your dog obeying the leash law.

From Inverness, follow Sir Francis Drake Boulevard to the fork; bear right on Pierce Point Road and go about four miles; park beside the road where you see the sign and walk about a half mile to the beach. (415) 663-1092.

• **Point Reyes Beach North** 🐾🐾🐾 1/2 *See* ❺ *on page 84.*

Point Reyes Beach North is a generous, functional beach. There's no long trail from the parking lot, no special tidepools or rocks, just a long, clean, beautiful running beach for the two of you. Officially, however, dogs must be leashed.

From Inverness, take Sir Francis Drake Boulevard. Follow signs for the lighthouse. Go about 10 miles. The turnoff for the beach is well marked. (415) 663-1092.

• **Point Reyes Beach South** 🐾🐾🐾 *See* ❻ *on page 84.*

Point Reyes Beach South is a little narrower and steeper than Point Reyes Beach North, and it has a few interesting sandstone outcrops with wind-carved holes. It has a bit less of that wide-open feeling. Leash the dog.

Follow the directions for Point Reyes Beach North; it's the next beach southward. (415) 663-1092.

RESTAURANTS

The Gray Whale: The pizzas, pastas, and sandwiches here are hearty as a whale. The Gray Whale boasts "the best vegetarian pizza in three counties." That's bad news for dogs who like their pizza slathered with sausage. Dine with doggy at the large side patio. 12781 Sir Francis Drake Boulevard; (415) 669-1244.

The Inverness Store: Lots of dogs visit this little grocery store, which has been around for more than 84 years. The folks here are kind to doggies, and welcome them to munch a lunch at the picnic table at the dike here. They even invite dogs and their people to bring a blanket and make it a real picnic. (No ants, though.) 12784 Sir Francis Drake Boulevard; (415) 669-1041.

Manka's Inverness Lodge: This magnificent lodge is home to a mouth-watering restaurant, if wild game is the type of dish that makes your mouth water. (See Places to Stay below for more information.)

PLACES TO STAY

The Ark: Don't expect 40 days and 40 nights of rain during your stay at The Ark. But be assured that even if it's raining cats and dogs, you'll still have a wonderful time here. That's because this two-room cottage is cozy and charming, with vast skylights, a soaring ceiling, a nifty loft, and the down-home comfort of a wood stove. It's furnished with lovely wood pieces and locally handcrafted items. The Ark is far removed from the "hustle-bustle" of downtown Inverness, and is adjacent to a wildlife preserve, replete with trees. If you enjoy singing birds, open a window and let the songs stream in. Or walk outside to the beautiful, private area surrounding the cottage.

The Ark was built in 1971 by a class of UC Berkeley architecture students under the guidance of maverick architect Sim Van der Ryn. The class was called "Making a Place in the Country." If you took a class in the result of this project, it would probably be called "Making a Place in Your Heart." Your dog won't soon forget a vacation here, and neither will you. As long as your dog doesn't take a stab at the subjects of "Making a Hole in the Yard" or "Making Pee-Pee on the Floor," he'll be as welcome here as the humans in his party.

The Ark sleeps up to six people. Rates are $130 for two people, $10 per additional person. There's a $30 fee per visit for dogs. A healthful, delicious breakfast is $5 extra. 184 Highland Way, P.O. Box 273, Inverness, CA 94950; (415) 663-984 or (840) 878-984.

Manka's Inverness Lodge: Often, humans and their dogs spend the night here, eat breakfast, and decide never to return home. It's an old hunting lodge, surrounded by woods and the beaches and mudflats of Tomales Bay—and the owners love dogs. They have a sweet yellow Lab, who goes by the dignified name of Louie. Louie's fellow canines can stay in the cabins or the garden suite. Rates are $135 to $365. Dogs are $50 extra for the length of their stay, and only one pooch per stay, please.

The food here is exceptional. The lodge's restaurant was recently given a four-star rating by the *Marin Independent Journal.* The vegetarian dishes are exotic and mouthwatering. But it's all the wild game dishes that make dogs vote it a four-paw restaurant. If dogs accompany you for a meal at the outdoor tables here, they'll drool over every mouthful you eat. Monday nights are excellent nights to come for a bite, because the wild game dishes are a mere $5 to $10 each.

Look for the uphill turn off Sir Francis Drake Boulevard and take Argyle Way about 400 yards to the lodge. P.O. Box 1110, Inverness, CA 94937; (415) 669-1034.

Rosemary Cottage: If you have a romantic, nature-loving bone in your body, you'll love a getaway at this quaint, French-country cottage. It's set in a secluded spot, with a wall of windows looking out at the stunning forest scenery of the Point Reyes National Seashore. A deck overlooks a sweet-smelling herb garden. The inside of the cottages is cozy and beautifully crafted, with a full kitchen and many homey details. Snuggle up near the wood-burning stove on chilly evenings after a day of whale-watching and dog-walking at nearby beaches. Hearth-type dogs love it here.

Rates are $170 for up to two people. Dogs are $30 extra for the length of your stay, so Joe Dog recommends getting your money's worth and staying a few nights. Breakfast is optional, and is $5 extra. 75 Balboa Avenue, P.O. Box 273, Inverness, CA 94950; (415) 663-984 or (840) 878-984.

KENTFIELD

PARKS, BEACHES, AND RECREATION AREAS

• **Northridge/Baltimore Canyon Open Space Preserve**
🐾🐾🐾🐾 🐕 *See ❼ on page 84.*
From this spot, access is good for a lot of fire roads through the ridges connecting with Mount Tamalpais and water district lands. Leashes aren't required on the fire roads, but bikes are also allowed on these trails, so be careful. You'll be starting out fairly high on the slope. Dogs must be leashed on regular hiking trails.

Two access points are at the ends of Crown Road and Evergreen Drive. (415) 499-6387.

LAGUNITAS

PARKS, BEACHES, AND RECREATION AREAS

• **Samuel P. Taylor State Park** 🐾🐾🐾 *See ❽ on page 84.*
An exception among the state parks: Dog access is generous. You can take a dog into the picnic areas, and that's worth doing here. The main picnic area right off Sir Francis Drake Boulevard is cool and often lively with the grinding call of jays. It's an easy place to bring out-of-state visitors who may just want to eat a sandwich, hug a redwood, and go home. There are hollow trees stretching 20 feet across that you can actually stand inside.

But best of all, you and your dog may spend a whole day on

the wide fire trails—roughly 10 miles of them—clearly differenti-
ated on the map you get at the entrance. Dogs may not go on the
foot trails, but the fire trails are delightful enough. You can take
the bicycle/horse trail from near the entrance along Papermill
Creek, rising for four miles to Barnabe Peak, at 1,466 feet. Unfortunately, your dog must stay leashed, but you may actually appreciate that when you see the excellent artist's drawing of a poison oak cluster on the park's map—it's everywhere.

The park has 60 campsites. Sites are $12 to $16. Dogs are $1
extra. From April through October, call Parknet for reservations
at (840) 444-PARK. The park's day-use fee is $5 for parking, $1 per
dog. The entrance is on Sir Francis Drake Boulevard about two
miles west of Lagunitas. (415) 488-9897.

RESTAURANTS

Lagunitas Grocery: Grab a sandwich at the deli inside and feast
on it at the outdoor tables with your dog. 7890 Sir Francis Drake
Boulevard; (415) 488-4844.

PLACES TO STAY

Samuel P. Taylor State Park: See Samuel P. Taylor State Park
on page 91 for camping information.

LARKSPUR

PARKS, BEACHES, AND RECREATION AREAS

• **Blithedale Summit Open Space Preserve** 😺 😺 😺 😺 🐕
See ❾ on page 84.

The access point at the end of Madrone Avenue—the north end
of this open space—is a delightful walk in hot weather, through
cool redwoods that let some light filter through. This isn't one of
those really dark, drippy canyons; you're at a medium-high altitude on the slopes of Mount Tamalpais. The trail follows Larkspur Creek, which retains some pools in summer. Cross the footbridge and follow the slightly rough foot trail. Unfortunately,
leashes are now the law on these trails. But you can let your dog
off his leash once you hit the fire road.

The drive up narrow Madrone Avenue is an adventure in itself;
redwoods grow right in the street. According to a sign at the entrance, the part of this space belonging to the city of Larkspur
requires dogs to be leashed. (415) 499-6387.

• **Creekside Park** 🐾🐾½ *See ⑩ on page 84.*

This is the small, attractive park where the multipurpose Bon Air Path starts. The 1.8-mile paved trail goes from Bon Air Road, following Corte Madera Creek, westward to the town of Ross and eastward to the Larkspur Landing shopping center, near the ferry terminal. There are lots of paths by Corte Madera Creek, as well as a kids' gym. You must leash your dog and be sure to keep him out of marshy areas. A bulletin board displays excellent bike trail maps and descriptions of local flora and fauna.

From Sir Francis Drake Boulevard, turn south on Bon Air Road; from Magnolia Drive, turn north. The park entrance is across from Marin General Hospital. You can get more information on the county's bike trails from the Bicycle Trails Council of Marin at (415) 456-7512. For more park information, call (415) 499-6387.

• **Piper Park (Canine Commons)** 🐾🐾🐾½ 🐕
See ⑪ on page 84.

Here's an ordinary people-style city park—athletic facilities, playground, picnic tables, community garden, the works—that has also included what your dog needs! It's got a small fenced area next to the community garden called Canine Commons, and it's just the ticket if your dog is a fetcher or an escape artist, hates the leash, or loves to meet other dogs. The drawback is its small size, a mere third of an acre—but we just got word that it's soon going to double in size! There's only one striving little tree. Still, it's better than nothing. Water, pooper-scoopers, and tennis balls are supplied.

The Larkspur City Recreation Department runs Piper Park. You can play or watch softball, volleyball, tennis, and even cricket. Outside Canine Commons, dogs must be leashed. The park is between Doherty Drive and Corte Madera Creek. Canine Commons is at the west end of the park. (415) 927-5110.

RESTAURANTS

Bread & Chocolate Bakery: If you enjoy either of the two aforementioned goodies, this bakery is a must-visit. Eat these or many other delicious goodies at the outside tables with your pooch. (Remember that dogs and chocolate don't mix, though.) 1139 Magnolia Avenue; (415) 461-9154.

The Left Bank: Your dog doesn't have to be a poodle to enjoy dining at this terrific French restaurant. Because it's a French place, management knows that dogs and restaurants really do mix. But because they're in America, they have to abide by local health regulations and keep doggies from dining inside. That's okay, though, because there are plenty of outside tables. When it's crowded, managers ask that you tie your dog to the railing that surrounds the outdoor area. You can still dine right beside your pooch, but at least he won't trip a *garçon*. 507 Magnolia Avenue; (415) 927-3331.

Marin Brewing Company: They brew their own beer here, and it's really good. Swig some with your dog and your sandwich at the nine outdoor tables. 1849 Larkspur Circle; (415) 461-4677.

MARSHALL

DIVERSIONS

Mingle with the mollusks: Your dog doesn't have to be a water dog to appreciate the fascinating sights and scents at Abalone Acres. Abalone in many stages of their young lives grow in kelp-filled tanks here. You can look around the outdoor facility and buy small homegrown abalone for a decent price: four (or approximately one pound, including shell) for about $22. Next door is the Hog Island Oyster Company, where you can buy oysters and mussels alive, alive-o.

Abalone Acres is on Highway 1, along rural Marshall's "main drag." The mailing address is P.O. Box 837, Marshall, CA 94940; (415) 663-1384.

MILL VALLEY

PARKS, BEACHES, AND RECREATION AREAS

• **Bayfront Park** 🐾 🐾 🐾 🐾 🐕 *See ⑫ on page 84.*

This good-looking park is well designed for every kind of family activity and for dogs. There's an exercise course, lawns are green and silky, and picnic areas are clean and attractive. The multiuse trails for bicycles, strollers, and whatnot may be used only by leashed dogs. (There are bikes galore.) But here's the canine payoff: It has a special dog run next to an estuary, where dogs are free to dip their paws.

The dog-use area starts where you see all the other dogs, and probably a sign or two by the time this edition hits the stores.

Beware, owners of escape artists: The area is a big three acres, but it's not fenced. No scoops or water are furnished, but the Richardson Bay Estuary is right there to jump into.

At the end of the run there's even a marsh that dogs can explore, if you're willing to put a very mucky friend back into the car with you. Luckily, this marsh is all organic muck, free from the dangerous trash that fills many unprotected bay marshes.

For a dog park, this one offers an unparalleled view of Mount Tam. Horses and bikes pass by harmlessly on their own separate trail in the foreground, and mockingbirds sing in the bushes.

Until recently, there had been a heap o' controversy over whether this should continue to be a dog run area. Some people thought soccer players of the young human persuasion should have the area, and that dogs should have to be leashed. But hooray, the dogs won! The city council approved a permanent dog run here. That's thanks to the work of a magnificent, high-energy group called Park People & Dogs. If you want to find out how you can help Park People & Dogs in its continuing efforts to make this park dog heaven, call Barbara Berlenbach at (415) 388-0071.

The parking lot is on Sycamore Avenue, just after you cross Camino Alto, next to the wastewater treatment plant. Keep your dog leashed near the steep-sided sewage ponds; dogs have drowned in them. Also, be sure to keep your dog leashed until you've reached the grassy dog run area; There's a $50 ticket if you get caught unleashed. (415) 383-1370.

- **Camino Alto Open Space Preserve** 🐾 🐾 🐾 ½ 🐕
  See ⑬ on page 84.

In this accessible open space, your dog may run free on a wide fire trail along a ridge connecting with Mount Tamalpais. You'll walk through bay laurels, madrones, and chaparral, looking down on soaring vultures and the bay, Highway 1, the hills, and the headlands. A small imperfection is that you can hear the whoosh of traffic. Just pretend it's the wind. Dogs must be leashed on the regular hiking trails here. Park at the end of Escalon Drive, just west of Camino Alto. (415) 499-6387.

- **Mount Tamalpais State Park** 🐾 🐾 🐾 *See ⑭ on page 84.*

Generally, dogs are restricted to paved roads here. But dogs may stay in one of the campgrounds, and there are also a few spots near the summit where you can take your dog. The views from here are something you'll certainly appreciate on a clear day.

Stop for lunch at the Bootjack Picnic Area, west of the Mountain Home Inn on Panoramic Highway and about a quarter mile east of the turnoff to the summit, Pantoll Road. The tables are attractively sited on the hillside under oak trees. This picnic ground is an access point for the Bootjack Trail and Matt Davis Trail. The Matt Davis Trail is off-limits, but you and your dog may— howlelujah!—use the 100 feet of Bootjack Trail that leads you into Marin Municipal Water District land, where leashed dogs are allowed. (You must travel north on the Bootjack Trail, though, not south; it's all state park in that direction.)

Heading northward, you can hook up with the Old Stage Fire Road and the Old Railroad Grade Fire Road, which are water district roads going almost the whole distance to the summit. You can also enter the Old Stage Fire Road right across from the Pantoll Ranger Station, at the intersection of Panoramic Highway and Pantoll Road. Pooches have special permission to cross the 100 feet or so of state park trail approaching water district trail.

The Bootjack Picnic Area parking lot charges $5 to park. (Once you pay in any state park lot, your receipt is good for any other spot that you hit that day.) The park has 16 developed walk-in campsites that allow dogs. They're at the Pantoll Station Campground. Sites are $12 to $16, plus $1 for your dog. All sites are first come, first served. (415) 388-2070.

•**Mount Tamalpais Summit** 🐾 🐾 🐾 *See ⓫ on page 84.*

The summit of Mount Tam is worth the $5 fee that you're charged merely to drive here. But in addition to the magnificent views, you may also take your dog on one trail up here ($1 dog fee).

You'll find a small refreshment stand, rest rooms, a visitors center, and viewing platforms. On clear days, you can see nine counties, whether you want to or not. In summer, white fingers of fog obscure a good part of your view as they creep between the "knuckles" of Marin's ridges.

It's too bad if your leashed dog doesn't care about views. But he will take eagerly to the smoothly paved Verna Dunshee Trail, about one mile long, running almost level around the summit. About three-quarters of this trail is also wheelchair accessible.

From U.S. 101, take the Stinson Beach/Highway 1 exit. Follow Highway 1 to Panoramic Highway, which will be a right turn. Continue on Panoramic to the right turn off to Pantoll Road; Pantoll soon becomes East Ridgecrest Road and goes to the summit, then loops back for your trip down. (415) 388-2070.

• **Mount Tamalpais–Marin Municipal Water District Land**
 🐾 🐾 🐾 *See* **16** *on page 84.*

Your very best bet for a dog walk high on the mountain is to find one of the water district fire roads near the summit. Your dog must be leashed, but at least she can go on the trails with you, and you both can experience the greenness of this wonderful mountain. At this elevation, the green comes from chaparral, pine, and madrone.

Just below the summit on East Ridgecrest Boulevard, watch for the water district's gate and sign. This is the Old Railroad Grade Fire Road, which descends 1,785 feet from the entry point just west of the summit. On the way it intersects with Old Stage Fire Road, then emerges at the Bootjack Picnic Area. En route, you'll cross three creeks. For obvious reasons, you'll be happier in warm weather taking this road down, not up; get someone to meet you in a car at the Bootjack picnic site.

Another spot to pick up a water district trail is off Panoramic Highway just west of the Mountain Home Inn. Look for the Marin Municipal Water District sign by the fire station. Park at the state park parking lot west of Mountain Home Inn and walk east along this fire road, called Gravity Car Road (though it's unmarked), through mixed pines, redwoods, fir, madrone, and scrub. Keep your eyes open for fast-moving mountain bikes. (415) 924-4600.

• **Old Mill Park** 🐾 🐾 🐾 *See* **17** *on page 84.*

Refresh your dog under cool redwoods right in the town of Mill Valley. The old mill, built in 1834, was recently restored. A wooden bridge over Old Mill Creek leads to well-maintained paths that run along the creek. The creek is dog-accessible, though pooches are supposed to be leashed.

One picnic table here sits within the hugest "fairy ring" we've ever seen—40 feet across. Boy dogs like to imagine the size of the mother tree whose stump engendered this ring of saplings. The park is on Throckmorton Avenue at Olive Street, near the public library. (415) 383-1370.

RESTAURANTS

The Depot Cafe and Bookstore: This place is Mill Valley's town square and everybody's backyard. You and your dog may sit at cafe tables, benches, or picnic tables and snack or just bask in the sun—if you don't mind skateboarders, bikes, chess players, crying kids, telephones, Frisbees, hackeysack, and guitar music happening right next to you. These are Marin kids, the kind who will reach out to your dog's face without a moment's hesitation. Mellow is the watchword here. Both sun and shade are available, at least after mid-afternoon. It's on the Plaza; (415) 383-2665.

Perry's Deli: The house-made soups at Perry's are delicious on a cool afternoon, but Joe prefers his fellow diners to order roast turkey sandwiches so he can catch the "droppings." Dine outside under the awning. 246 East Blithedale Avenue; (415) 381-0407.

Piazza d'Angelo: This Italian lunch and dinner spot has 15 tables on two outside patios, one shaded, the other not. Dogs are welcome at either as long as it's not too busy. The premier dish for people here is the tortelloni della casa, and they'll even bring a bowl of agua for your dog. 22 Miller Avenue; (415) 388-2185.

PLACES TO STAY

Mount Tamalpais State Park: See Mount Tamalpais State Park on page 95 for camping information.

MUIR BEACH

PARKS, BEACHES, AND RECREATION AREAS

•**Muir Beach** 😺😺😺😺 🐕 *See* ⑱ *on page 84.*

Muir Beach allows obedient, leash-free doggies these days! With so much of the Golden Gate National Recreation Area's lands being taken away from leashless dogs, this is a refreshing addition to this book. It's small, but a real gem, with rugged sand dunes spotted with plants, a parking lot and large picnic area, a small lagoon with tules, and its share of wind. Redwood Creek empties into the ocean here. Leashless dogs (under voice control, as leashless dog should always be) are permitted from the shoreline to the crest of the dunes. They must be leashed from the dune crest inland to Big Lagoon, and in parking lots and picnic areas.

You can reach Muir Beach the long way, hiking about five miles from the Marin Headlands Visitors Center (see Rodeo Beach, page

115), or the easy way, via Highway 1. From Highway 1, watch for the turnoff for the beach. (415) 388-2596.

NOVATO

Novato is one of the Marin cities whose dog ordinance is the county's: Dogs must be on leash or under verbal command. Its city parks require leashes, though.

But that last rule will soon have an exception in the form of a leash-free dog park. After four years of hard work, a group called D.O.G.B.O.N.E. (Dog Owners Group Bettering Our Novato Environment) has succeeded in getting a terrific two-acre site for a dog park! It's in the San Marin area of Novato, a couple of lots past Morningstar Farms (the horse place) on the left side of North Novato Boulevard as you head toward Stafford Lake. Townies will know what I'm talking about. Others will get better directions in this book's next edition, when the park is a reality.

At press time, the group had just received the city's blessing, as well as a mandate to have the park ready to go in two years. The group now has to raise big bucks for grading the property, irrigating it, fencing it, and putting in a few doggy essentials. When the fencing goes up and a few dog things go in, the city says the park can open, even before all the other tasks are done. That means the park could be open as early as summer of 1998! To get an update or find out how you can help, call Lauren Cobb, founder of D.O.G.B.O.N.E., at (415) 898-5843, or write (donations are welcome) to D.O.G.B.O.N.E. at P.O. Box 359, Novato, CA 94948.

PARKS, BEACHES, AND RECREATION AREAS

• **Deer Island Open Space Preserve** 🐾 🐾 🐾 🐾 🐕
See ⑲ on page 84.

This preserve is called an island because it's a high point in the floodplain of the Petaluma River, an oak-crowned hill surrounded by miles of dock and tules. You can easily imagine it surrounded by shallow-water Miwuk canoes slipping through rafts of ducks. The trail is a 1.8-mile loop of gentle ups and downs above ponds and marshy fields. There are some sturdy old oaks among the mixed deciduous groves, and lots of laurels. The trail is partly shaded and bans bikes. Dogs have to be leashed on the trails, but are permitted off leash on fire roads here.

From U.S. 101, exit at San Marin Drive/Atherton Avenue; drive east about 1.5 miles and take a right on Olive Avenue, then a left on Deer Island Lane. Park in a small lot at the trailhead, by a small engineering company building. (415) 499-6387.

• Indian Tree Open Space Preserve 🐾🐾🐾½ 🐕
*See **20** on page 84.*

This open space and Verissimo Hills Open Space Preserve (see page 102) are good to know about because they're just east of Stafford Lake County Park. You needn't leash on fire roads here, but watch out for horses. Leashes are the law on the preserve's trails.

From U.S., exit at San Marin Drive/Atherton Avenue; drive west on San Marin. After San Marin turns into Sutro Avenue, take a right onto Vineyard Road. Park along the dirt county road that begins at the trailhead. (415) 499-6387.

• Indian Valley Open Space Preserve 🐾🐾🐾🐾 🐕
*See **21** on page 84.*

Lots of dogs come here to trot around in leashless ecstasy on the fire road. On hiking trails, they have to trot around in leashed ecstasy. The hiking trail here is partly sunny, partly shaded by laurels, and much-revered by canines.

From U.S. 101, exit at DeLong Avenue and go west on DeLong, which becomes Diablo Avenue. Take a left on Hill Road and a right on Indian Valley Road. Drive all the way to the end; park on this road before you walk left at the spur road marked "Not a Through Street," just south of Old Ranch Road. Cross Arroyo Avichi Creek right at the entrance (dry in summer). (415) 499-6387.

• Loma Verde Open Space Preserve 🐾🐾🐾½ 🐕
*See **22** on page 84.*

There are two access points to this open space where dogs are allowed off leash on fire roads. One, south of the Marin Country Club, is a waterless, tree-covered hillside with a fire road. Bikes are allowed, so be sure to keep your leash-free dog under voice control. It's a good road if you like easily reachable high spots; there are fine views of San Pablo Bay. Exit U.S. 101 at Ignacio Boulevard. Go west to Fairway Drive and turn left (south), then left on Alameda de la Loma, then right on Pebble Beach Drive. Access is at the end of Pebble Beach.

The second access point is through the Posada West housing development. From Alameda del Prado, turn south on Posada del Sol. The trail opening is at the end of this street. (415) 499-6387.

• **Lucas Valley Open Space Preserve** 🐾🐾🐾🐾 🐕
See **23** on page 84.

This space of rolling, oak-dotted hills affords great views of Novato and Lucas Valley developments. There are a dozen access points, most from Lucas Valley and Marinwood.

One access point is reached by turning left (north) off Lucas Valley Road on Mount Shasta Drive, followed by a brief right turn on Vogelsang Drive. Park near this dead end and walk in. Keep in mind that all Marin open space preserves require pooches to be on leash except on fire roads. (415) 499-6387.

• **Miwuk Park** 🐾🐾🐾 See **24** on page 84.

This is one of the best city parks we've visited. Dogs must be on leash, but it offers a great combination of dog pleasures and human amenities. Paved paths, good for strollers, wind through pine trees. There are bocce ball courts, horseshoes, a kids' gym, and a lovely shaded picnic area with grills.

Outside the Museum of the American Indian, located in this park, is an intriguing display of California native plants that the coastal Miwuk used for food, clothing, and shelter.

Best of all for canines, Novato Creek flows deep and 30 to 40 feet wide—even in summer. A woman we encountered with a golden retriever told us that the muddy bottom can sometimes be soft and treacherous, so keep a close eye on your dog if he goes swimming. The park is at Novato Boulevard and San Miguel Drive. (415) 897-4323.

• **Mount Burdell Open Space Preserve** 🐾🐾🐾🐾 🐕
See **25** on page 84.

Mount Burdell is the largest of Marin's open space preserves. You'll share it with cattle, but there's plenty of room. There are 8 or 10 miles of cinder and dirt paths, including part of the Bay Area Ridge Trail, that wind through its oak-dotted grasslands. (Dogs have to be leashed on trails, but are permitted to run leashless on fire roads here.)

A creek is located about one-eighth of a mile up the trail starting at San Andreas Drive, but it's dry in summer. In winter, you might find the preserve's Hidden Lake. In summer, there are lots of foxtails and fire danger is high. No fires are ever allowed. Camping is allowed by permit, but there are no facilities.

From San Marin Drive, turn north on San Andreas Drive. Park on the street. (415) 499-6387.

• **Verissimo Hills Open Space Preserve** 🐾🐾🐾 🐕
See ㉖ on page 84.

The golden hills with clumps of oak have narrow foot trails only; bikes are prohibited. As you enter the area, you'll see a fork in the trail. Take the trail uphill to the left. This path features fine views of the hills as well as nearby residential areas. (Note that this open space preserve is co-managed by the Marin Municipal Water District, which means that if you're in doubt, leash. Be sure to close the gate to keep cattle inside.) Dogs are permitted off leash on fire roads only. Leashes are the law on regular trails.

From U.S. 101, exit at San Marin Drive/Atherton Avenue; drive west on San Marin. Turn right (west) on Center Road. Go all the way to the end, where you can park. (415) 499-6387.

DOGGY DAYS

Enter him in the Olympics: Picture this: Your dog proudly marches up the Steps of Champions while Olympic music fills the air. An Olympic official says a few words of praise and hangs a bronze-ish, silver-ish, or even gold-ish Olympic medal around your dog's neck. The crowd cheers. It's a glorious moment.

This is the stuff dog dreams may be made of (actually, we think they're made of chasing cats and eating steak and rolling in cow patties, but that's just one theory). Every spring, the Marin Humane Society makes this dream come true for hundreds of pooches at the Bay Area Canine Games, also known as the Doggy Olympics. And your dog doesn't have to be an athlete to compete. Sure, there are the usual physical challenges, like the 50-yard dash and the obstacle course. But the Olympics is also for the average dog in your life. Competitions like the Fastest Eater, Best Crooner, and Loudest Barker make the Olympics an event where just about any dog can have his day. If your dog puts his paw down when it comes to competing, bring him along as a spectator.

The Olympics are held on the spacious grounds of the Marin Humane Society, at 171 Bel Marin Keys Boulevard, Novato, CA 94949. Write or call (415) 883-4621 for entry fees and details of this year's event. Proceeds benefit shelter animals.

OLEMA

PARKS, BEACHES, AND RECREATION AREAS

• **Bolinas Ridge Trail** 🐾🐾🐾 *See* ㉗ *on page 84.*

This Golden Gate National Recreation Area trail, part of the Bay Area Ridge Trail, is not for sissies—canine or human. It climbs steadily up for 11 miles from the Olema end, giving you gorgeous views of Tomales Bay, Bolinas, and the ocean, and ends up at the Bolinas-Fairfax Road below Alpine Lake.

You must keep your dog leashed. One good reason for this is that there are cattle roaming unfenced along the trail. And the trail is very popular with non-sissy mountain bikers. (The trail is wide, but made of dirt and rock.) From the western end, you'll walk through rolling grassland with cypress clumps. Rock outcrops sport crowns of poison oak, so watch it.

You may be able to cope with 11 miles of this, but remember your dog's bare pads and don't overdo it. Also, it isn't much fun for man or beast to walk 11 miles attached by a leash.

Unfortunately, only the Bolinas Ridge Trail is open to dogs; you can't take any of the spur trails going south.

The western end begins about one mile north of Olema on Sir Francis Drake Boulevard. There's roadside parking only. (415) 556-0560 or (415) 663-1092.

• **Limantour Beach** 🐾🐾🐾 *See* ㉘ *on page 84.*

This bountiful beach at Point Reyes National Seashore is most people's favorite, so it's often crowded. From the main parking lot, walk a quarter of a mile through tule marsh, grasses and brush, and scattered pines, past Limantour Estero. (Dogs are prohibited on the side trails.)

Rules for leashed dogs are clearly marked—a refreshing exception to the obscure and contradictory rules in so many parks. For example, approaching Limantour Beach on the path, you'll see a sign that says dogs are prohibited to your right, allowed to your left. This beach is plenty big, so it's an excellent arrangement that keeps dog owners and dog avoiders equally happy. You may walk with your dog to Santa Maria Beach.

From Highway 1, look for the turnoff to Bear Valley Road, which runs between Olema and Inverness Park. Take Bear Valley from either direction to Limantour Road; turn south on Limantour all the way to the beach. (415) 663-1092.

PLACES TO STAY

Olema Ranch Campground: It's hard to find a campground that's decent for both RVs and tent campers, so we were mighty pleased to find Olema Ranch. RV folks get all the hookups they need, and tenters get a choice of scenic meadow or forest campsites. Many sites come with water. The campground features amenities like a kitchen, laundry facilities, and a supply store, so we're not exactly talking the big wilderness adventure here. But still, it's a terrific spot to set up a tent with a dog who doesn't mind a little civilized camping.

Rates are $18 to $25. Dogs are $1 exra. 10155 Highway 1, P.O. Box 175, Olema, CA 94950; (415) 663-8401 or (840) 655-CAMP.

POINT REYES STATION

RESTAURANTS

Bovine Bakery: The bread here will make you drool, which will make your dog embarrassed. Dine on bread or pizza or "killer monster cookies" at the bench in front. 11315 Highway 1; (415) 663-9420.

Cafe Reyes: The patio on the cafe's side is big and very attractive, with excellent views of local scenery. Even dogs seem to enjoy its ambience. The food is great, too. Bring it to the seven umbrella-topped tables and wolf it down with your pooch at your side. The cuisine is best described as Tex-Mex with a California leaning. Try one of the Thai burritos for a true international experience. You can also get baked goodies and strong coffee, for those lazy, foggy days here. There's not really a street address. It's on Highway 1 and is big and wooden. You can't miss it. (415) 663-9493.

PLACES TO STAY

Jasmine Cottage and Gray's Retreat: These two glorious getaway cottages are the cat's meow for dogs and their people. Located on a serene stretch of rolling pastureland in Point Reyes Station, the cottages have a sweet country theme and seem perfectly at home in their surroundings. Dogs love it here, because the cottages are each adorned with their own private enclosed patio and garden. They're wonderful places to relax outside with your pooch.

The cottages also have fully equipped kitchens that come with a real bonus: a lovely picnic basket and all the gear that goes with it (excluding the food). Now there's no excuse for not taking your pooch on a picnic. In addition, each cottage has a fireplace, and the two share a secluded garden hot tub.

Jasmine Cottage is the smaller of the two romantic hideaways. It's sequestered in a country garden at the top of a hill and has small flower gardens, vegetable gardens, and even a flock of chickens, who provide guests with their morning eggs. (A full, simple breakfast is included in your stay at this cottage.) The chickens are in a protected area, but if your dog has a hankering for KFC, best keep her away. When we visited, Joe Dog went cuckoo over the cock-a-doodle-doos. We had to drag him kicking and screaming back inside the cottage for fear he would give a hen a heart attack.

Gray's Retreat is just as enchanting, but chicken-free and bigger. It's more geared toward families, since it sleeps up to six and comes with a high chair and a portable crib. Breakfast is not provided, but the kitchen is stocked with enough basic dry goods (including pancake mix) that with a few groceries, you can have yourself a feast.

If you'll be visiting with two pooches, you'll have to stay at Gray's Retreat. Jasmine Cottage permits only one pooch. Each dog pays a $15 fee for the length of her stay at either location. The cottage rate is $165 nightly for the first two people. Additional people are $15. The weekly rate is $990. The mailing address is P.O. Box 56, Point Reyes Station, CA 94956; (415) 663-1166.

DIVERSIONS

If only dogs could read: The Brown Study Bookshop sent me a letter that ended like this: "We welcome genteel canines, whether a reading rover or a browsing bowser—or just a patiently waiting companion. Se habla milkbone." So of course, next time we found ourselves pawing around for a good book, Joe hounded me to drive with him to this wonderful little bookstore. He immediately fell in love with the place. Dogs get lots of loving, some water, and a crunchy biscuit. I think he's trying to learn to read now. He used to chew books, now he's simply making dog-eared pages. Anything to go back.

This store really is a treat—for dogs and humans. There's a big selection of new and used books, with a strong outdoor book section. Combine a visit here with a hike and a lunch, and you've got yourselves a doggone great day. 11315 Highway 1; (415) 663-1633.

ROSS

PARKS, BEACHES, AND RECREATION AREAS

• **Natalie Coffin Greene Park** 🐾🐾🐾 *See* **29** *on page 84.*

Leashed dogs are welcome at this enchanted mixed forest of redwood and deciduous trees. The picnic area has an old-fashioned shelter built of logs and stone.

The park borders generic Marin Municipal Water District land, and from the park, you can pick up the wide cinder fire road leading to Phoenix Lake, a five-minute walk. Bikers, hikers, and leashed dogs are all welcome on this road, but the lake is a reservoir, so no body contact is allowed—for man or beast.

The road continues, depending how far you want to walk, to Lagunitas Lake, Bon Tempe Lake, Alpine Lake, and Kent Lake. (No body contact in any of them; sorry, dogs.) Combined, the water district offers 94 miles of road and 44 miles of trail in this area, meandering through hillsides, densely forested with pine, oak, madrone, and a variety of other trees. For a trail map, send a self-addressed, stamped envelope to Sky Oaks Ranger Station, P.O. Box 865, Fairfax, CA 94978, Attention: Trail Map.

At the corner of Sir Francis Drake Boulevard and Lagunitas Road, go west on Lagunitas all the way to the end, past the country club. You'll find a parking lot and some portable toilets. (415) 453-1453.

SAN ANSELMO

San Anselmo Avenue provides you and your mellow pooch with a laid-back stroll, and you can both cool your paws in San Anselmo Creek, which runs through town. Your well-behaved pooch can even be off leash, provided she's under voice control. There's a group called Friends of San Anselmo Dogs that's trying to get a permanent pooch park started at Red Hill Park, behind the Red Hill Shopping Center at the end of Shaw Drive. At press time, the dogs had only temporary status. By the next edition, we're hoping to find a four-paw dog park here. For more information on this noble effort, call (415) 258-4600.

PARKS, BEACHES, AND RECREATION AREAS

• **Creek Park** 🐾🐾🐾 *See* ㉚ *on page 84.*

San Anselmo Creek runs between Sir Francis Drake Boulevard—which has a wide variety of antique shops—and San Anselmo Avenue, the main shopping street. A bridge connects the two streets.

Creek Park is small, but handy and clean. It's next to a free public lot with some shady spaces. Along the creek banks on the Sir Francis Drake side are picnic tables on a lawn with beautiful willows and maples. Lots of people lounge on the grass. Wooden steps lead down to the water. There's plenty of shade in which to picnic or lie on the grass, while resting between shopping binges for antiques.

Turn into the parking lot from Sir Francis Drake Boulevard, near "The Hub" (intersection of Sir Francis Drake and Red Hill Avenue). (415) 258-4645.

• **Loma Alta Open Space Preserve** 🐾🐾🐾🐾 🐕
See ㉛ *on page 84.*

A little canyon amid bare hills, lined with oaks, bay laurel, and buckeye, this is an exceptional open space preserve. There's plenty of shade. The trail follows White Hill Creek, which is dry in the summer. Leashes are required on the trails, but obedient dogs can throw their leashes to the wind on the fire road.

You can park at the trailhead at the end of Glen Avenue, a turn north off Sir Francis Drake Boulevard. (415) 499-6387.

• **Memorial Park** 🐾🐾🐾🐾 🐕 *See* ㉜ *on page 84.*

This pleasant and popular city park has tennis courts, three baseball diamonds, and a children's play area. Next to the diamonds is a fenced dog-exercise area, where leash-free dogs romp joyfully, fetching, chasing Frisbees, or socializing. There's even a creek next to the dog run. A volunteer group, Memorial Park Dog Owners Association, publishes a newsletter and keeps an eye out for scooper-scofflaws. The park is off Sunnyhills Drive. (415) 258-4645.

• **Sorich Ranch Park** 🐾🐾🐾🐾 🐕 *See* ㉝ *on page 84.*

The biggest and by far the wildest city park in San Anselmo is Sorich Ranch Park, an undeveloped open space soaring up to a ridgetop from which you can see a distant make-believe San Francisco skyline across the bay. From the very top of the ridge, you also can see Mount Tamalpais and most of San Rafael, including the one-of-a-kind turquoise and salmon Marin County Civic Center, designed by Frank Lloyd Wright. (Some Marinites are glad there's only one.)

The entrance from the San Anselmo side is at the end of San Francisco Boulevard, and the path is pretty much straight up. But if you aren't up to a 10-minute puffing ascent, you can just stroll in the meadows at the bottom. No leash is required, and the park is uncrowded and often pleasantly breezy. There's no water available, and it can be scorching in summer. (415) 258-4645.

RESTAURANTS

Creekside Bistro: Dogs are welcome at the front patio, where they can dine on tasty bistro cuisine at an abundance of clean white metal tables. 626 San Anselmo Avenue; (415) 459-5708.

SAN RAFAEL

This charming town may soon go to the dogs, thanks to an enterprising organization called Field of Dogs. At press time, founder Mario Di Palma and his group had been working to open a dog park for more than five years. Most of the approvals had been granted at this time, but the group is still awaiting a final vote by the county board of supervisors. When the park is approved, it will be on an acre of land at the civic center. The park, which will be aptly named Field of Dogs (I love it) will be fenced, and have water, scoopers, shade trees, and trash cans. Joe Dog is keeping his paws crossed that Di Palma's dream comes true. So is Di Palma. "It's been a real battle," says Di Palma. For more information, or to make a donation for much needed park funding (the group has to raise the money for fencing and everything else itself), call Di Palma at (415) 454-4851.

Thanks to an enlightened high-tech company based here, San Rafael has already gone to the dogs in an unusual way: Autodesk, Inc., the world's fourth-biggest PC software company, permits employees to bring their dogs and other pets to work. Some 75 employees frequently show up at work with pooches in hand. It's apparently a real selling point when recruiting—and keeping—employees.

Sure, there are occasional problems when a dog hikes his leg on someone's chair or decides to gnaw on a computer cable, but generally pooches are seen as enjoyable additions to the company.

We give Autodesk a four-paw rating, and hope other companies will follow its lead.

PARKS, BEACHES, AND RECREATION AREAS

• **Boyd Park** 🐾 🐾 ½ *See* ㉞ *on page 84.*

This is not a very doggy park, until you drive past the Dollar mansion (now the Falkirk Community Cultural Center) into the hills on Robert Dollar Scenic Drive to the undeveloped portion. The only parking is at a turnout off the drive, but at that spot, the drive becomes a dirt fire trail, closed to autos, that mounts the ridgecrest in a steady uphill climb through brush, oak, and madrone.

Leash your pup and start walking. You'll get a breathtaking view of the Richmond–San Rafael Bridge, the Bay Bridge, the Oakland skyline, and Mount Tam. Robert Dollar Scenic Drive begins at the end of Laurel Place. (415) 485-3333.

• **China Camp State Park** 🐾 🐾 🐾 *See* ㉟ *on page 84.*

You shouldn't miss a drive through this lovely park, although it's not terribly hospitable to dogs except at Village Beach, the site of the 1890s Chinese fishing village for which the park is named. As you drive in, you'll see a rare piece of bay, marsh, and oak-covered hills as the Miwuks saw it. The hills, like islands, rise from salt marsh seas of pickleweed and cordgrass. You'll see the "No Dogs" symbol at every trailhead, in case you're tempted. However, with your dog, you may visit any of three picnic grounds on the way, via North Point San Pedro Road. Buckeye Point and Weber Point both have tables in shade or sun overlooking San Pablo Bay, mudflats at low tide, and the hills beyond the bay. Bullhead Flat lets you get right next to the water, but there's no shade at the tables.

Watch for the sign to China Camp Village, a left turn into a lot, where there's some shade. You'll see the rickety old pier and the wood-and-tin village. Park, leash your dog, and walk down to the village and the beach. On weekdays, this park is much less crowded. There are more picnic tables overlooking the water by the parking lot, an interpretive exhibit (open from 10 A.M. to 5 P.M., and open to the air so that your dog can casually stroll in with you if it isn't crowded), and, on weekends, a refreshment stand serving shrimp, crab, and beer. You can eat at picnic tables right on the beach—small, but pleasantly sheltered by hillsides, with gentle surf.

Swimming is encouraged here, and it's often warm enough. Derelict fishing boats and shacks are preserved on the beach. You can walk all the way to a rocky point at the south end, but watch out for the luxuriant poison oak in the brush along the beach. You may occasionally find broken glass.

There are 31 primitive walk-in campsites here. As in all state parks, dogs must always be leashed or confined to your tent. Sites are $12 to $14. Dogs are $1 extra. Reserve through Parknet at (840) 444-PARK. From U.S. 101, take the North Point San Pedro Road exit and follow it all the way into the park. (Don't go near McNears Beach County Park just south of China Camp. Dogs are strictly forbidden.) (415) 456-0766.

• **John F. McInnis County Park** 🐾 🐾 🐾 🐕
See 36 on page 84.

This is an all-around, got-everything park for people. Among its riches are two softball fields, two soccer fields, tennis courts, a picnic area, a scale-model car track, a nine-hole golf course, miniature golf, batting cages, and a dirt creekside nature trail.

Best of all for trustworthy dogs, they can be off leash, so long as they're under verbal command and out of the golf course. This park isn't particularly pretty, but it's very utilitarian. From U.S. 101, exit at Smith Ranch Road. (415) 499-6387.

• **San Pedro Mountain Open Space Preserve** 🐾 🐾 🐾 ½ 🐕
See 37 on page 84.

A narrow footpath rises moderately but inexorably upwards through a madrone forest. But if you make it up far enough, you'll be rewarded with terrific views of the bay and Marin's peaks. Deer are plentiful, so it's kind to leash your dog if you don't trust him completely to stay by your side.

Park at the entrance at the end of Woodoaks Drive, a short street off North Point San Pedro Road just north of the Jewish Community Center of Marin. (415) 499-6387.

• **Santa Margarita Island Open Space Preserve** 🐾 🐾 🐾 ½
See 38 on page 84.

What a wonderful, secret place this is. Gallinas Creek, fortified by levees, is lined with rickety piers and small boats, like a bit of the Delta. You can cross to a tiny island via a footbridge and climb the hill you'll find here, covered with oaks and boulders, or walk around the edge on a dirt path. Watch for poison oak on the hill. Though of course it isn't true, you can feel as if no one has been here before you except Coast Miwuks.

From North Point San Pedro Road, turn west on Meadow Drive. Where it ends, at the western end of Vendola Drive, is the foot-bridge. You can park on the street. Carry water if you plan to stay long. (415) 499-6387.

• Santa Venetia Marsh Open Space Preserve 🐾🐾🐾½
See ㊴ on page 84.

Dogs are very lucky to be able to visit this saltwater marsh. Only leashed pooches on their best behavior should come here, because the preserve is home to two endangered species who don't need barking, chasing dogs to do them in.

Mmm, doggy, the scents can be mighty strong here sometimes. They're so doggone nose-flaring good your dog may not even notice he's wearing a leash. You may not feel the same about the odor, but hey, just keep saying to yourself "it's a natural smell."

It's cool and breezy here, but gentler than any San Francisco Bay shore park. The grasses and pickleweed make a pretty mixture of colors, and swallows dart above the ground hunting insects.

Vendola Drive has two distinct parts, and you can get to the marsh from the end of either. At the western end of the creekside segment of Vendola, at the corner of Meadow Drive, is a foot-bridge leading to Santa Margarita Island (see page 110). (415) 499-6387.

• Terra Linda-Sleepy Hollow Divide Open Space Preserve
🐾🐾🐾½ 🐕 *See ㊵ on page 84.*

There are many entrances to this ridgeline preserve, but generally the best are the highest on the ridge. We'll describe the one that starts you at a good high point, so that you don't have to climb. From the entrance at the end of Ridgewood Drive, you can walk into Sorich Ranch Park (see page 107).

From this ridge, you can see the city of San Rafael, Highway 101, the wonderful turquoise-roofed Marin County Civic Center, the bay, and the hills of Solano County. No leash is necessary on fire roads, unless you're worried about your dog tangling with deer. But pooches must be leashed on trails.

Park near the very end of Ridgewood Drive. The entrance is unmarked, and you have to step over a low locked gate. (415) 499-6387.

RESTAURANTS

Cento Stelle: We really enjoy eating at Cento Stelle, which in Italian means a hundred stars. Besides being in love with the name, we're also in love with the very good Italian food. Dine with dog at the four sidewalk tables. 901 Lincoln Avenue; (415) 485-4422.

Chinook Restaurant & Cafe: Dogs are thrilled to be able to join the humans who eat at this fine-dining establishment. The cuisine here is very California, very delicious. For the more casual mutt, there's also deli food. Dine at the six outdoor tables. 1130 Fourth Street; (415) 457-0566.

Erik's Drive-In: Formerly an A&W burger joint, Erik's maintains the drive-in burger tradition. Dogs whose manners require they eat in the car will appreciate this. But Erik's also has eight outdoor tables for dogs who dig dining al fresco. 836 Second Street; (415) 454-6605.

Phyllis' Giant Burgers: Dogs dig this drive-in burger joint. Order your meat-eater one of the giant burgers. Or if your pooch is in a no-beef mode, try a veggie burger. 2202 Fourth Street; (415) 456-0866.

Shaky Grounds: This restaurant's name reminds Joe too much of the Loma Prieta quake, so he has a hard time getting really relaxed here. Of course, the grounds probably refer to the coffee they serve, but that doesn't make Joe very relaxed either. Fortunately, you can also order pastries, smoothies, soups, salads, and sandwiches. Nothing melts Joe more than having a few sips of warm chicken soup from his porta-bowl. 1840 Fourth Street; (415) 256-2420.

Villa Romana: The Italian food here may not remind you of the Old Country, but it's a decent place for a pizza lunch with the pooch. Dine at the two sidewalk tables. 901 B Street; (415) 457-7404.

PLACES TO STAY

China Camp State Park: See China Camp State Park on page 109 for camping information.

Villa Inn: Rates are $60 to $83. Dogs require a $20 deposit. 1600 Lincoln Avenue, San Rafael, CA 94901; (415) 456-4975.

SAUSALITO

Even if you live here, you should play tourist and stroll around Sausalito's harbor in the brilliant sea light (or luminous sea fog). On weekends, it's especially pleasant early in the day, before the ferries disgorge their passengers. The city's attitude toward dogs is relaxed. It's the perfect place to stop and sniff around for awhile. Be sure to fortify yourselves with a big breakfast at one of Sausalito's many fine outdoor eateries (see page 116) before heading to the blustery Marin Headlands.

PARKS, BEACHES, AND RECREATION AREAS

•**Dunphy Park** 🐾🐾🐾 *See* **41** *on page 84.*

This is a small but accessible park by the bay, and it comes complete with grass, willows, picnic tables, and a volleyball court. Best of all, there's a small beach, and canine swimming is fine. You can watch sailing and windsurfing from here, too. Dogs officially must be on leash. The parking lot is at Bridgeway and Bee Streets. (415) 289-4125.

•**Marin Headlands Trails** 🐾🐾🐾🐾 🐕
See **42** *on page 84.*

From Rodeo Beach (see page 115), you can circle the lagoon or head up into the hills, as long as your pooch is leashed. You're in for a gorgeous walk—or a gorgeous and challenging walk, depending on the weather. Look at a map of the Bay Area, and it will be obvious why the headlands' trees all grow at an eastward slant. In summer especially, cold ocean air funnels through the Golden Gate, sucked in by the Central Valley's heat—chilling the headlands and the inhabitants of western San Francisco with fog and wind. The Bay Area may be "air-conditioned by God," but the headlands sit right at the air inflow, and it's set on "high." Never come here without at least one jacket.

Your dog will love the wind. The combination of fishy breeze and aromatic brush from the hillsides sends many into olfactory ecstasy. What looks from a distance like green fuzz on these headlands is a profusion of wildflowers and low brush. Indian paintbrush, hemlock, sticky monkeyflower, ferns, dock, morning glory, blackberry, sage, and thousands more species grow here—even some stunted but effective poison oak on the windward sides. (On the lee of the hills, it's not stunted.) Groves of eucalyptus grow on the crests. You hear a lovely low rustle and roar of wind, surf, birds, and insects—and the squeak and groan of eucalyptuses rubbing against each other. Pinch some sage between your fingers and sniff; if you can ever leave California again after that, you're a strong person.

From the beach and lagoon, you can hike the circle formed by the Miwuk Trail starting at the eastern end of the lagoon, meeting the Wolf Ridge Trail, then meeting the Coastal Trail (à la the Pacific Coast Trail), back to where you started. Or you can pick up the Coastal Trail off Bunker Road near Rodeo Beach. There are trailhead signs.

Sights along these trails include World War II gun emplacements, the Golden Gate Bridge, and San Francisco. As the trail rises and falls, you will discover a blessing: You'll be intermittently sheltered from the wind, and in these pockets, if the sun warms your back, you'll think you've died and gone to heaven.

Dogs used to be able to run off leash on all these trails, but no longer. The Golden Gate National Recreation Area, which oversees this 12,000-acre chunk of heaven, has become stricter of late. The only trail where good dogs can be leashless is the Oakwood Valley Trail, on the left side of Tennessee Valley Road, a little bit before the Miwok Stables. Dogs can be off leash on the trail or adjacent to it, anywhere north of the small cattle pond. They have to be leashed south of the pond, and they're not permitted to do the dog paddle, backstroke, or any other swimming styles in the pond. The trail doesn't make for an arduous hike, but at least we can still take our dogs for some much-needed off-leash romping.

If you want to hike from Rodeo Beach to Muir Beach (see page 98), remember that dogs have to be leashed the entire way now. But the great thing is that you can travel nearly the whole width of the headlands with your dog. This is tick country, so search carefully when you get home. (415) 331-1540.

• **Remington Dog Park** 🐾 🐾 🐾 🐾 🐕 *See ❹❸ on page 84.*
Your leash-free dog can exercise his paws while you both exercise your social skills at this delightful park. Remington Park is named after the dog whose owner, Dianne Chute, helped raise the money to put the park together a few years back. It's more than an acre, all fenced, on a grassy slope with trees. Dogs have the time of their lives tearing around chasing each other, and humans have a great time chatting. The park comes complete with

an informative bulletin board, a leash rack, benches, scoopers, and water. There's even a tent you can hide under in foul weather! They make everything cozy here.

Best of all, on Friday evenings, about 100 human patrons and their dogs gather for cocktail hour, with wine, cheese, bread, and of course, doggy treats. It sounds very Marin, but it's really just very civilized. On a recent summer evening, the park was host to a Mexican happy hour. Margaritas, chips, and salsa made the atmosphere even more festive than the usual Friday night gathering. If Joe could talk, he would have said "Ole!" Or at least "Make mine without salt."

From the day it was finished, Remington and his dog friends have made terrific use of this place. "It's the social hub of Sausalito," says cartoonist Phil Frank, "where the elite with four feet meet." What a boon to freedom-loving Sausalito dogs, who otherwise must be leashed everywhere in town. D.O.G. (Dog Owners Group) of Sausalito maintains the park and publishes a newsletter. Write to D.O.G., 690 Butte Street, Sausalito, CA 94965, or call (415) 332-6086.

From U.S. 101, take the Sausalito/Marin City exit, driving west to Bridgeway. Turn right on Bridgeway and drive south the equivalent of a long city block. Turn right at Ebbtide Avenue and park in the large lot at the end of Ebbtide.

•Rodeo Beach and Lagoon 🐾 🐾 🐾 🐾 🐕
See ㊹ on page 84.

Rodeo Beach is small but majestic, made of the dark sand common in Marin. Large rocks on shore are covered with "whitewash," birders' polite name for guano. Voice-controlled dogs can go off leash from the shoreline to the crest of the dune. Water dogs enjoy this beach, but letting your dog swim in Marin County surf is always risky—currents are strong, and trying to rescue a dog who is being swept away is to risk your own life. Also, while on the beach, watch your dog like a hawk and don't turn your own back on the surf. Especially in winter, a "sneaker" wave can sweep you and your dog away.

Doggies must be leashed from the dune crest inland to Rodeo Lagoon, and of course in the parking lot and picnic areas. If your dog promises not to bark and disturb wildlife, he can join you, on leash, on an interesting walk around Rodeo Lagoon. The lagoon is lined with tules and pickleweed. Ocean water splashes into the lagoon in winter and rainfall swells it until it overflows, continually mixing salt and fresh water. Birds love this fecund lagoon. It can be almost too much for a bird dog to take. An attractive wooden walkway leads across the lagoon to the beach.

From the Marin Headlands Visitors Center, follow the signs west. (415) 331-1540.

RESTAURANTS

Just a few of Sausalito's pooch-friendly restaurants:

Gatsby's: They serve fresh California cuisine here, but if you want to get really decadent, try the Chicago-style deep-dish pizza. It's as close to the real thing as you can get way out west. Dogs can join you at the four sidewalk tables. 39 Caledonia Street; (415) 332-4500.

Tommy's Wok: This fun Chinese restaurant is located just a bone's throw from Remington Park (see page 114), so it's a great place to dine after your dog burns up all his energy. The food is delicious, leaning more toward Szechuan dishes, but accommodating Cantonese-loving palates as well. Dine with your good doggy at the four outdoor tables. 3001 Bridgeway; (415) 332-5814.

Winship's Restaurant: Dogs like coming to the two outdoor tables here for a big breakfast, but the fare later in the day is good, too. It's the usual tasty soup, salad, sandwich, pasta menu, but this stuff always tastes even better with your dog at your side. 670 Bridgeway; (415) 332-1454.

DIVERSIONS

Seize the Bay: Ahoy, dogs, if you love the Bay, then Carpe Diem and take a ride on the Blue & Gold Fleet's ferry. Lucky dogs get to go from Sausalito to San Francisco and Tiburon. Please see page 181 in the San Francisco chapter for more information.

STINSON BEACH

It's fun to poke around Stinson, which is swarming with surfers and tourists on beautiful days. There's a relaxed attitude toward dogs at the outdoor snack shop tables. Bolinas Lagoon, stretching along Highway 1 between Stinson Beach and Bolinas, is tempting but environmentally fragile, so you should picnic along the water only if your dog is controllable. You'll also be taking a chance with muddy paws in your car. Don't go near Audubon Canyon Ranch, where herons and egrets nest.

PARKS, BEACHES, AND RECREATION AREAS

•**Stinson Beach** 🐾 🐾 🐾 ½ *See* ㊺ *on page 84.*

Highway 1 to Stinson and Bolinas is worth the curves you'll negotiate. Don't be in a hurry. On sunny weekends, traffic will be heavy. Try it on a foggy day—it's otherworldly. Anyway, dogs often don't care whether or not the sun is shining.

Before setting out, we asked around. "Go to Stinson," said a friend. "There are dogs everywhere." "Dogs aren't allowed on Stinson Beach," said a Golden Gate National Recreation Area ranger. "Stinson is swarming with dogs," said another friend.

A kind woman in the Muir Woods bookstore solved the mystery. "No dogs on Stinson," she said sternly, "but there's this little part at the north end that isn't Stinson. We call it Dog Beach."

Indeed, the county-managed stretch where private houses are built at the north end does allow dogs on leash. This is itself a bit of a contradiction, because as you walk along with your obediently leashed dog, dogs who live in the houses lining the county stretch, and who don't have to wear leashes, come prancing out like the local law enforcement to check out the new kid. Leashed and leashless, dogs are indeed everywhere at Stinson. It's merry and there's plenty of room for them.

You and your dog will be equally happy on Stinson Beach, with its backdrop of low hills and lining of dunes. Keep the dog off the dunes where they're roped off, being "repaired" by the forces of nature. Dogs are allowed in Stinson Beach's picnic area by Eskoot Creek, a pretty setting redolent with tantalizing smells.

Take the beach turnoff from Highway 1. Turn right at the parking lot and park at the far north end. Walk right by the sign that says "No Pets on Beach"—you can't avoid it—and turn right. Where the houses start is the county beach. You'll see a sign dividing the two jurisdictions saying "End of Guarded Beach." (415) 868-0942.

TIBURON

The town of Tiburon is almost too Disneyland-perfect, with its green lawns and fountains, brick sidewalks, and lack of smells.

On a sunny day you can't beat the clean, safe street atmosphere for eating and strolling. Dogs, of course, must be as polite and well behaved as their owners. Tiburon did a good job of planning for parking: There's almost none except for one large lot costing $2 just for the first hour, which means that cars aren't driving around searching for a spot. Just give up and park there.

The town has also arranged for fog banks to lie harmlessly to the west—usually over Sausalito. You and your dog can walk onto the ferry dock and watch boats of the Red & White Fleet come in and out, destination San Francisco or Angel Island. Dogs aren't allowed on Angel Island, but they can take pleasure with you sniffing the exciting scent of boat motor oil on the dock.

If you get a sudden impulse to take off for San Francisco, do it! One recreational secret of the Bay Area is that you may take your dog with you on the Red & White Fleet ferries, except to Angel Island or Alcatraz (see page 181).

PARKS, BEACHES, AND RECREATION AREAS

•**Richardson Bay Park** 🐾🐾🐾 *See* **46** *on page 84.*

Generally known as the Tiburon Bike Path, this is a terrific multiuse park, unusual because it can be safely enjoyed by both bicyclists and dogs. It stretches two-thirds the length of Tiburon's peninsula and has parking at both ends. The larger lot is at the northern end. A dirt road, Brunini Way (no vehicles), leads into the park at the north end. You'll find a quiet, natural bay shoreline with a bit of marsh. There's some flotsam and jetsam, but only the highest quality, of course.

Keep walking and you'll enter McKegney Green, the wide bike path that runs for two miles along Tiburon Boulevard toward downtown. (It doesn't go all the way, though.) Your dog must be leashed. The path, marked for running trainers, swings past benches overlooking the bay and a kids' jungle gym.

Soon the path splits and goes past both sides of a stretch of soccer fields, fenced wildlife ponds (no dogs), and a parcourse. You can take your dog on either side, but be aware that bicyclists use both. You'll also share this path, on a fair weekend day, with roller skaters and parents pushing strollers. On the green are sunbathers and kite fliers.

The view: Mount Tamalpais and Belvedere, with the Bay Bridge, San Francisco, and the Golden Gate Bridge peeking out from behind it. Bring a jacket—it can be breezy here—and carry water for your dog if you're walking far. The only fountains are for people. Going toward town on Tiburon Boulevard, turn right at the sign that says Blackie's Pasture Road. It leads to the parking lot. (415) 435-7373.

RESTAURANTS

Paradise Hamburgers and Ice Cream: This place furnishes bike racks and lots of outdoor tables. There's always a Fido bowl of water outside the door. The owners adore dogs and occasionally give a pooch a special treat. 1694 Tiburon Boulevard; (415) 435-8823.

Tutto Mare: You and your well-behaved pooch will love it at this restaurant. If it's not too crowded, dogs can join you at the tables on the rear lower deck, right on the San Francisco Bay. (You can also dine at the front patio, but it's not as scenic.) The lower deck is shaded by the floor of the upper deck, so your pooch won't melt on a hot summer day. The food here is a tasty blend of Italian and California cuisine. The wood-fired pizzas are our favorite, but the grilled sea bass is also mouthwatering. It's tempting, but don't fill up on the delicious focaccia they serve with everything.

Dogs are often given bowls of water if they look thirsty. This is the restaurant Craig and our small wedding party, including the dogs, boated to after we got married on the bay. The dogs were more than welcome here, and Joe the landlubbing dog was more than happy to be on dry, solid land again. 9 Main Street; (415) 435-4747.

DIVERSIONS

Bless your dog: For Paws pet store holds a Blessing of the Animals ceremony on Memorial Day weekend. In past years, blessings have been bestowed by ordained Episcopalian priests; a woman once brought a bottle of water from the River Jordan. 90 Main Street. (415) 435-9522.

Disguise your dog: Many dogs actually seem to enjoy getting dressed up for the Doggy Costume Contest at For Paws pet store on the Sunday before Halloween. They prance around in little butterfly or ballerina costumes like everyone is staring at them. And of course, everyone is staring at them.

The competition is fierce for four costume awards; some 400 dogs attended last year, and owners work all year on their canine costumes. If your dog thinks dressing up is beneath her, there's a special Nude Beach area for water dogs and sophisticates—inflatable pools supplied with balls. In 1991, one of the judges was Grace Slick. So long as your dog likes crowds of other dogs looking silly, you shouldn't miss this. A $5 donation is suggested for the Marin Humane Society. 90 Main Street. (415) 435-9522.

Seize the Bay: Salty sea dogs love this: Poochies are welcome to ride on the Blue & Gold Fleet ferry between here and such dog-friendly destinations as Sausalito and San Francisco. Please turn to page 181 in the San Francisco chapter for more information on this briny adventure.

WOODACRE

PARKS, BEACHES, AND RECREATION AREAS

• **Gary Giacomini Open Space Preserve** 🐾 🐾 🐾 🐾 🐕
See 🅸 on page 84.

The most recent addition to Marin's open space lands is this 1,600-acre gem. The preserve stretches for seven miles along the southern edge of the San Geronimo Valley. Stands of old-growth redwoods shade the ferny lower regions of the park. The higher you go, the more grassy it gets. Dogs like Joe (i.e., male) prefer the trees, but they can get the best of both worlds by following one of the wide fire trails and sniffing out various areas along the way.

Pooches may go leashless on the fire roads, but not on the more narrow hiking trails. Come visit before the rest of the doggone world finds out about this hidden treasure.

From U.S. 101, take Sir Francis Drake Boulevard west to San Geronimo Valley Drive and turn left. You can park at the intersection of Redwood Canyon Drive, just west of Woodacre, and begin your hike at the nearby trailhead. This is a fun route to take with your dog, since it brings you from thick forest to the top of the ridge. (415) 499-6387.

NAPA COUNTY

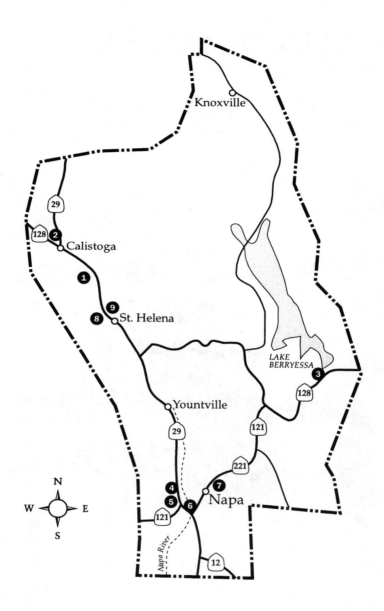

4
NAPA COUNTY

Napa dogs don't whine. They wine. And since there are plenty of dog-friendly restaurants here, they often wine and dine.

This is the home of California's most famous wine-making valley, and dogs get to experience some of the fringe benefits of this productive area. A few attractive wineries invite well-behaved dogs to relax and sniff around with their owners, but most don't want to publicize their dog policy. When you do find a dog-friendly winery, don't let your dog do leg lifts on inappropriate items, because Bacchus will get you. And your little dog, too.

The county's parks come up a little on the dry side. With the county's lush, fertile, and inviting vineyards, it seems like there's so much land that dogs would be in heaven here. Not true.

Only nine public parks and a few miscellaneous sites in Napa County allow dogs. The city of Napa has four parks where dogs are allowed, and all four permit them off leash in certain sections. You may incur the grapes of your dog's wrath if you don't take her to visit one of these leash-free lands next time you're in town.

CALISTOGA

PARKS, BEACHES, AND RECREATION AREAS

• **Bothe-Napa State Park** 🐾🐾 *See* ❶ *on page 122.*

Dogs are relegated to paved roads and campgrounds here, and it's a crime because of all the alluring trails. Hiking the highways can be fun, though. Joe seemed especially captivated by a man who was burning bacon over the campfire, his wife yelling that this was some vacation.

A wilderness haven this park is not, at least for you and your dog. Dogs must be leashed at all times. One of the two roads they're allowed on parallels Highway 29 and is so close you can see the drivers' eyes, often bloodshot from too much wine-tasting.

On the positive end, the roads are stunning in autumn when the leaves change color. And dogs are allowed to camp with you, on leash. Dogs are also allowed in some of the picnic areas just off the roads.

The day-use fee is $5. Dogs are an additional $1. There are 50 campsites. Fees are $15 to $16 a night, plus $1 extra for the dog. Call Parknet at (800) 444-PARK for reservations. The park is on Highway 29, halfway between St. Helena and Calistoga, just north of Bale Lane. The entrance is on the west side of the road. 3801 North St. Helena Highway (Highway 29). (707) 942-4575.

• **Pioneer Park** 🐾 🐾 *See* ❷ *on page 122.*

This is a small park, but its location so close to the heart of Calistoga makes it a great place to stop for a relaxing picnic with your leashed pooch. The two-acre park has plenty of shade trees and enough open area so your canine won't feel claustrophobic.

Going north on Foothill Boulevard, turn right on Lincoln Avenue. In two blocks, turn left on Cedar Street. The park will be on your right within a block. (707) 942-2800.

RESTAURANTS

Home Plate: Far from the tourist parking woes in town, this inexpensive, unassuming short-order restaurant makes some of the best grilled cheese sandwiches that ever melted in a mouth. Dine at one of three big outdoor tables. 2448 Foothill Boulevard (Highway 128); (707) 942-5646.

Lord Derby Arms English Pub and Restaurant: You drink one of 11 imported beers offered on draft here, and your dog can drink a fine bowl of water supplied by the staff. "We're very dog-friendly here," one staffer told us. "Dogs are some of our best customers." The large outside deck, also known as the beer garden, has 10 shaded tables and is comfortable on all but the hottest of afternoons. Food is served until late at night, and you can choose from typical English pub grub like fish-and-chips or bangers and mash. 1923 Lake Street; (707) 942-9155.

PLACES TO STAY

Calistoga Ranch Campground RV Resort: There's a lake here where dogs love to swim, but otherwise you're asked to leash them on the hiking trails and in the camping areas. The owners keep guinea hens to chase the rattlesnakes away, and you don't want your puppy to tangle with either creature. There are 144 RV sites. Fees are $19 to $25 a night for up to four people. It's $1 extra for a dog. 580 Lommel Road, Calistoga, CA 94515; (707) 942-6565.

Hillcrest II Bed and Breakfast: On the outside it's a good-looking, large, modern house. But on the inside, it's filled with antiques and other family heirlooms of the locally famed Tubbs family. Debbie O'Gorman, owner of Hillcrest II, is the last of the Tubbs family to live in the Napa area, and she's tastefully stocked the house with items from the family mansion, which burned down in 1964. There's even an old Steinway grand piano waiting to be played in the sitting room (which also has a fireplace).

All this is well and good with dog guests, but what they really adore is that the house is set on 36 acres where they're allowed to romp without a leash if they're well behaved. This is a dog's dream come true, because there just aren't leash-free stomping grounds like these in Napa County, unless you own big property. Fisherfolks and their dogs love it here, too, because there's a fishing pond on the property and it's stocked with all kinds of fishies, including catfish and bluegill. The property is at the base of Mount St. Helena, and the house is on a hilltop (thus the name), so the views are breathtaking.

Humans enjoy using the 40-foot-long pool. Dogs enjoy dipping their paws in the pond. Humans can also use the kitchen and barbecue areas, which is convenient if you don't want to go out to eat every day. A delectable continental breakfast is served on weekends.

Debbie, who has two friendly dogs of her own, asks that you bring a bed for your dog, if he sleeps on the floor, or a blanket to place under him if he sleeps on human furniture.

Rates are $45 to $90. 3225 Lake County Highway, Calistoga, CA 94515; (707) 942-6334.

Meadowlark Country House: The simple elegance of this secluded 20-acre estate makes guests feel right at home. The house where dogs with people get to stay has a light and airy feel and attractive decor, but it's really the surrounding property that makes this place so special. Beware, though. Cats and guinea hens also make their home around the house, so if your dog is a chaser, hang on to that leash.

You and your leashed pooch can hike on the estate's trails, past pastured horses, ancient oaks, and fields replete with wildflowers (and meadowlarks, thus the name). It's quiet here—a perfect place for a hilltop picnic with the pooch. If it's warm, the humans in your party can cool their heels (and knees and shoulders) in the beautiful swimming pool, which is surrounded by a cobble-stone walk. If all this isn't enough to fill your day, take a quick drive down the road and spend some time at the Petrified Forest (see Diversions, page 127).

Rates are $125 to $150. A delicious, large breakfast is included in the price. 601 Petrified Forest Road, Calistoga, CA 94515; (707) 942-5651 or (800) 942-5651.

Napa County Fairgrounds: A far cry from the great outdoors, this flat landscape with few trees is at least a good, fair-priced campground if all the inns and motels are booked. There are 50 sites, including some decent places to park your recreational vehicle. Sites are $10 to $18. Dogs (one per site) are $1 extra. 1435 Oak Street, Calistoga, CA 94515; (707) 942-5111.

Pink Mansion: This enchanting old place is an 1875 Victorian—very picturesque and very pink. The owners love dogs. "It's so stupid that so many hotels don't allow these wonderful animals. They add so much," says Jeff Seyfried, one of the owners. If you have a bird dog, think twice about staying here, since also in residence are some doves and a chicken. Water dogs will enjoy watching you splash around in the comfy heated indoor pool and adjacent hot tub, but they mustn't set paw in the water. Dogs are allowed in only one room here, so book ahead lest another dog beats you to the phone. Rates are $95 to $195. Pooches are $15 extra. 1415 Foothill Boulevard (Highway 128), Calistoga, CA 94515; (707) 942-0558.

Triple S Ranch: Once a working ranch, this hidden 11-acre spread in the hills above Calistoga still retains that old ranch feel. The nine rustic yet cozy cabins have only one large room each, so they feel kind of like bunkhouses. But each comes with a private bathroom, so you won't have to wander out to the outhouse in the middle of the night.

What really sets dogs' tails to wagging is that if they're obedient, they get to run around the ranch's property without a leash. That's right, a leash-free doggy haven. (Watch out for foxtails.) Don't be surprised if your dog doesn't want to leave this place. You'll probably be feeling much the same yourself. It's hard to kiss all this—and a pool, and a fun restaurant with some of the best onion rings around—good-bye.

Rates are $60. 4600 Mountain Home Ranch Road, Calistoga,

CA 94515; (707) 942-6730.

Washington Street Lodging: Relax in any of several cabins, each with its own little kitchen. You're just a couple of blocks from Calistoga's main drag here. Joan, the animal-loving owner, has cats, but she says if they don't like your pooch, or vice versa, they'll make themselves scarce. She also has a happy basset hound who will probably become your fast friend when you visit.

Your stay here includes a continental breakfast and a doggy treat or two. Cabins are $90, and dogs are charged a $15 fee per visit. 1605 Washington Street, Calistoga, CA 94515; (707) 942-6968.

DIVERSIONS

The two places dogs can actually roam among the trees in this town happen to be at two private roadside attractions. Call them kitschy, call them tacky—they're more fun to explore than most public parks in this county.

Sniff out a petrified forest: You and your leashed dog can roam among trees entombed by a volcanic explosion 3.4 million years ago. During a summertime visit, Joe found out why they call it the Petrified Forest. For him, it had nothing to do with the fact that we were surrounded by trees of stone. The sign announced in big bold letters, "ONCE TOWERING REDWOODS—NOW THE ROCK OF AGES." But Joe didn't know the true meaning of petrified until we encountered—the elves.

They were the Elves of Ages, the ceramic kind you find on suburban lawns and know beyond a doubt they'll be discovered by archaeologists a million years from now, the ones with the leering grins and bewitching eyes that children find enchanting by day and have nightmares about at night. They appeared everywhere Joe looked—sitting beside giant ceramic storybooks, standing beside stony trees.

The elves were at eye level for an Airedale, and they were all staring at him. Every time he saw a new one, he backed away with his tail between his legs and twisted his head around to make sure it wasn't following him. I couldn't help wondering how Airedales have remained so popular for frontline duty during wars.

But then came the petrifying elf. He didn't look any different from the others. But as soon as Joe laid eyes on him and his donkey companion, his tail went down and he turned 90 degrees. For at least two minutes, he was too frightened to look at the elf, growling instead at a manzanita tree. When he peeked and the elf was still staring at him, he decided enough was enough and bolted—leash and all.

He was waiting by the wishing well when I finally caught up to him. He would have left the park if he could have negotiated the turnstile by himself.

The Petrified Forest is at 4100 Petrified Forest Road, off Highway 128. It's actually in the outskirts of Sonoma County, but its address is in Calistoga. The unpaved trail is a quarter-mile loop. Admission is $3 for adults. There are dozens of tables around the gift shop, so pack a picnic. The forest is open from 10 A.M. to 5:30 P.M. in summer, 10 A.M. to 4:30 P.M. in winter. (707) 942-6667.

See Old Faithful in your own backyard: You know you're in for a treat when a big sign greets you at the entry to Old Faithful Geyser: "Many Notable People Have Come to SEE HEAR AND LEARN the mysteries of this WONDER OF NATURE which captures the imagination. IT'S AMAZING."

And indeed, when dogs see the 350-degree-Fahrenheit plume of water gushing 50 to 70 feet into the air, they generally stare for a few seconds with their mouths agape. But the sight of tourists jumping in front of the geyser for a quick photo before the eruption subsides quickly bores them. Dogs then try to wander to the snack bar and persuade the person on the other end of the leash to buy a couple of hot dogs. But even more fascinating is the scent of goat and pig in nearby pens.

If your dog is the brave sort, don't hesitate to bring him to visit Clow, the fainting goat. Clow butts her head against her fence at first, but she's only playing. After a few minutes, she was calming Joe's fears by licking him on the nose. Soon he was in love. Valentino, the Vietnamese potbellied pig, is no longer here. (I hope he didn't go the way of so many of his oversized brethren.) Joe is relieved, since Valentino scared the heck out of him.

Old Faithful erupts every 40 minutes, and the eruptions last about two to three minutes. Picnic tables are plentiful, so bring a snack or buy one here between eruptions. A sign at the site warns that dogs aren't allowed in the geyser viewing area, but you can bring your dog—securely leashed—within a safe distance of the geyser and not get scolded or scalded.

The geyser and goats are between Highways 128 and 29 on Tubbs Lane and are open 9 A.M. to 6 P.M. in summer, 9 A.M. to 5 P.M. in winter. Admission is $6 for adults. (707) 942-6463.

LAKE BERRYESSA

PARKS, BEACHES, AND RECREATION AREAS

• **Lake Berryessa** 🐾🐾 *See* ❸ *on page 122.*

Lake Berryessa, the largest man-made lake in Northern California, offers 165 miles of shoreline for human and canine enjoyment. Most of the resort areas on the lake allow leashed dogs. Better yet, they allow them off leash to swim. The summer heat is stifling here, so your dog will want to take advantage of the water.

Most resorts rent fishing boats and allow dogs to go along on your angling adventure. The fishing is fantastic, especially for trout in the fall and black bass in the spring. It's cooler then, too, so you won't have to contend with so many water-skiers, and your dog won't roast.

If you just want to hike and swim for an afternoon, explore the Smittle Creek Trail. The entrance is just north of the lake's visitors center, on Knoxville Road. The trail takes you up and down the fingers of the lake. Dogs must be leashed, except when swimming.

To get to Lake Berryessa from the Rutherford area, take Highway 128 and turn left at the Lake Berryessa/Spanish Flat sign. It's a very curvy route, so take it easy if you or your dog tend toward car sickness. For more information about the lake, call the Bureau of Reclamation Visitor Information Center at (707) 966-2111. For questions about lakeside businesses, call the Lake Berryessa Chamber of Commerce at (800) 726-1122.

PLACES TO STAY

Here are some of the Lake Berryessa resorts that permit pooches. Prices and amenities vary depending on the season and the extent of the drought, so call the individual resorts for information.

Berryessa Marina Resort: Dogs are $1 extra per day. (707) 966-2161.

Rancho Monticello Resort: Dogs stay for free. (707) 966-2188.

Spanish Flat Resort: Dogs stay for free, but they aren't allowed on rental boats. (707) 966-7700.

Steele Park Resort: Dogs are allowed in the campground, but not in the motel. They're $1 extra. (800) 522-2123.

NAPA

The city of Napa has some 40 parks. Dogs are allowed in a whopping four, each of which has an off-leash section. You'll see dogs in some of the bigger parks, such as the Lake Hennessey Recreation Area, but they're not officially sanctioned, so we can't officially mention them.

PARKS, BEACHES, AND RECREATION AREAS

• **Alston Park** 🐾🐾🐾 🐕 *See ❹ on page 122.*

With 157 acres of rolling hills surrounded by vineyards, Alston Park seems to stretch out forever. The lower part of the land used to be a prune orchard, and these prunes are just about the only trees you'll find here.

From there on up, the park is wide-open land with a lone tree here and there. Without shade, dogs and people can fry on hot summer days. But the park is magical during early summer mornings or any cooler time of year.

Miles of trails take you and your dog to places far from the road and the sound of traffic. Dogs are supposed to be off leash only in the lower, flat section of the park. Signs mark the area. It's better than nothing, and it's reasonably safe from traffic. A water fountain and a water closet also grace the entrance.

From Highway 29, take Trower Avenue southwest to the end, at Dry Creek Road. The parking lot for the park is a short jog to your right on Dry Creek Road and across the street. It's open dawn to dusk. (707) 257-9529.

• **Century Oaks Park** 🐕 🐕 *See ❺ on page 122.*

This park is a cruel hoax on canines. Dogs are restricted to a dangerous dog run—a tiny postage stamp of an area without fences, just off a busy street. And as for the park's name, which promises granddaddy oak trees, we're talking saplings here— maybe a dozen in the whole dog run area. We don't know how many are in the rest of the park, because dogs aren't allowed there even on leash.

The dog run area (we suggest keeping all but the most highly trained dogs on leash here) is on Brown's Valley Road, just off Westview Drive. Park on Westview Drive and walk around the corner to the dog run. The short walk to the park, with its shade and shrubs, is more enjoyable than the park itself. It's open dawn to dusk. (707) 257-9529.

• **John F. Kennedy Memorial Park** 🐾 🐾 🐾 🐕
  See ❻ on page 122.

Throw your dog's leash to the wind here and ramble along the Napa River. Dogs are allowed in the undeveloped areas near the park's boat marina. The only spot to avoid is a marshland that's more land than marsh during dry times.

Dogs enjoy chasing each other around the flat, grassy area beside the parking lot. There's also a dirt trail that runs along the river. You can take it from either side of the marina, although as of this writing, the signs designate only the south side as a dog-exercise area. The scenery isn't terrific—radio towers and construction cranes dot the horizon—but dogs without a sense of decor don't seem to mind.

Dogs like to amble by the river, which is down a fair incline from the trail. But be careful if you've got a water dog, because jet skiers and motor-boaters have been known to mow over anything in their path. There's no drinking water in the dog area and it gets mighty hot in the summer, so bring your own.

Take Highway 221 to Streblow Drive, and follow the signs past the Napa Municipal Golf Course and Napa Valley College to the boat marina/launch area. Park in the lot and look for the trail by the river. The park is open dawn to dusk. (707) 257-9529.

• **Shurtleff Park** 🐾 🐾 🐾 🐕 *See ❼ on page 122.*

The farther away from the road you go, the better it is in this long, narrow park. It gets shadier and thicker with large firs and eucalyptus trees. Dogs are allowed off leash as soon as you feel they're safe from the road.

The park is almost entirely fenced, but there are a few escape hatches. Two are at the entrance and two others are along the side that lead you into the schoolyard of Phillips Elementary School. This isn't normally a problem, unless your dog runs into the daycare center at lunchtime, as Joe once did. A teacher escorted him out by the scruff of his neck before he could steal someone's peanut butter sandwich.

You'll find the park on Shelter Street at Shurtleff, beside Phillips Elementary School. It's open dawn to dusk. (707) 257-9529.

RESTAURANTS

Brown's Valley Yogurt and Espresso Bar: Cool off with a cold frozen one at the outside tables shaded by a wooden awning. 3265 Brown's Valley Road; (707) 252-4977.

Downtown Joe's: Joe Dog thinks the name of this place is first-rate. (Don't tell Joe, but it's named after chef-owner Joe Ruffino, not him.) This microbrewery is housed in a 100-year-old landmark building on the Napa River. Turns out he has good taste. Joe and Nisha loved it here. And here's a great deal for dogs: Last time we talked with dog-loving general manager Linck Bergen, he'd just bought some doggy water bowls and oodles of dog bones for his canine customers. Linck gets two paws up from Joe Dog.

Dogs get to sit with you at the edge of the area with outdoor tables (not in the covered section, though) or they can stretch out beside you on the comfy lawn. (Sadly, the sweet dog who originally told us about this place was subsequently treated very rudely by a waiter, and refuses to come back. When I brought it up to a manager, he said he would talk to his staff to make sure it didn't happen again. So you should be okay here, but I thought a heads-up wouldn't be a bad idea, just in case.)

You get to sip good beers made right on the premises. They even make a red ale called Tail Waggin' Ale. For a while, I thought Joe was foaming at the mouth with enthusiasm for the place, but I soon discovered he'd just dipped his snout into a near-empty, still-foamy glass of Tail Waggin' someone had left behind.

Foodwise, Downtown Joe's has something for every taste. Joe Dog likes to smell the porterhouse steaks, but he gets stuck with us ordering things like salads, fresh seafood (Tomales Bay oysters are always in season here), and pastas. 902 Main Street; (707) 258-2337.

Honey Treat Yogurt Shop: The nonfat frozen yogurt here will make you feel 10 pounds lighter and 10 degrees cooler after a long walk with the dog. Slurp it up at the outdoor tables. 1080 Coombs Street; (707) 255-6633.

Napa Valley Traditions: Enjoy fresh baked goods and cappuccino at four outside tables shaded by two trees and an awning. Your dog will find as much to enjoy here as you will—inside, they also sell dog biscuits and dog soap. 1202 Main Street; (707) 226-2044.

Racer's: General manager Linck Bergen wrote to tell us about his fun and unique dog-friendly restaurant. We raced on over to check it out, and it sure is a hoot. However, this may not be the restaurant for you if your dog has a passion for chasing cars; the theme here is racing cars. There's race car memorabilia everywhere, including a real live race car on the wall. And before you blame your chili-eating dog (the chili is super here) for certain strange noises, be aware that every so often racing sounds emanate from the speakers.

Of course, you'll be eating at the 25 tables in the outside area if you visit with your dog, so you may not get the full racing spirit. But you'll still have a good time sipping a "performance" microbrew and downing a burger or pizza. Thirsty dogs can always get a cool bowl of water here. 1201 Napa Street/Town Center; (707) 252-5475.

Rio Poco: Great burritos and easy take-out packages make eating on the outside bench a pleasure. Veteran's Park may beckon from across the street, but unfortunately you're not allowed in with your dog. 807 Main Street; (707) 253-8203.

PLACES TO STAY

Budget Inn: Rates are $40 to $85. Only one small pooch per room, and they're $10 extra. 3380 Solano Avenue, Napa, CA 94558; (707) 257-6111.

ST. HELENA

PARKS, BEACHES, AND RECREATION AREAS

• **Baldwin Park** 😊 😊 *See* ❽ *on page 122.*

Baldwin Park has everything you could want in a park, except size. But what it lacks in acreage, it makes up for in dog appeal. Set off a small road, it's almost entirely fenced and full of flowering trees, oaks, and big pines. A dirt path winds through green grass from one end of the park to the other, passing by a water fountain and a conveniently placed garbage can.

Unfortunately, dogs must be leashed, but it's still a pleasant place to stretch all your legs after a tour through the Wine Country. The park is on Spring Street between Stockton Street and North Crane Avenue and is open dawn to dusk. (707) 963-5706.

• **Lyman Park** 😊 😊 *See* ❾ *on page 122.*

You'll think you're on a movie set for some old-time village scene when you and your dog wander into this small, cozy park on historic Main Street. Leashes are mandatory, but the park has a gazebo, lots of trees and benches, a flower garden, and—best of all for dogs—an antique horse/dog water fountain. The top part is for horses, the lower bowl for dogs. Horses aren't allowed here anymore, so if your dog is huge, he might as well sip from the equine bowl.

The park is nestled snugly between the police station and a funeral home, at 1400 Main Street, and is open dawn to dusk. (707) 963-5706.

RESTAURANTS

Taylor's Refresher: The folks here are so doggone dog-friendly that you shouldn't drive by without stopping to pay homage to their kindly ways. Dogs have a choice of two items they can have for free: a Milkbone or a hot dog. Yes, a real live in-the-flesh (so to speak) hot dog. "I love seeing dogs munching their favorite treats here," says Sara Toogood, a manager who also house-sits all kinds of critters. Humans will enjoy ice cream, burgers, and other fun lunch items, but unlike dogs, they have to pay. 933 Main Street; (707) 963-3486.

Tomatina: The little sister of the more expensive and upscale Tra Vigne Ristorante (see below), Tomatina is just what the vet ordered if you have a pooch and a pedigreed palate, but a more paltry pocketbook. Lots of families come here. The pastas, pizzas, and salads are delicious. Munch with your dog at the four tables on the patio. 1016 Main Street; (707) 967-9999.

Tra Vigne Ristorante: This is one of the most attractive restaurants with some of the best food in the Bay Area. The wood-burning oven gives even the most simple pasta, pizza, and meat dishes a taste that's out of this world. Your dog can dine with you at the 20 tables in the large, garden-like lower courtyard. (The terrace is out because you have to go through the restaurant to get there, and that's a no-no.) The two of you are sure to drool over the gourmet cuisine. 1050 Charter Oak Avenue (you'll see the restaurant from Main Street, though); (707) 963-4444.

Valley Deli: Eat good deli food at a couple of sidewalk tables. 1138 Main Street; (707) 963-7710.

PLACES TO STAY

El Bonita Motel: This little motel provides decent lodging at very reasonable prices for this area. Rates are $75 to $219. Dogs are $5 extra. 195 Main Street, St. Helena, CA 94574; (707) 963-3216.

Harvest Inn: Dogs who stay in this Tudor-style lodging can wander the inn's 21 acres of gardens, vineyards, fields, and ponds (on leash). Rates are $149 to $399. Dogs are $20 extra daily. They prefer small dogs here. One Main Street, St. Helena, CA 94574; (707) 963-WINE.

DIVERSIONS

Grape Expectations: There are miles and miles of lush vineyards in Napa Valley and more than 70 wineries. But sadly, despite all the fine wine tours available, you'll be hard-pressed to introduce your dog to the joyous process of fermentation, since very few wineries permit pooches inside. However, many do have outdoor areas where you may be allowed to brunch with your pooch and have your own private wine tasting (provided your dog isn't planning on driving home).

Finding a dog-friendly winery can be hit or miss, so call ahead if you have a particular place in mind. For general info on Napa Valley, call (707) 226-7455. Here's one of the friendlier places that allows dogs to dine in the picnic area:

Cuvaison: You'll find three small picnic areas with a total of 11 outdoor tables here. Water is available. The person I spoke with even said, "Dogs are welcome in the tasting room if it's not too crowded." The winery is open 10 A.M. to 5 P.M. daily. 4550 Silverado Trail in Calistoga; (707) 942-6266.

YOUNTVILLE

Unlike the Yountville town government, which bans dogs from its parks, restaurateurs here have the right idea. Several exquisite restaurants welcome dogs to their patios, which are generally shaded and very accommodating to people and their canines. The only word of warning is to avoid these restaurants when they're packed with people from the tour buses that occasionally descend upon the town. It's just too crowded for dogs, who usually get tripped on and later photographed as tourist souvenirs.

RESTAURANTS

Compadres Mexican Bar & Grill: Tropical landscaping, intoxicating jasmine and honeysuckle, and umbrellas over tables make this one of the most pleasant restaurants for spending a few hours with your dog. Try the *pollo borracho*, a whole chicken cooked with white wine and tequila. 6539 Washington Street, at the Vintage 1870 complex; (707) 944-2406.

Napa Valley Grill: California cuisine reigns here, with fresh seafood as the focal point. Several outdoor tables with oversized umbrellas keep you and your dog cool. 6795 Washington Street; (707) 944-2330.

Piatti Restaurant: The atmosphere at the 10-table semienclosed patio is enchanting, and the food is just as wonderful. Choose from a couple of dozen house-made pastas, rotisserie-cooked chicken, fresh-caught fish, pizzas from a wood-burning oven, and many other delectable items. As long as it's not too crowded, your dog is welcome to dine at your side. 6480 Washington Street; (707) 944-2070.

Yountville Pastry Shop: Eat pastries, sandwiches, or pizza on the wooden outdoor patio. 6525 Washington Street, at the Vintage 1870 complex; (707) 944-2138.

PLACES TO STAY

Vintage Inn: Dogs who get to stay here are lucky dogs indeed. This inn ("inn" is an understated description of this place) puts dogs and their people in the lap of luxury, with a perfect blend of old-world charm and new-world design. The airy, beautiful, multilevel villas have fireplaces, and many have views of nearby vineyards. Dogs swoon over the grounds, which have pools, gardens, courtyards, and even a fountain. Rates are $150 to $300, and include a "California Champagne breakfast." Dogs pay a $25 fee per visit. 6541 Washington Street, Yountville, CA 94599; (707) 944-1112.

SAN FRANCISCO COUNTY

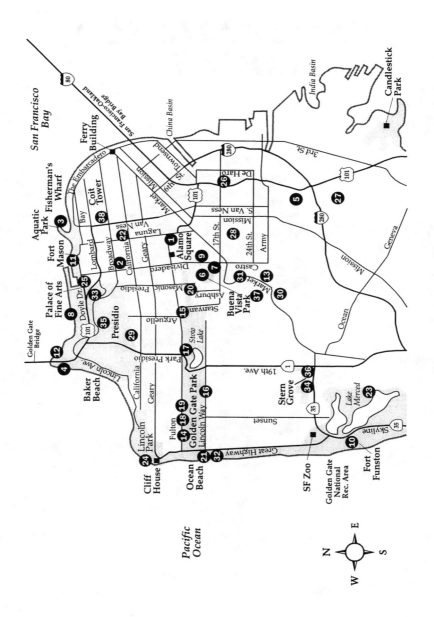

5
SAN FRANCISCO COUNTY

It's very likely that San Francisco is the most dog-friendly large city in the world. Sure, Parisians allow their poodles inside restaurants, but they don't have 18 parks and beaches where well-behaved dogs can run around in leash-free ecstasy. And no public transportation anywhere compares with San Francisco's, where pooches can ride cable cars, ferries, and buses. In addition, the finest hotels here permit pooches, as do some of the most popular tourist spots, including Fisherman's Wharf and Ghirardelli Square.

To top it all off, San Francisco is usually air-conditioned by the Big Dog in the Sky. So when temperatures are soaring around the rest of the area, it's often cool and foggy here.

But not everything is perfect in the City by the Bay. In fact, of late, many dog people have been howling mad over a few doggy digressions that have taken place here recently.

The Golden Gate National Recreation Area (GGNRA), which oversees a few pooch-friendly lands here, has closed off a two-mile strip of Ocean Beach to off-leash dogs (see Ocean Beach, page 157) and had made moves (and may once again) to reduce or eliminate Crissy Field's leash-free area (see page 143). A professional dog walker (who also happens to be an animal saint, according to many) is fighting the GGNRA in court over citations she got for walking dogs off leash in Presidio National Park (see page 159). A city supervisor is trying to dramatically increase dog patrols at parks to make sure dogs aren't off leash outside of designated areas. And at press time, dog people at Corona Heights Park/Red Rock Park (see page 143) were still fighting to maintain a leash-free area there.

Even with these problems, compared to most cities, San Francisco is still a blissful place to be a dog. And a few organizations have popped up in the last couple of years to make sure San Francisco keeps its Top Dog status. I'll mention organizations devoted to a specific park in the appropriate park's description.

An umbrella organization called the San Francisco Dog Owners Group (SFDOG) keeps track of all the dog park battles going on in the city (and occasionally in other parts of the Bay Area), and helps dog people network and support each other. The organization sponsors a fun monthly event called Critical Mutt, where dogs and their people get together and walk around to show their strength in numbers (à la bicyclists' Critical Mass). It's held on the last Saturday of every month at Crissy Field. SFDOG also puts out a newsletter that keeps people in touch with the issues. Membership is $10 (more if you feel like it, less if you can't afford it), and includes the newsletter. Write SFDOG, P.O. Box 31071, San Francisco, CA 94131, or call (415) 332-5800. Or you can check out SFDOG's Web page at www.sfdog.org.

SAN FRANCISCO

San Francisco is the only city in San Francisco County, but it's the only city this magical county needs.

PARKS, BEACHES, AND RECREATION AREAS

• **Alamo Square Park** 🐾🐾½ *See* ❶ *on page 138.*

A postcard comes to life in this park for you and your leashed dog. This is where the famed Painted Ladies hold court over the city. These six brightly colored Victorian homes are even better in person than they are on a postcard.

Walk up the east side of the park, near Steiner Street, to enjoy the view of the old houses with the modern city skyline in the background. Even if your dog doesn't care about architecture, she'll love the grassy hills that make up this park. There's plenty of room to roam and she'll find plenty of other dogs cavorting.

The park is bordered by Fulton, Hayes, Scott, and Steiner Streets. (415) 831-2700.

• **Alta Plaza Park** 🐾🐾🐾½ 🐕 *See* ❷ *on page 138.*

Smack in the middle of Pacific Heights, this park is where all the best breeds and most magnificent mutts gather daily. They flock to the hill on the north side of the park and conduct their dog business in the most discriminating fashion. It's not uncommon to see 25 dogs trotting around the park. Owners often address each other by their dogs' names—"Shane's mom! How *are* you?"

The park's off-leash run is actually on the other side of the playground and tennis courts, on the second level up from Clay Street. You can distinguish it by the two concrete trash cans that warn non-dog owners, "Dog Litter Only." Bushes line the paved walkway, and it's far enough from traffic that you don't have to worry about cars.

The park is bordered by Jackson, Clay, Steiner, and Scott Streets. (415) 831-2700.

• **Aquatic Park** 🐾🐾1/2 *See* ❸ *on page 138.*

You've got tourist friends in town and don't feel like taking them for the usual amble through Fisherman's Wharf? Here's a great plan that lets you be semi-sporting about the whole thing while you take your dog for a jaunt. Drop off your friends at Aquatic Park, point them toward the tourist attractions, and walk your dog right there.

Aquatic Park is just a few minutes from Ghirardelli Square, Fisherman's Wharf, a cable car line, and the Hyde Street Pier. It's also a decent place for a leashed dog to romp, with its large grassy field and plenty of pine trees, benches, and flowers. But stay away from the little beach—dogs aren't allowed. If you feel like shopping for T-shirts, jewelry, or arts and crafts, you can take your dog along Beach Street, where dozens of sidewalk vendors sell their wares (see page 182).

The park is on Beach Street between Hyde and Polk Streets. (415) 556-8371.

• **Baker Beach** 🐾🐾🐾🐾 🐕 *See* ❹ *on page 138.*

This beach brings your off-leash dog as close as she can get to the ocean side of the Golden Gate Bridge. And what a sight it is. Though in summer you shouldn't hold out much hope for a sunny day here, this sandy shoreline is ideal for a romp in the misty air. And dogs really appreciate Baker Beach in the summer. It's almost always cool and breezy.

If you like to sunbathe without a bathing suit and want to take your dog along, the very north end of the beach (closest to the bridge) is perfect. It's the only official nude beach in Northern California where dogs are welcome (as long as they're under voice control). But just make sure he doesn't get too up close and personal with your exposed co-bathers.

The south end is also intriguing, with trails meandering through wooded areas, and lots of picnic tables for leisurely lunches. Battery Chamberlain, with its 95,000-pound cannon aimed toward the sea, looms nearby.

From either direction, take Lincoln Boulevard to Bowley Street, then make the first turn into the two parking lots. The first one will put you closer to the off-leash area, which starts at the north end of the lot, closest to the Golden Gate Bridge. (415) 556-8371.

• **Bernal Heights Park** 😃 😃 😃 ½ 🐕 *See* **⑤** *on page 138.*

On a recent visit to this park, a dozen wolf-shepherds were the only dogs atop the amber hill. They ran and played in such pure wolf fashion that it was hard to believe they weren't the genuine item. The icy wind hit the power lines overhead and made a low, arctic whistle. The scene left an indelible impression that even in the middle of a city like San Francisco, the wild is just beneath the surface.

The rugged hills here are fairly rigorous for bipeds, but dogs have a magnificent time bolting up and down. Humans can enjoy the view of the Golden Gate and Bay Bridges. The vista makes up for the austere look of the treeless park. Dogs are allowed off leash on the hills bordered by Bernal Heights Boulevard. It can be very windy and cold, so bundle up.

Enter at Carver Street and Bernal Heights Boulevard, or keep going on Bernal Heights Boulevard until just past Anderson Street. (415) 831-2700.

• **Buena Vista Park** 😃 😃 😃 😃 🐕 *See* **⑥** *on page 138.*

The presence of vagrants who sometimes congregate at the front of the park has scared off lots of would-be park users, but it shouldn't. They're generally a friendly lot, posing no threat to folks exploring the park's upper limits with a dog.

This park is a real find for anyone living near the Haight-Ashbury district. Hike along the myriad dirt and paved trails winding through the hills, enveloped by eucalyptus and redwood trees. Some of the gutters are lined with pieces of tombstone from a nearby cemetery. The cemetery's occupants, who died in the 1800s, were moved to the oh-so-quiet town of Colma earlier this century. The gutters give the park a historical, haunted feeling.

From the top of the park, you can see the ocean, the bay, the Marin headlands, and both the Golden Gate and Bay Bridges. Birds sing everywhere, and there are lots of benches to rest on. Dogs are allowed off leash at the woodsy west side of the park, near Central Street.

A note: Sometimes people meet for assignations at the top of the park. If this bothers you or your dog, avoid this lovers' lane.

Enter at Buena Vista Avenue West and Central Street, or from Haight Street. (415) 831-2700.

• **Corona Heights Park/Red Rock Park** 😊 😊 😊 ½ 🐕
See **7** *on page 138.*

The rust-colored boulders atop this park cast long, surreal shadows at dawn. If you and your dog are early risers, it's worth the hike to the summit to witness this. And there's a fine view any time of day of downtown and the Castro district.

Unfortunately, dogs aren't allowed off leash on hikes up the hill. Until recently, the off-leash area was a roomy square of grass at the foot of the park. But now the off-leash space is in question. The city moved it (who knows why) to a smaller, less-attractive, foxtail-filled area at the side of the big hill here. At press time, the only thing in this area were fence posts that block neighbors' magnificent views. A group called Corona Heights Dog Owners Group (CHDOG) has stepped in to try to work with the city to get a better space. CHDOG is also taking up a few other issues with the city. To check on the status of the leash-free area, call CHDOG president Neva Beach at (415) 863-4636. Or you can write to CHDOG at 183 Delmar Street, San Francisco, CA 94117.

Wherever the leash-free section ends up, your best bet is to park at Museum Way and Roosevelt Avenue. This is at least in the vicinity of any future leash-free area. After a bit of leashless playing (if we're lucky enough to have such an area by the time you read this), you can don a leash and take your pooch up the hill. Fences keep dogs and people from falling down the steep cliffs. Keep in mind that there's virtually no shade, so if you have a black rug of a dog, think twice about climbing the hill on hot, sunny days.

The park is at Museum Way and Roosevelt Avenue. (415) 831-2700.

• **Crissy Field** 😊 😊 😊 😊 🐕 *See* **8** *on page 138.*

There's nothing quite like Crissy Field at sunset: As the orange sun disappears behind the Golden Gate Bridge, you'll be viewing one of the most stunning blends of natural and man-made wonders in the world.

Crissy Field, part of the Golden Gate National Recreation Area, is a jewel of a park any time of day. Obedient, leash-free dogs can chase and cavort up and down the beach and jump into the bay whenever they feel like it. It's one of very few spots in the Bay Area where they are allowed to swim in the bay. This is a particularly good place to bring a dog who has no desire to brave the waves of the Pacific. The surf here doesn't pound—it merely laps.

As you walk westward, you'll see the Golden Gate Bridge before you, Alcatraz and bits of the city skyline behind you. Sailboats sometimes glide so close you can hear the sails flagging in the wind. There's a stretch of trees and picnic tables a few minutes into your walk, where you'll find water and a good place to relax while your dog investigates the scents. There's also a heavily used jogging and biking path parallel to the beach, but dogs should be leashed there. Dogs also need to be leashed a little bit before the old Coast Guard station. You'll see the signs. The area to the west has been designated as a protected area for birds.

Not long ago, park users had to battle the GGNRA to maintain the park's leash-free status. They won. But at press time, the GGNRA had announced a plan to dramatically alter the park to the tune of a $25 million restoration, which includes a 20-acre marsh. Dogs are still supposed to be able to run free here, but there's worry that any doggy–marsh animal conflict could put an end to that. Keep your paws crossed that this works out, and let's be careful out there.

Enter on Mason Street in the Marina district and drive past the warehouses. Go right on Mitchell Street and through a big, rough parking lot. If you go too far to the east, you'll run into a sea of windsurfers, so try starting your walk close to the western edge of the parking lot. The beach is bordered by delicate dunes that are undergoing restoration in many places, including the entrance, so keep canines off. (415) 556-8371.

• **Duboce Park** 🐾 🐾 *See ❾ on page 138.*

If peering into people's windows is your dog's idea of fun, this urban park is his kind of place. A couple of large buildings have ground-floor windows that seem to fascinate dogs. Perhaps there's a cat colony inside.

Your dog will probably find other dogs to play with here. They're supposed to be leashed, since they're never more than a few fast steps from the nearest street. The park is grassy and has pines and a variety of smaller trees around some of its borders. There's also a children's playground at the west end.

The park is at Duboce Avenue between Steiner and Scott Streets. (415) 831-2700.

• **Fort Funston** 🐾🐾🐾½ 🐕 *See* ⑩ *on page 138.*

If there were a heaven on Earth for dogs, this would be it. This scenic ocean park will make your jaw drop with awe the first (and second and third) time you see it. Trails wind through magnificent bluffs overlooking the mighty Pacific. Even on gloomy days, you're bound to find plenty of ecstatic dogs and their people cavorting around this elysian piece of nature and having a wonderful time.

Fort Funston provides the perfect mingling of environment and companionship. And dogs who are very obedient and promise not to chase horses or birds can experience it all sans leash. Unfortunately, because of people who don't clean up after their dogs and let them wreak havoc and tear up sensitive dune habitat, the Golden Gate National Recreation Area is occasionally forced to consider making Fort Funston a leashes-only park. That would be a mighty big doggy disaster, so be careful out there. (A wonderful organization, the Fort Funston Dog Walkers, works hard to keep Fort Funston dog heavenly. The group supplies pooperscoopers and sponsors monthly cleanups and other events to help the park. If it weren't for this group, dogs would probably have to be leashed here. Membership is $10 annually, and includes an occasional newsletter. To find out more about the organization and how you can help, write or call Linda McKay, 241 Tocoloma Avenue, San Francisco, CA 94131; 415-468-1262.)

There are a few areas where you can start your walk, but the easiest access is from the main parking lot, next to the take-off cliff for hang gliders. Before you begin, walk your dog (still on leash, since it's a parking lot) to the watering hole—actually a bowl underneath a drinking fountain—and fill her up.

Now that you're all watered and ready for adventure, turn around and take the first trail to the north of the parking lot, the Sunset Trail. You'll meander through dunes and ice plant, encountering every kind of happy dog imaginable. You'll soon come to the main entrance to Battery Davis, which was built in 1939 to protect San Francisco from enemy ship bombardment. It was recently sealed shut because of some rotten sorts who hung out there, but you can still get the feel for the place.

Continue along on trails on either side of the battery. Both eventually end up in the same place. If you take the trail at the rear of the battery, you'll quickly be able to see the Golden Gate Bridge and the Cliff House. At that point, you'll also see a trail that takes you back into a mini-forest. Don't go all the way down, though, or you'll end up on the street.

You can get to the beach by following the narrow trails through the dunes shortly after the cypress groves. You'll notice that one trail takes you between two cliffs, where you won't be stepping on coastal dune plants. Take it all the way down to the beach. Depending on the tide, you can walk for miles or just a few feet.

You can go back the way you came, or walk along the ocean and take the steep trail back up to the main parking lot. (At press time, the stairs between the parking lot and the beach were closed because of weather damage, and there was no telling when they'd be fixed.) By this time, you and your dog will both be thirsting for that water fountain.

If you visit frequently, expand your explorations. Many trails wander throughout Fort Funston, and you and your dog will want to sniff out every inch of this place. (Be careful to avoid poison oak and areas marked as off-limits. A few spots have signs about staying out of dunes and away from bank swallow habitat. Please heed them. This is a delicate area.)

Because of the closure of a big chunk of Ocean Beach to off-leash dogs (see page 157), Fort Funston is getting very heavy use lately. On nice days, it can be impossible to find parking in the huge lot. "I just don't know if Fort Funston can support too many more people and dogs," said Fort Funston Dog Walkers organizer Linda McKay. And because of the larger number of dogs, skirmishes can ensue. Be sure that if you bring your dog here he gets along with other dogs. A man with a rottweiler recently had to carry his dog out because he was picking too many fights. (The dog, not the man.) McKay asks that people visit the park in the early morning if possible, so the park doesn't get overloaded in the afternoon.

To get to Fort Funston, follow the brown signs on the Great Highway. It's about one-half mile south of the turnoff to John Muir

Drive. (If you get to the Daly City limits, you've gone too far south.) There's also some roadside parking near that intersection. Once on the main drive into the park, bear right (going left will take you to the interesting new Fort Funston Visitors Center, but dogs have no desire to visit, since they're not allowed). Continue past a little building with paintings of hang gliders, and drive into the main parking lot. (415) 556-8371.

• **Fort Mason** 🐾 🐾 🐾 *See* ⑪ *on page 138.*

This park, perched high above the bay, is full of surprises. Depending on the disposition of your dog, some of the surprises are great fun. One can be downright frightening.

The best stands right in the middle of the wide-open field that constitutes the main part of the park. It's a fire hydrant, and it sticks out like a sore yellow thumb from its flat green surroundings. Joyous male dogs bound up and pay it homage time and time again.

The object that seems to take dogs aback, although people find it riveting, is a gigantic bronze statue of Phillip Burton. Several feet taller and broader than life, with outstretched hand, it can send a dog fleeing as far as his mandatory leash will allow.

Lower Fort Mason is also interesting to investigate. You can walk alongside the piers and sniff the bay, or peer at the liberty ship *Jeremiah O'Brien.*

Enter the lower Fort Mason parking lot at Buchanan Street and take the stairs all the way up to upper Fort Mason. (Huff, puff.) Or park along Bay Street or Laguna Street and walk in. (415) 556-0560.

• **Fort Point National Historical Site** 🐾 🐾 *See* ⑫ *on page 138.*

Beneath the Golden Gate Bridge, this mid-nineteenth-century brick fortification stands as a reminder of the strategic military significance San Francisco once had. Now it serves as a tourist attraction and one of the best places to view the skyline, Alcatraz, and the bridge. It's also a magnificent spot for your dog to stand mesmerized by the crashing surf.

By itself, Fort Point doesn't offer much for dogs. They must be leashed and there's only a small patch of grass. We recommend Fort Point as the goal of a long hike that starts at Crissy Field (see page 143). After walking to the west side of Crissy Field, leash your dog when you get to the old Coast Guard station and follow the Golden Gate Promenade toward the bridge.

Along the way, you'll come to an old pier. There are actually two piers, but the one you're allowed on is closer to the bridge. Stroll to the end for a close-up view of sailboats being tossed about on the bay. When you finally reach Fort Point, it's a tradition among dog people to continue to the westernmost point and touch the fence. There's no telling why, but you may as well try it.

To get to Fort Point without a long hike, follow the signs from Lincoln Avenue as you approach the Golden Gate Bridge. (415) 556-8371.

•**Glen Canyon Park** 🐾 🐾 🐾 *See* ⑬ *on page 138.*

From the cypress forests to the streams and grassy hills, this park was made for you and your dog. The nature trail in the middle of the park follows a muddy creek and is so overgrown with brush and bramble that at times you nearly have to crawl. It's as though the trail were blazed for dogs. There are so many dragonflies of all colors and sizes near the creek, and so much lush vegetation, that you may wonder if you've stepped back to the age of the dinosaurs.

Park at Bosworth Street and O'Shaughnessy Boulevard and walk down a dirt trail past a recreation center, through the redwoods and loud birds. Stay away from the paved road—it can look deserted for hours on end, then a car suddenly whizzes by. Your dog is supposed to be leashed, but you should still be aware of the road. In a few minutes, you'll come to a long, low building. At this point, you can go left and up a hill for some secluded picnic spots or keep going and take the nature trail. When you finally emerge from the dragonflies and dense greenery, take any of several trails up the open, rolling hills and enjoy a panorama of the park.

At press time, a group called the Glen Park Dog Owners Group (GPDOG) was on the verge of getting the okay to have leash-free access in the canyon before 8 A.M. and after 5 P.M. If this happens, it will be a really terrific place to take a pooch.

The park is at Bosworth Street and O'Shaughnessy Boulevard. (415) 831-2700.

•**Golden Gate Park** 🐾 🐾 🐾

This famed city park provides much dog bliss, but only in the places where dogs are supposed to be leashed. Several areas are set aside for leashless dogs (see below), but dogs in the know like to avoid those places, for good reason. For information about any area in the park, call (415) 831-2700.

•Golden Gate Park Dog Run 🐾🐾🐾 🐕
*See **14** on page 138.*

This fenced-in dog exercise area has the dubious distinction of being right next to a field full of buffalo. Some dogs adore the location, especially when the wind is blowing in just the right direction. It's the only fenced-in dog run in the city, so it's really the only game in town for escape artists. But the park's fans aren't just dogs who walk on the wild side. All sizes and shapes of dogs come here for playtime. So many dogs use it that much of it is grassless and dusty.

If you're a new dog owner in the city, this is a good place to come and learn about the world of dogs. People here always talk with each other, and they're usually talking about dogs. There's a steady stream of dog advice on tap.

The place can sometimes get a little rough around the edges when the usual dog crowd isn't around. People who like their dogs tough will occasionally drop in and hang out with something to swig while their dogs strut around. It's not usually a problem, though, especially during the normal dog rush hours (before work and after work for 9-to-5ers, and all day on weekends).

We've found more amorous dogs here than in any other park, so if your dog isn't in the mood (or you don't want her to be), this isn't the place to take her. For some reason, Joe gets accosted by both boy and girl dogs at almost every visit, so it's not one of his favorite places. He's flattered, but he's not that kind of dog.

The Dog Run is at 38th Avenue and Fulton Street. Park on Fulton Street and walk in, or take 36th Avenue into the park and go right at the first paved road. Drive all the way to the end, and there it is.

•Golden Gate Park (northeast corner) 🐾 🐕
*See **15** on page 138.*

Then there are the narrow fields at the northeast corner of the park, up by the horseshoe courts. It's a strange little area with hills and dales and dirt paths. Homeless people live here, and some don't keep good house. You'll see the campfire remains, old sleeping bags, and trash of every type. It's best to avoid this place, except in the middle of the day.

Enter at Stanyan and Fulton Streets.

• **Golden Gate Park (south side)** 🐾 🐾 🐕
See **16** *on page 138.*

The two other areas set aside for dogs are slivers along the south end of the park. One is between Fifth and Seventh Avenues and bounded on the north and south by Lincoln Way and Martin Luther King Jr. Drive. The other is on the south side of the polo field, between 34th and 38th Avenues and Middle and Martin Luther King Jr. Drives. Bring your dog to these sections if he's very good off leash. They're too close to busy traffic for less disciplined dogs.

• **Golden Gate Park (Stow Lake/Strawberry Hill)** 🐾 🐾 🐾
See **17** *on page 138.*

One of the "in" places in Golden Gate Park is the summit of the man-made mountain at Stow Lake. It's truly a sniffer's paradise. Dogs who like to look at ducks will also enjoy it. The path winds up Strawberry Hill to a breathtaking 360-degree view of the city. Unfortunately, dogs are not supposed to be off leash. It's best to avoid this walk on weekends, when bikers and hikers are everywhere.

Stow Lake is between 15th and 19th Avenues. From John F. Kennedy or Martin Luther King Jr. Drives, follow the Stow Lake signs.

• **Golden Gate Park (by the Polo Field)** 🐾 🐾 🐾
See **18** *on page 138.*

Dogs who prefer playing Frisbee (on leash) go to the meadow just east of the polo field. It's known for wide-open dells, good bushes, and plenty of gopher holes for old sports. Your best bet here is to go early in the morning.

• **Golden Gate Park (horse paths)** 🐾 🐾 🐾 *See* **19** *on page 138.*

Dogs who like to promenade—to see and be seen—take to the horse paths that radiate out from the stables. Or you can simply walk along the track that circles the field. One word of caution: The stables are rife with cats. Dogs need to know this. Leashes are mandatory, and remember, the mounted police station is uncomfortably close by.

• **Golden Gate Park (The Panhandle)** 🐾 🐾 🐾
See ㉠ on page 138.

That long, thin strip of park that extends eight blocks from the east end of the park to Baker Street is a great hangout for cool dogs. It's got a real Haight-Ashbury influence in parts, and although dogs must be leashed, they love to saunter around visiting other dogs wearing bandannas.

• **Golden Gate Park (Beach Chalet)** 🐾 *See ㉑ on page 138.*

Other lesser-known areas include the paths in back of the Beach Chalet—the soccer fields between the windmills near the ocean. The paths, which run along the edge of the fields, can be a little unsavory, but to leashed dogs, they're full of nothing but good smells. There's also the hilly, piney area up behind the archery field. We haven't heard of any accidental impalements up there, but be careful.

• **Lafayette Park** 🐾 🐾 🐕 *See ㉒ on page 138.*

This four-square-block park gets lots of dog traffic. For some reason, even though they have a legal grassy, off-leash section, dogs prefer to play on the paved paths in front of the playground. At least it's good for their nails.

The park is hilly and green and studded with palm trees, pines, and well-trimmed bushes. The official dog-run area is near Sacramento Street, between Octavia and Gough Streets. As you enter the park from the main Sacramento Street entrance, it's on your right. But most dogs gather atop the hill to the left, around two huge, smelly garbage cans.

The park is bounded by Laguna, Gough, Sacramento, and Washington Streets. (415) 831-2700.

• **Lake Merced** 🐾 🐾 ½ *See ㉓ on page 138.*

As the city's largest body of water, Lake Merced is favored by Labrador retrievers, Irish setters, and the like. An ideal spot to explore is the footbridge area near the south end of the lake. There are a couple of sandy beaches there that are safe from traffic, but dogs are supposed to be leashed anyway. Once you cross the bridge, you'll find an inviting area with lots of little trees.

You'll enter a small grassy section and come to a narrow dirt trail overlooking the lake's northeast bowl. We don't recommend letting dogs off the leash until you're at least a couple of hundred feet into the park, because menacing traffic is so close by. There are birds galore and purple wildflowers in spring. The park is a tease, though, because there's no way to get to the lake from here—it's down a very formidable slope covered with impenetrable brush.

The off-leash section of Lake Merced is at the north end, at Lake Merced Boulevard and Middlefield Drive. Park at Middlefield and Gellert Drives and cross Lake Merced Boulevard—very carefully. At times it's like a race car track. (415) 831-2700.

• **Land's End/Lincoln Park** 🐾 🐾 🐾 ½ *See* ㉔ *on page 138.*

This is probably the most spectacular park in San Francisco. You won't believe your eyes and your dog won't believe his nose. And neither of you will believe your ears—it's so far removed from traffic that all you hear are foghorns, the calls of birds, and the wind whistling through the pines and eucalyptus.

Unfortunately, leashes recently became the law at this Golden Gate National Recreation Area gem. Problems with mountain bikes and wildlife encounters led to the decision. But it's still a magnificent place to peruse with a pooch.

The towering cliffs, high above the crashing tide below, overlook virtually no civilization. For miles, all you can see is ocean, cliffs, trees, wildflowers, and boats. It looks more like Mendocino did 100 years ago—at least until you round one final bend and the Golden Gate Bridge jars your senses back to semi-urban reality.

If you want to venture the entire length of the dirt trail, keep two things in mind: Don't wear tight pants—you'll have to do some high stepping in some spots, and you don't want your legs packed into your Levi's—and don't bring a young puppy or an out-of-control dog. The cliffs here can be dangerous, especially where the trail becomes narrow.

There are many entrance points, but we like to start from the parking lot at the end of Camino del Mar. Go down the wooden steps to the wide dirt trail and turn right. As you hike, you'll come to occasional wood benches overlooking wildly beautiful seascapes. Take a moment to sit down. Your dog will appreciate the chance to contemplate the wondrous odors coming through her bulbous olfactory sensor.

As you continue, you'll pass a sign that makes its point efficiently and effectively: "Caution! Cliff and surf are extremely dan-

gerous. People have been swept from the rocks and drowned."
You'll have no problem if you proceed on the main trail and ignore the temptation to follow the dozens of tiny paths down the
cliff face. (Naked men often hang out at a beach or two down
there, so if your dog blushes easily, you'll have extra reason to
stay on the wider paths.)

In a little while, you'll come to the second such sign. This time,
instead of continuing on the main path (it gets extremely precarious, even for the most surefooted), take the trail to your right. It's
a fairly hard slope, but it's safe and gets you where you want to
go.

Rest at the bench halfway up, if you feel the need. The trail will
soon bring you down and around to an incredible view. Keep going
and turn around when you're ready to go home. Try not to end
up on the golf course, though. Golfers don't appreciate canines at
tee-off time.

A very convenient entry point is at the parking lot on Point
Lobos (which is what Geary Street turns into toward the ocean)
just above the Cliff House and Louie's. But we like to park in the
lot at the end of Camino del Mar, a little street just above that lot.
You'll pass a sign for Fort Miley on your right just after you enter
Camino del Mar. Leashed dogs are allowed on this large patch of
trees on a hill, and the views are stunning. It's a good place to
visit to get away from the weekend crowds who can descend on
Land's End. (415) 556-8371.

• **Marina Green** 🐾 🐾 ½ *See* ㉕ *on page 138.*

The clang of halyards against masts creates a magical symphony
from the nearby marinas here on windy days. Your dog's first re-
action may be a puzzled 30-degree head tilt.

Most of us know the Marina Green for its high-flying kites and
hard-running joggers. But it's also a decent place to take your dog,
as long as he's leashed. It's too close to the rush of cars on Marina
Boulevard to be comfortable off leash, anyway.

The grass is always green here, as the park's name indicates.
It's a treat for eyes overdosed on dry yellow grass and paws laden
with foxtails. There's also an attractive heart parcourse and a great
view of Alcatraz.

Enter on Marina Boulevard, anywhere between Scott and
Buchanan Streets. (415) 556-0560.

• **McKinley Square** 🐾 🐾 🐕 *See* ㉖ *on page 138.*

The view from this little patch of land is, shall we say, interesting. You can see for miles and miles, and the view includes several other leash-free parks, such as Buena Vista, Corona Heights, Mission Dolores, and Bernal Heights Parks. But you can also see such lovely sights as Highway 101, with its cars rushing madcap-fashion just a couple of hundred feet down the hill from you. And if you ever craved a view of San Francisco General Hospital's most austere, Dickensian brick buildings, this is the place to come. If you had really long arms, you could almost reach out and touch them. Actually, depending on the direction of the wind, on some days *they* reach out and touch *you*—the steam from the hospital's huge chimneys has been known to slip right up to this hilltop park.

Dogs are permitted off leash in the back section of the park, between the playground and the community gardens. Signs will point you in the right direction. It's nothing beautiful, just a wide path with a little running room on a hillside dotted with brush and occasional trees.

The off-leash section is on 20th Street and San Bruno Avenue, just a few blocks from the heart of the Potrero Hill business district. (415) 831-2700.

• **McLaren Park** 🐾 🐾 🐾 🐕 *See* ㉗ *on page 138.*

You and your dog can enter this park anywhere and find a trail within seconds. The surprise is that most of the trails run through remote wooded areas and windswept hills with sweeping views.

It's an ideal place to visit if you're taking someone to play soccer or softball at the Crocker-Amazon Playground. They play, you walk up a hill behind the soccer fields and roam with your leashed dog. Better yet, drive to the northern part of the park, to the section bounded by John F. Shelley Drive. Dogs are allowed off leash here, where they're far enough from traffic. Certain parts can be crowded with schoolchildren or company picnickers or ne'er-do-wells, so watch where you wander.

There are many entry points, but we prefer Brazil Avenue, which turns into Mansell Street in the park. (415) 831-2700.

• **Mission Dolores Park** 🐾 🐾 🐕 *See* ㉘ *on page 138.*

You can get a little history lesson while walking your dog here.

A statue of Miguel Hidalgo overlooks the park, and Mexico's liberty bell hangs at the Dolores Street entrance.

History may not impress your dog, but a wide-open space for running off leash will. It's behind the tennis courts.

There are two problems with this area, though. One: It's easy for your dog to run into the road. Even if she's the voice control type, she could find herself in Church Street traffic just by running a little too far to catch a ball. And two: You have to be on the lookout that your dog doesn't run over people who live in the park. Joe once slid into a sleeping homeless woman and scared her so badly she screamed and ran away.

Enter anywhere on Dolores or Church Streets, between 18th and 20th Streets. (415) 831-2700.

• Mountain Lake Park 🐾🐾🐾½ 🐕 *See ㉙ on page 138.*

In this sociable park, your dog can cavort with other dogs while you shoot the breeze with other dog people. The off-leash area is between two signs on the east side of the park. There's a bench for humans and a pretty good safety net of trees and grass between dogs and the outside world.

The favorite game among dogs here involves a big green bush. One dog usually starts running around it for no apparent reason. Circle after circle, he'll attract more and more dogs into chasing him until almost every dog is swirling around in a dizzying loop. Watch too closely and you can get seasick.

Dogs find the rest of the park mildly entertaining, although they have to be leashed. The lake that's the park's namesake is little more than a pond. Ducks and a couple of swans live here, and the temptation may be too much for your dog. We've seen dogs drag their owners ankle-deep into the muddy pond in pursuit of a duck dinner. The park is also home to an attractive playground and a decent heart parcourse.

To reach the dog-run area, enter on Eighth Avenue at Lake Street. (415) 831-2700.

• Mount Davidson 🐾🐾🐾 *See ㉚ on page 138.*

Hiking to the peak of this park can be a religious experience—literally. As you emerge from the tall pine and eucalyptus trees leading to the 927-foot summit, a concrete structure looms in the distance. As you get closer you'll see that it's a gigantic cross, 103 feet tall. It's so huge, and in such a prominent spot—at the end of a long, wide path surrounded by trees—that it can be a startling sight. On his first encounter, Joe backed out of his collar and collided with a tree. Since leashes are the law here, we had to quickly put him back together.

In 1934, President Roosevelt became the first person to flick the switch and light the cross. It's visible for miles, especially vivid under its nighttime floodlighting. On a night hike up Mount Davidson, you can follow the glow to the top. There was recently lots of controversy about keeping the cross (a religious symbol) in the park (a city-run property). That church and state mixing thing just wasn't making some folks happy. Thank God (so to speak), an Armenian group bought the property surrounding the cross. The cross, an intriguing landmark for generations—much more than a religious icon—will remain.

Since you enter the park at such a high altitude, it's only about a 10-minute pilgrimage to the peak. But you can make it a much longer walk by experimenting with different trails.

Enter at Dalewood Way and Lansdale Avenue. (415) 831-2700.

•**Noe Courts** 🐾 🐾 See ③ on page 138.

This partially fenced park is very small and green, but it's at the center of a very large and red-hot battle. For years, dog people have let their pooches run around here off leash even though it isn't officially a leash-free park. Then some parents stepped in and started calling police because they said their tots were being mowed over by dogs running into the playground. Unfortunately what ensued was a kids-versus-dogs fight, with some dog people seeing parents as "evil dog haters" and some parents seeing dog people as inconsiderate menaces. Of course, there are many parents who are also dog people, and many in both camps who empathize with each other's plight.

A group of park users has formed the Noe Courts Coalition, with the goal of mixing kids and dogs safely in the same park. Among their proposals is to allow leash-free pooches before 9 A.M. and after 5 P.M. To check on the status of the park or find out how you can help make it a more dog-friendly spot, call (415) 675-0110. Or you can write for more info (or send donations) to the Noe Courts Coalition, P.O. Box 460520, Noe Valley Station, San Francisco, CA 94146-0520.

The park is on Douglass Street, between 24th and Elizabeth Streets. (415) 831-2700.

•Ocean Beach 🐾🐾🐾🐾 🐕 See ❸❷ on page 138.

This broad, four-mile-long beach with a crashing surf isn't exactly Palm Beach. It's usually cold and windy and full of seaweed, jellyfish, jagged bits of shells, and less savory deposits from the Pacific. In other words, dogs think it's grand.

They used to think it was even better, since until recently, it was all a leash-free poochy paradise. But in 1997 the Golden Gate National Recreation Area (GGNRA) closed off a two-mile strip of beach to off-leash dogs. GGNRA heads said they had to do this because a threatened bird, the western snowy plover, hangs out in the dunes and beach here. They said they'd determined dogs were hurting the plover population by walking in areas where they live and by chasing them. Dogs shouldn't chase any birds, and in my opinion the rangers should have come out and ticketed people whose dogs were bird chasers. But the GGNRA folks enacted this sweeping policy without giving dog people a chance to show responsibility. A group of bird-loving dog people, called Rovers for Plovers, wasn't able to make them budge. Rovers for Plovers believes that if the bird is really in decline (and they have great doubts about the method used to count the birds), there are many reasons, including bulldozing the dunes for sand control, and homeless people living in the dunes. To get in touch with Rovers for Plovers, call Jocelyn Kane at (415) 731-1885.

The sections where your dog can still be off leash are from stairwell 21 (a little north of Lincoln Way) north to the beach's northern end just below the Cliff House, and from Sloat Boulevard south (where it eventually becomes part of Fort Funston's beach area). Unfortunately, the northern end is the most crowded. Dogs like Joe may be tempted to eat picnics or do leg lifts on backpacks resting on the ground. And the southern end is narrow and not as accessible as other parts. The area between stairwell 21 and Sloat, which is where dogs would do best off leash, is now a leash zone. Be careful to use your leash here, because the rangers are out in force. I've seen them give many a ticket ($50 per dog), and I've seen the dog people give the rangers many a hard time. "I've been in law enforcement 25 years, and have dealt with all kinds of people, but the dog people are the toughest to deal with," said one GGNRA ranger/park policeman, who genuinely feels sympathetic for dog folks.

You can park along the ocean, between the Cliff House and

Balboa Street. Walk south on the sidewalk until you hit the beach. Or park in the spaces between Fulton Street and Lincoln Way. There's also a parking lot at Sloat Boulevard and one a little south of Sloat. At press time, though, both of these were closed because of damage from erosion (they're up on the dunes, essentially, and the dunes done come down with all the rain). GGNRA folks weren't sure when this big problem would be fixed, so you might need to park elsewhere. (415) 556-8371.

•**Palace of Fine Arts** 🐾🐾🐾 *See* ❸❸ *on page 138.*

The glory of ancient Rome embraces you even as you approach this relic of the 1915 Panama-Pacific Exposition. From the huge colonnaded rotunda to the serene reflecting pool, the place drips with Romanesque splendor.

The Palace is especially grand under its night lighting. It's also an ideal place to take your dog while the kids go to the Exploratorium, located inside. Walk around the paved path that winds through the grand columns and around the pond. But keep your eyes peeled for people feeding the multitudes of pigeons, ducks, and geese. Dogs like Joe love to break up the feeding frenzy with an abrupt tug on the mandatory leash. Feathers fly and dried bread scatters everywhere.

The best place to enter for the full Roman effect is on Baker Street, between North Point and Jefferson Streets. Dogs are not allowed inside the buildings, although Joe did sneak into the Exploratorium one fine afternoon. (It's a long story.) He got as far as the tornado demonstration machine when he was nabbed and whisked away. (415) 831-2700.

•**Pine Lake Park** 🐾🐾🐾 *See* ❸❹ *on page 138.*

Adjacent to its more famous cousin, Stern Grove (see page 160), Pine Lake Park can be even more fun for dogs because it has Laguna Puerca, a small lake at the west end of the park. Swimming isn't allowed, but there's always the muddy shore for wallowing.

The lake is in a valley at the bottom of steep slopes, so there's not much need to worry about traffic. Leashes are supposed to be on at all times, in any case. At the lake's east end, there's a big field where dogs can really cut loose—as far as leashes allow.

Enter at Crestlake Drive and Wawona Street and follow the paved path, which quickly turns into a dirt trail. (415) 831-2700.

• **Presidio National Park** 🐾🐾🐾🐾 🐕 *See* ㉟ *on page 138.*

Dogs and their people like to pretend that the Presidio is their very own country estate, complete with acre after rolling acre (1,480 in all!) of secret pathways, open meadows, and dense groves of eucalyptus and pine. It's truly a magnificent spread.

The conversion of the land from the Army to National Park land hasn't changed the dog rules here. Pooches can breathe a sigh of relief, because they're still permitted (many were in doubt for a while). Not only are they permitted, but they're allowed off leash in a nice chunk of the park. A wide strip of land on the north side of West Pacific Avenue, from just west of Presidio Avenue all the way to Arguello Boulevard (but excluding the children's playground and ball fields), is the leash-free area. And it's an enchanting spot, made of big pines, little wildflowers, and long stretches of flat fields that blossom into rolling, densely shaded hills.

A controversy surrounding a professional dog walker who was issued tickets for walking dogs off leash in another part of the park was still brewing in court at press time. It's pitted dog people against the national park people. Again. This time it's especially contentious, since the dog walker, Michelle Parris, runs a dog rescue service with the money she makes walking dogs. They couldn't have picked on a worse person.

Now that the Presidio is a park, it's expected to draw more visitors than either Yosemite or Yellowstone National Parks. But there are still some out-of-the-way areas, such as the leash-free land, that even the most adventurous tourists will have a difficult time finding. A fun leashed tour starts when you park just north of the Arguello Boulevard entrance, at a roadside parking area on the west side of Arguello. Follow the path in and go down the hill as it gets wider. It will loop past wildflowers and seasonal sweet peas. Bear left at the first major fork and hike through a thick forest area, then bear right when that path gives you a choice. You'll hike up and down a gentle sequence of hills. Pull over and enjoy the larger hills to the west. Dogs thrill at speeding up and down them for no apparent reason. You'll run into a few more side trails along the way. Explore them as you wish, watching out for traffic on nearby roads.

In these hills, in the spring, you'll come across patches of bright yellow jonquils, many of them in formations resembling letters of the alphabet. An elderly British fellow who kept a good rapport with other dog owners used to plant them as a memorial to dogs who had gone to the Big Dog Run in the Sky. There's a "G" for a dog named George at the foot of the first large hill. The sweet old man, now deceased himself, liked to plant the flower bulbs in the spots favored by the deceased dogs. His spirit lives on with the dogs he memorialized in this piece of dog heaven on Earth. (415) 556-8371.

• **Stern Grove** 🐾 🐾 🐕 *See* **36** *on page 138.*

Until the 1991 concert season, dogs were welcome at all Stern Grove music festivals. Unfortunately, complaints about hygiene and noise changed this policy. Though dogs aren't allowed at the concert meadow, as of this printing, they are still tolerated around the peripheral hills, on leash. Bring a picnic, a bottle of wine, a rawhide bone, and, of course, a pooper-scooper.

Stern Grove is a treasure of trees, hills, meadows, and birds. There's even a spot where dogs are allowed off leash. Unfortunately, it's one of the least attractive areas in the park—very close to the street—although trees act as an effective barrier. And if you perch on the inner edge, the dog-run area isn't a bad place to listen to a concert. The violins get a little tinny at that distance, but your dog won't care.

For the dog-run area, enter on Wawona Street between 21st and 23rd Avenues. (415) 831-2700.

• **Twin Peaks** 🐾 🐾 *See* **37** *on page 138.*

So dogs aren't allowed at the Top of the Mark. So what. The view from up here will put all those "No Dogs Allowed" establishments to shame, and it's cheaper to entertain guests up here—it's free, in fact.

The summits of the twin peaks are higher than 900 feet. It's usually cold up here, so bundle up. You can drive to the northern peak and park in the lot. It's very touristy, and on this peak, signs tell you what you're looking at—Tiburon, Nob Hill, Mount Diablo, Japantown, and Mount Tamalpais. Your dog won't get much exercise, though, since all he can do is walk around the paved viewing area on leash. And frankly, Joe is bored by the marvelous vistas.

For your dog's sake, try exploring the other peak. It's a bare hill with wooden stairs up one side. While dogs must be on leash, it's not bad exercise. And the view—at almost 20 feet higher than the first peak—is magnificent. From here you can see other potential walks for you and your dog on the lower hills, where the views are almost as dynamic and the air is a little warmer. Be sure to keep him on leash, because the road is never far away.

The twin peaks are on Twin Peaks Boulevard, just north of Portola Drive. (415) 831-2700.

• **Washington Square** 🐾🐾 *See* ❸❽ *on page 138.*

Grab a gelato, leash your dog, and relax in this park in the middle of North Beach. There are plenty of benches and enough trees to make your dog comfortable with his surroundings. The park is only about one block square, but it's great for a stroll when you're hitting the cafes of San Francisco's Little Italy. And if you have a child with you, so much the better. There's a small playground that's popular with local parents.

Washington Square is right across from the ornate Saints Peter and Paul Catholic Church, and the Transamerica pyramid looks close enough to reach out and touch.

Enter the park at any of its four borders: Columbus, Union, Stockton, or Filbert Streets. Try not to drive to North Beach. Even during the day, parking's a bear. (415) 831-2700.

RESTAURANTS

Angelina's Caffe: Conveniently located one-half block from Cal's Discount Pet Supply, Angelina's is a good place for you and your dog to take a break from shopping. It's got everything from soup to pine nuts, plus a large variety of coffees. Enjoy them at one of six sidewalk tables. You can also stock on up on Italian souvenirs here, but watch out for the red, white, and green hats. 6000 California Street; (415) 221-7801.

Bepples Pie Shop: Joe thinks the cherry pie here is tops. He's right. Eat a piece at the little bench outside each of San Francisco's dog-friendly Bepples locations: 2142 Chestnut Street, (415) 931-6226, and 1934 Union Street, (415) 931-6225.

Blue Danube Coffee House: Have your cake and eat soup and sandwiches, too, at five tables outside this charming cafe. You can even indulge in a wide selection of beer or wine, but you'll have to drink alone if your dog is under 21. On sunny days, it may be hard to find an empty spot. 306 Clement Street; (415) 221-9041.

Brain Wash Cafe: The folks at this South of Market cafe-

Laundromat are so doggone dog-friendly that they'll even let you . . . well, we'll let you find out. Dine at the outdoor tables with your pooch, and before you know it, you'll be ready to fold your clothes, gulp the last of your espresso, and head home. This is a really fun time for dogs who don't mind the whoosh of traffic from busy Folsom Street. 1122 Folsom Street; (415) 861-1383.

Cafe Francisco: Take your dog to one of the two outside tables at this North Beach-Fisherman's Wharf cafe, and dine on fresh Mediterranean food and good brunch cuisine. 2161 Powell Street; (415) 397-2602.

Caffe Centro: The bistro dinners are so good you'll wish you could afford to come here with your dog every night to dine at the eight outdoor tables. Try the seared tuna Nicoise or the saffron fettuccine with grilled prawns. You can also get gourmet breakfasts and lunches at this South of Market cafe. 102 South Park; (415) 882-1500

Caffe Freddy's: This is a real find in North Beach, especially if you want a touch of California influence to your Italian food. Pizzettas are the specialty here. A favorite has goat cheese and smoked salmon, but there are eight other kinds. And if you want to feel what it's like to drink from a bowl, order Freddy's special coffee-in-a-bowl. It's lip-licking good. 901 Columbus Avenue; (415) 922-0151.

The Cannery: This old Del Monte packing plant is home to three delightful restaurants with courtyard tables for you and your dog, and there's often entertainment here. The restaurants usually don't have courtyard service after dark because it's too cold, so call first to find out. The Cannery is at 2801 Leavenworth Street. Here are two of its dog-friendly restaurants:

•*Cafe Rigatoni:* Eat delicious Italian food outside with your dog. It's *benissimo*. (415) 771-5225.

•*Las Margaritas Restaurant:* Seven kinds of margaritas, mesquite-grilled shark, and a great view of the courtyard below make this one of the more popular Mexican restaurants this side of the Mission district. (415) 776-6996.

Crêpevine: Mmmm. MMMMMmmm. MMMMMM. That's the way Joe groans with desire when he comes here and looks at all the happy folks sitting at the outdoor tables dining on their steaming hot crepes. You can choose from a variety of delicious crepes or create your own concoction. Joe highly recommends the spinach-cheese-mushroom deal. Crêpevine has a cozy, bohemian feel, even outside. 624 Irving Street; (415) 681-5858.

Curbside Cafe: The servers here are very dog-friendly, and the continental cuisine is top-notch. Try not to let your dog block the sidewalk, since it's a tight squeeze here. 2417 California Street; (415) 929-9030.

Foggy's: If your dog is a poodle or Border collie or some other brilliant breed, she can sit at the wooden tables outside this Fisherman's Wharf coffeehouse and play chess with you. Dine on gourmet salads and sandwiches between your opening move and when your dog wins paws down. 540 North Point Street; (415) 474-2070.

42 Degrees: This sumptuous, unique restaurant has one of the most picturesque courtyard patios we've ever laid eyes on. Joe was overjoyed when we checked it out, because not only was it attractive, it was also popular with the pooches. "We get a lot of dog lovers here," a manager told us. I can see why. Dogs get water if they're thirsty, and if the restaurant has dog biscuits (and it usually does), they get those, too. Humans drool over 42 Degrees because of the amazing food. There are so many styles and choices of cuisine that the place can't be categorized. You can have French food, Italian food, Spanish food, Mideast food, and lots more. Everything here is top-notch. The outdoor seating is available only for lunch. 235 16th Street; (415) 777-5558.

Ghirardelli Square: What was once a chocolate factory is now one of the classiest tourist shopping centers in the country. More important than that, it's got a lot to offer residents and their dogs. Ghirardelli Square is at 900 North Point Street. Here are some restaurants with outdoor cafes:

• *Boudin Sourdough Bakery & Cafe:* Dine on pastries, croissants, cheesecake, or huge sandwiches as you gaze across Beach Street at the bay. (415) 928-7404.

• *Ghirardelli Fountain & Candy:* Here's where you can get some of that famous rich Ghirardelli ice cream with all the fixings. Just remember: The more your dog gets, the fewer sit-ups you have to do. Stay away from chocolate, though. It can be very bad for dogs. (415) 474-3938.

• *Ghirardelli's Too!:* This more healthful alternative to the previous entry offers nonfat yogurt desserts. (415) 474-1414.

Harry Denton's Bar & Grill: Your dog is a lucky dog to be able to hang out with you at this landmark San Francisco restaurant. The food has no pretenses. It's just extremely tasty and hearty with a San Francisco flair (no snide remarks, please). Your dog will be your best friend forever if you order Harry's famous pot roast. Dine with your pooch at the four tables in front. 161 Steuart Street; (415) 882-1333.

Horse Shoe Coffeehouse: Enjoy good coffee and pastries at a down-to-earth cafe with two sidewalk tables. 566 Haight Street; (415) 626-8852.

Hungry Joe's: Joe Dog loves this yummy greasy spoon–style restaurant every bit as much as the people who eat here seem to love him. "Oh, that's Joe? Is he hungry?" they'll say upon meeting him, and they'll then laugh at their humor and give him an onion ring, french fry, or lick of milk shake. The food is good, filling, and fits most budgets. Dine with your happy dog at Hungry Joe's two or three outdoor tables. 1748 Church Street; (415) 282-7333.

Il Fornaio: Your dog can't exactly sit right beside you at this splendid Cal-Ital restaurant, but she can sit quite close if you call ahead of time and tell them you'd like to bring your dog. If space permits, they'll reserve you a seat at the edge of the very popular patio, so you can be as near as possible to your pooch, who has to be tied to a tree or pole a few short arm's lengths away. If you bring your dog a couple of pieces of your delicious pasta or a bite of your chicken fresh from the wood-burning rotisserie, she probably won't mind the slight distance. The restaurant serves a good breakfast, too, and has tasty take-out pastries to boot, should you want to take your party elsewhere. 1265 Battery Street; (415) 986-0100. (Reminder: Call first!)

Java Beach: After a morning of combing Ocean Beach, you can catch some rays and eat some lunch on one of the benches outside this mellow soup, sandwich, and salad shop. 1396 La Playa at the Great Highway; (415) 665-5282.

Jayman's: If you're in the Castro with your dog and you're in the mood for a tall cool one, step up to the two sidewalk tables here and get yourselves a couple of frozen yogurts. 3600 16th Street; (415) 626-5410.

La Canasta: This Mexican take-out restaurant is where we get our favorite burritos. When Joe is with us, we like to sit on the bench outside while we wait—and often while we eat. 2219 Filbert Street; (415) 921-3003.

La Mediterranée: Dog owners are lucky—there are two of these top Mideast/Greek restaurants in the city; each puts tables outside in decent weather and has a dog-loving staff. Joe highly recommends the Mideast vegetarian plate, even for meat eaters. The restaurant at 2210 Fillmore Street, (415) 921-2956, has only a couple of tiny outdoor tables. (The area inside is fairly tiny, too.) The location at 288 Noe Street, (415) 431-7210, has several roomy sidewalk tables, some of which are covered by an awning.

Martha & Bros. Coffee Company: Strong coffee on a hard bench may not be an ideal way to start the day, but it will wake you up enough to take your dog for a long walk. 3868 24th Street; (415) 641-4433.

Mocca on Maiden Lane: Now your dog can dine in one of the most posh streets of the Union Square area. Just a bone's throw from the finest stores in San Francisco, Mocca is a European-style cafe famed for its many types of salads. Dine at the zillions of umbrella-topped tables right on the street, which is closed to traffic. 174 Maiden Lane; (415) 956-1188.

The Orbit Room: Situated between Hayes Valley and the Castro, this trendy spot serves sandwiches, bagels, salads, coffee drinks, and beer. There are two outdoor tables where dogs are welcome and glassed-in windows so you and your hip pooch can see the hipsters as they mix and mingle. And if you're in the mood to do your laundry between sips of Italian soda, you can take care of business at the Little Hollywood Laundrette next door. 1900 Market Street; (415) 252-9525.

Pier 39: If your dog doesn't mind flocks of tourists, there's a wide selection of decent eateries with outdoor tables for the two of you here. Your dog gets to smell the bay and sniff at the sea lions below. Pier 39 is off the Embarcadero, near Jefferson Street. These are some of the restaurants where you and your dog are allowed:

 •*Burger Cafe:* Every burger imaginable is waiting for your dog to drool over. The mushroom cheeseburger is a big hit. (415) 986-5966.

 •*Chowder's:* Fried seafood and several types of chowder make Pier 39 really feel like a pier. (415) 391-4737.

•*Eagle Cafe:* Eggs, potatoes, burgers, cheese—good heavy food for a cold day is yours for the asking. Management asks that you tie your dog to a pole near the tables, rather than have him underfoot. (415) 433-3689.

•*Le Carousel Patisserie:* The next best thing to being on the carousel at the end of the pier (sorry, no pooches on the painted ponies) is this restaurant with a carousel theme and painted ponies everywhere. It also has a large deli with a selection of cakes and pastries, and plenty of outdoor tables. (415) 433-4160.

•*Sal's Pizzeria:* You and your dog can get a real taste of San Francisco by biting into any of Sal's special pizzas. The 49er Special has sausage, pepperoni, onions, and mushrooms. The Earthquake, with sausage, salami, mushrooms, and tomatoes, was a hit with Joe. (415) 398-1198.

Polly Ann Ice Cream: Here, dogs are treated like people, in the best sense. Every dog gets a free mini-doggy cone. It's vanilla, it's creamy, and dogs think it's to die for. Even if you have several dogs, the owners welcome them all and dole out the goods with a smile. They're especially happy if you buy some ice cream for yourself, of course. The doggy cone tradition has been alive for more than 30 years. (Joe and Nisha's first date together was videotaped here as part of KRON-TV's delightful *Outdoor Journal* show. Little did they know . . .) 3142 Noriega Street; (415) 664-2472.

Pompei's Grotto: If your dog likes the smell of seafood, he probably won't mind joining you at an outdoor table at this famous restaurant on the main drag at Fisherman's Wharf. The fish is fresh and the pasta delicious. And if your dog is thirsty, one of the friendly servers will probably offer her a cup of water. 340 Jefferson Street; (415) 776-9265.

Real Food Deli: You'd think a place like this would have only the healthiest, most vegetarian cuisine. It does have gourmet natural food, like grilled tofu brochettes, but it also has decadent dishes, like prosciutto sandwiches. Desserts soar to the same extremes. Three outdoor tables make eating with your dog a pleasure. 2164 Polk Street; (415) 775-2805.

Rustico: This eatery in Potrero Hill features pizza, pasta, panini, soup, and salads. There are lots of outside tables. 300 DeHaro Street; (415) 252-0180.

Sally's Deli and Bakery: Right next door to Rustico (page 166), this spot serves brunch on the weekends in addition to breakfast and all kinds of salads and sandwiches during the week. 300 DeHaro Street; (415) 626-6006.

Simple Pleasures Cafe: This is a quaint cafe with a warm and cozy atmosphere, and food to match. You and your dog can sit at the outdoor tables and catch live folk and jazz music Wednesday through Saturday nights. It may be cold, so bring lots of money for hot chocolates. 3434 Balboa Street; (415) 387-4022.

South Park Cafe: Vive la France! You and your dog may think you're in the Left Bank of Paris when you come to the South Park Cafe. The three sidewalk tables look out at beautiful, small, sycamore-studded South Park, which is a great place to visit for a quick leg stretch after a meal here. And the food is *tres magnifique*, with such yummies as roasted duck breast with honey-lime sauce, crispy croque monsieur, and tarte au beurre noisette. Even if you can't pronounce half of the foods, you'll drool over them. Joe Dog liked the idea of ordering spicy blood sausage with mashed potatoes and carmelized apples, but I can't stomach the thought of sausages, much less bloody ones. 108 South Park Avenue; (415) 495-7275.

Suisse Italia: You and your hungry pooch can eat here and feel like you've gone far away from the Financial District without ever officially leaving at all. The half-dozen outdoor tables are under a canopy and look out on tree-filled Walton Square. The cuisine is a little European, a little Californian, and a lot good. 530 Davis Street; (415) 434-3800.

Tart to Tart: If you want to satisfy a sweet tooth (with your dog as accomplice), the outdoor tables are perfect for your desires. 641 Irving Street; (415) 753-0643.

Tassajara Bread Bakery: The goods here are as wholesome and natural as the bread Tassajara made famous. Although this Upper Haight cafe is usually crowded, there are plenty of outdoor tables. 1000 Cole Street; (415) 664-8947.

Toy Boat Dessert Cafe: You may not be able to say it 10 times fast, but you and your dog won't feel a need to speak when you're at the outside bench eating rich and creamy desserts. 401 Clement Street; (415) 751-7505.

Trio Cafe: Sandwiches, soups, and salads—the basics here are some of the best. Eat them at the shaded outdoor tables. 1870 Fillmore Street; (415) 563-2248.

PLACES TO STAY

Best Western Civic Center Motor Inn: This isn't in a great part of town, but you and your dog should feel safe outside—at least by day. Rates are $65 to $95. Dogs are $25 extra (per night, and in this neighborhood!). 364 Ninth Street, San Francisco, CA 94103; (415) 621-2826.

Campton Place: The European ambience and superb service make this a luxury hotel your dog will never forget. Your room comes with your choice of newspaper, a nightly turn-down service, a terry cloth robe, a hair dryer, and an in-room safe, to name a few of the unique extras. Pooches who weigh more than a large Thanksgiving turkey will pant with joy when they learn Campton Place has relaxed its size limitation for well-behaved pooches. It used to be that dogs over 25 pounds weren't permitted at this luxury hotel. But now, as long as your pooch "isn't really big," size won't be an issue, according to a dog-loving front-desk agent. And think of the fun your springer will have strolling through stately Union Square, only half a block away. Rates are $230 to $1,000. 340 Stockton Street, San Francisco, CA 94108; (415) 781-5555.

Clift Hotel: This first-rate, top-notch, crème-de-la-crème hotel is also one of the most dog-friendly hotels anywhere. When you call to make your reservation, ask for your pet to be put on the Very Important Pet list. Every VIP gets a basket of pet treats sent to his room on arrival. They don't even blink at dogs here. "We've had pigs, Bengal tigers, you name it, we've seen it," a concierge told us. Your dog can even get his own doggy bathrobe here. Dog walking is also available. And if you have a human child, the Clift has all kinds of goodies for them, as part of its Young Travelers Program.

The hotel itself is to die for. It was built in 1915, and, as its elegant brochure states, "embraces the grand traditions of the past while initiating unparalleled levels of service and comfort." Some members of the staff have been with the hotel for nearly a half century, if that tells you anything. The attention to detail is everywhere, from the way your bed is turned down at night to the way the picture-perfect Art Deco lounge is arranged. Rates are $255 to

$655. Dogs are $40 extra per night. 495 Geary Street, San Francisco, CA 94102; (415) 775-4700.

Grosvenor House: Don't let the name fool you. This is a 200-room hotel, not a house. But the large, attractive rooms and suites are kind of like home, with most featuring cute little kitchens. The Grosvenor is on Nob Hill, an address that can impress. If you're thinking about staying here with your dog, though, you should know that you'll be charged a $175 pooch fee. That's a fee, not a deposit. Ouch! But if your stay is long enough, that doesn't sting quite as much. (By the way, to spare your dog the same embarrassment Joe Dog experienced when we visited here, you should know that the Grosvenor does not sound like it's spelled. The "s" is silent.) Rates are $99 to $189. 899 Pine Street, San Francisco, CA 94108; (415) 421-1899 or (800) 999-9189.

Hotel Nikko: Small dogs are welcome to spend the night with you at this lovely contemporary Japanese-style hotel three blocks west of Union Square. Rates are $175 to $2,500. 222 Mason Street, San Francisco, CA 94102; (415) 394-1111.

The Inn of San Francisco: This grand Victorian bed-and-breakfast was built in 1872, making it one of the oldest Victorians in the city. The style of Victorian is Italianate, for those of you who know your architecture. It's been fully and lovingly restored to its original grandeur, and as long as your dog promises not to poop in the beautiful English garden and to be a quiet guest, he's welcome here. Lucky dog! Classical music wafts through the inn's main area, mingling with the scent of roses. The woodwork is ornate, the carpets are oriental, and the fireplaces are marble. The 27 guest rooms are furnished with antiques and have marble sinks with polished brass fixtures. Most have private baths. The more deluxe rooms have featherbeds, and either a hot tub, spa, or fireplace. The flowery garden sports a gazebo, which is home to the inn's hot tub. A light but tasty breakfast buffet is served in the grand double parlors.

Rates are $85 to $235. The inn is located in the Mission District, where the sun shines more than anywhere else in San Francisco. The neighborhood here is not exactly Luxuryville, but you could do worse. 934 South Van Ness Avenue, San Francisco, CA 94110; (415) 641-0188 or (800) 359-0913.

Laurel Motor Inn: The owners love dogs, so many visiting dogs choose to stay here. It's conveniently located in a lovely neighborhood just far enough from downtown to be able to get great views of it from some of the rooms. It's also just a bone's throw from the magnificent Presidio National Park (see page 159). Rates are $80 to $104. 444 Presidio Avenue, San Francisco, CA 94115; (415) 567-8467.

Mansions Hotel: Step back in time in this elegant, mysterious old mansion, circa 1890. It's full of art treasures and beautifully attired mannequins. People tell tales of a resident ghost. The hotel has been described as "San Francisco's most San Francisco Hotel." The *San Francisco Examiner* said the Mansions is "elegance carried to the Nth degree." The *Wall Street Journal* says that "Upstairs, Downstairs is still a way of life at the Mansions Hotel." (The service is wonderful, something out of the past.) The hotel has five mini-museums, including the International Pig Museum and the Magic Museum. Dogs are allowed in only a few of the 21 opulent guest rooms, but at least they're allowed. Because the hotel itself is a work of art, bring only a very docile dog. Rates are $89 to $350. The price, amazingly enough, includes the Mansions' famous nightly magic show, complete with a performing ghost, and a delicious breakfast. (If you attend the magic show, be sure there's someone to watch your dog for you.) 2220 Sacramento Street, San Francisco, CA 94115; (415) 929-9444. The Mansions' Web site: www.themansions.com.

Ocean Park Motel: This Art Deco gem is San Francisco's very first motel. It was completed in 1937, one month before the Golden Gate Bridge. "When we took the place over (in 1977), Deco was pretty much a lost art," says owner Marc Duffett. "But my wife and I put everything into this place to preserve the Deco flair and at the same time make it homey."

Conveniently located just a long block from Ocean Beach (see page 157) and the San Francisco Zoo, this pleasant motel provides a quiet, safe atmosphere away from the hectic pace (and price) of downtown. You can hear the foghorns from the motel's relaxing hot tub. You can also hear the trolley cars, but it's not bad. And there's a special little play area for kids (the Duffetts have two and know the importance of playgrounds).

Joe and I stayed here with Laura (my human child) for a few days recently when our house was having the lead paint scraped from it, and we had a lovely time. Joe felt right at home after a couple of days, and I'm not sure he wanted to leave. He likes carpeting, something we lack in my house. Rates are $47 to $140. Two-room suites with three queen-sized beds and a kitchen are $100 to $140. Dogs are $5 extra. A few rooms don't have phones, so if you want a real break from the world, ask for one of these. 2690 46th Avenue, San Francisco, CA 94116; (415) 566-7020.

Pan Pacific Hotel: Before I begin, I want to let you know that only dogs under 25 pounds can stay here. Now I don't have to break your heart at the end of the description, should you have a Labrador retriever and a hankering for elegance.

The service at this downtown luxury hotel is impeccable. Your room is made up twice a day (more if you request), you have access to a free chauffeur-driven Rolls Royce, and there's even someone to draw a bath for you if you want. Speaking of baths, the bathrooms are delectable, with floor-to-ceiling marble, deep soaking tubs, and terry robes. The rooms are gorgeous, and come with such extras as in-room safes, voice mail, and in-room fax machines. The Pan Pacific also has a fitness center and a really good restaurant, but dogs will have to settle for their own version of this: a walk and a bowl of dog food in your room. Rooms are $199 to $1,700. Dogs pay a $50 fee per stay. 500 Post Street, San Francisco, CA 94102; (415) 771-8600 or (800) 327-8585.

San Francisco Marriott: The higher priced the room, the higher it will be in this towering pink downtown hotel (which many confuse with a giant Wurlitzer organ), so if your dog has vertigo, you'll save yourself some money. But the views from the top are magnificent. The city skyline, the bay, and the Bay Bridge are all in your scope. This modern hotel has 1,500 guest rooms and 136 suites, so there should be something here to suit every dog. For humans, there's a business center, an indoor pool, and a great health club with whirlpools, saunas, and a steam room. For dogs, there's you. Dogs have to sign a liability form, but there's no deposit. Rates are $149 to $225. 55 Fourth Street, San Francisco, CA 94103; (415) 896-1600 or (800) 228-9290.

San Francisco Marriott Fisherman's Wharf: Stay here and you and your pooch are just two blocks from all the T-shirt and souvenir shops that have taken over Fisherman's Wharf. Actually, some fishing boats still live at the Wharf, and some local crabs still frequent the restaurants, so it's not as commercialized as it looks at first (and second) glance. The rooms are decent, and your stay includes use of the hotel's health club and sauna. Rates are $149 to $300. 1250 Columbus Avenue, San Francisco, CA 94133; (415) 775-7555 or (800) 228-9290.

Sir Francis Drake Hotel: This famous Union Square hotel is a historic landmark, if your dog cares about such things. If there's someone in your party who can hang out with your pooch, check out Harry Denton's Starlight Room, a luxurious nightclub on top of the hotel. The views are truly to pant for.

Every one of the 412 rooms has voice mail, which is a big plus when your dog is expecting an important call. The cable car stops just a bone's throw away, so take your dog on a ride around this enchanting city. (See page 179, "Ride halfway to the stars," for more about dogs on cable cars.) Rates are $165 to $650. Dogs require a $100 deposit. 450 Powell Street, San Francisco, CA 94102; (415) 392-7755.

Travelodge by the Bay: Some rooms here have their own private patios. A few even have extra-length beds, should you find that you're tall. This motel (formerly the Rodeway Inn) is just three blocks from the part of Lombard Street that's known as "the crookedest street in the world." Rates are $65 to $135. Dogs require a $20 deposit. 1450 Lombard Street, San Francisco, CA 94123; (415) 673-0691.

The Westin St. Francis: At this luxurious Union Square hotel, "small, well-behaved dogs are as welcome as anybody," according to a manager. And "small" is not in the eye of the beholder. It's 15 pounds or under. That's about the size of Joe's head, so he won't be staying here any time soon. The cable car stops in front of this historic landmark, so there's no excuse for not taking your little dog on it. (See page 179, "Ride halfway to the stars," for more about dogs on cable cars.) The St. Francis also has a business center and a fitness center, for dogs with people on the go. Rates are $209 to $1,850 (super-duper suites are the pricey ones). 335 Powell Street, San Francisco, CA 94102; (415) 397-7000.

DOGGY DAYS

Celebrate a dog's life: At the San Francisco SPCA's Animal Wingding, you can also celebrate a cat's life, a llama's life, even an iguana's life. (If your dog goes for cats, though, you may want to keep him home so he doesn't put an end to those cat lives some are celebrating. The temptation is too much for poor Joe Dog, so he doesn't get to attend.) This huge, daylong street fair is the ultimate pet experience, with oodles of vendors, dozens of pet-related activities (including a pet star search), and the Parade of Life, a fun, colorful homage to the creatures who share our homes.

You can also take tours of the SPCA, and see its absolutely astounding, luxurious new dog and cat "apartments." The event takes place in early June in the streets around the SPCA, which is located at 2500 Alabama Street. This is not an event for dogs who are crowd-shy: Some 40,000 people attended the last Wingding. Hot dog! For more information, call (415) 554-3026 or (415) 554-3050.

Have a ball: The dog's version of the famous Black & White Ball is truly a spectacle to behold. At the Bark & Whine Ball, well-heeled dogs and their people shine. This is definitely one of those events to see and be seen. No one even shrugs when they see someone dancing with their dog. The ball features good music, passed hors d'oeuvres (dogs love this, but it's really for humans), and wine. It's held at the delightful Old Fed building. Tickets to this SPCA benefit (held in late February) are $75 per human. For more information, phone the SPCA at (415) 554-3050.

Show some poochy pride: Pet Pride Day, sponsored by the San Francisco Department of Animal Care and Control, is a day filled with pets on parade, pets in costumes (if the event falls near Halloween, the costumes get especially interesting), pets "pawditioning" for prizes, and many pet-oriented exhibits. Donations go directly to the department's adoption and outreach programs. Pet Pride Day is held in Golden Gate Park's Sharon Meadow the last Sunday in October. For more information, call (415) 554-9414.

Shake paws with Santa Claus: Whether your dog has been naughty or nice this year, he can have a one-on-one powwow with Santa Claus at the SPCA. In early November, pooches line up to see Santa and have their pictures taken with him. It's very cute. Better than watching the kids do it. Photos are $10, or two poses for $15. The SPCA is at 2500 Alabama Street. Call for this year's Santa date(s). (415) 554-3050.

Take your pooch out to a ball game: You won't strike out with your dog if you bring her to the Dog Days of Summer at Candle-stick, er, 3-Com, er, soon-to-be Pac Bell Park. In fact, you'll score a home run. If you thought hot dogs and baseball go together, you should see just plain dog dogs and baseball. It's a match made in dog heaven!

At Dog Days of Summer, your pooch gets to accompany you to a baseball game on a set day in August. You'll sit together in "The Dog Zone" and watch the Giants pound the heck out of the visiting team (we hope). But that's not all. Before the game, you and your dog can take part in a poochy parade around the field! Not many dogs (or humans) can say they've cruised around a pro-ball park. There's also a dog costume contest, should your dog be feeling creative. Cost for the day is $9 per human. Dogs don't pay a dime. Two dollars from each ticket goes to the San Francisco SPCA. Dogs have to wear ID and rabies tags. For other rules and info, call (415) 330-2516. To order tickets, call (415) 467-8000.

DIVERSIONS

Be a stage parent: Anyone who watches KOFY-TV (aka "the WB-20") is familiar with the hairy beasts who sit in easy chairs every half hour for station identification. Maybe you've longed to launch your own dog into the living rooms of thousands of viewers, but never thought you had a chance.

The good news is that your dog doesn't need connections, an agent, or a Screen Actors Guild card to be a star. Just send KOFY-TV a photo of your dog, along with your daytime phone number. If they're interested, they'll call and set up a taping date. "They're always looking for unique breeds," advises Frank Pappas, aka the TV 20 Dog Guy, but any mutt with a lovable face can qualify.

An added benefit to being taped is that you can finally find out just what makes those TV dogs whirl their heads toward that TV set at the perfect moment. Write to KOFY-TV 20, Attention: Pets, 2500 Marin Street, San Francisco, CA 94124; (415) 826-8900.

Catch a rising star: If your pooch has his paws on the ground but his head in the stars, give the San Francisco Sidewalk Astronomers a call. Since 1986, once or twice a month, depending on what's happening in the sky, astronomer John Dodgson and friends have been setting up telescopes at city intersections (at such well-traveled areas as Ninth and Irving, and 24th and Noe) and hosting stargazing parties. Passersby can scan the universe through

Dodgson's 18-inch telescope lens. (The telescope is so big it requires climbing up a six-foot ladder to peer through it.)

The group sets up at dusk, sometimes positioning telescopes on three different corners, and stays out for hours. On a given night, more than 100 people might check out the constellations. "If people want to walk by with their dogs, they're welcome to join in," Dodgson says. Best of all, it's free. To find out when and where the Sidewalk Astronomers will be stargazing next, call (415) 681-2565.

Celebrate great music and dance: Your dog's in for culture shock if you bring him to Golden Gate Park to catch top artists Saturday afternoons in the summer. Grab a picnic blanket, a leash, and lunch and head for the Golden Gate Park Music Concourse, in front of the Academy of Sciences. You'll see top dancers from around the world and hear some of the best jazz, classical, and ethnic music around. Just be considerate, and if your dog is the barking type, leave her at home. Admission is free. For more information, call (415) 831-2700.

From April through October on Sundays from noon to 3 P.M., the Golden Gate Band serenades parkgoers with a wide range of music. The band is a lively group with talent for both oompah rhythms and delicate tunes. For more information on the band, call (415) 831-2700.

Cruise the Castro: Your well-behaved dog is welcome to join you on a fascinating walking tour focusing on the gay and lesbian history of the Castro district. Tour leader Trevor Hailey will guide you and a small group to historically significant Castro settings while giving a superb narrative of how the Castro came to be what it is today. Trevor starts with the Lavender Cowboys of the 1849 Gold Rush and takes you through the impact of the 1906 earthquake, World War II, and the Summer of Love.

The only restriction on dogs who go on the Cruisin' the Castro tour is the brunch, which comes with the tour's $35 fee. Brunch is inside a restaurant, and pooches are not permitted. Trevor suggests, if possible, coming with a friend and taking turns eating brunch and walking the dog. You'll miss out on a little of the history Trevor relates at mealtime, but at least you won't miss out on the tasty brunch.

All tour takers, including dogs, get a miniature rainbow flag as part of the deal. Tours are given Tuesday through Saturday. For more information, write Trevor Hailey at Cruisin' the Castro, 375 Lexington Street, San Francisco, CA 94110, or call (415) 550-8110.

Explore a military pet cemetery: If only human cemeteries were so full of bright flowers (albeit many made of plastic or silk) and thoughtful epitaphs as this military pet cemetery located at the Presidio National Park (see page 159), death might not seem so somber. When you enter the little cemetery surrounded by a white picket fence, a sign tells you, "The love these animals gave will never be forgotten." You'll want to bring your leashed dog friend with you.

"Sarge," reads one simple epitaph. "Our pet George. George accepted us people," says another. Several markers bear only a large red heart, which means the pet was unknown but loved even after death. This is where cats, birds, dogs, and even Freddy Fish—whose grave is marked by a lone plastic rose—can live together in harmony. Take Lincoln Boulevard and turn north onto McDowell Avenue. The cemetery is just south of the corner of McDowell and Crissy Field Avenues. (415) 561-4516.

Find an apartment with your dog: With San Francisco's real estate market so tight (the estimated occupancy rate is 99.25 percent!), finding an apartment is grueling enough. Add a dog to the mix and you may as well move back to your hometown. But thanks to a wonderful new program of the San Francisco SPCA, dog people are finding it easier to rent apartments in the city these days. The Open Door Program helps landlords and potential tenants come together in several ways, including providing a listing of available pet-friendly housing, and giving renters tips on how to present their pooch in the right manner (making a doggy resume really helps). This is a hugely popular, free service, garnering 500 phone calls a month. There have been many terrific success stories. Maybe you'll be next. I sure wish they had this program when I was renting. For a complete packet of Open Door info, call (415) 554-3098.

Forget Greyhound; take a Tortoise: Traveling dogs delight in the knowledge that the Green Tortoise, last of the hippie bus companies that thrived in the 1970s, permits well-behaved pooches on its West Coast route. Green Tortoise buses are the ultimate way to travel by bus. Riders are generally a friendly, eclectic lot, which includes tots, retirees, yuppies, punksters, hippies, and students. At night, the whole bus converts to one big bed, with a few sort of private bunks. And if you cross into Oregon, you'll get treated to one of the best breakfasts (cooked by volunteers from the bus, under the guidance of a breakfast guru) and saunas and cold-creek dips of your life—all on the pastoral acreage of the owner of Green Tortoise.

All this makes up for one item that's lacking on Green Tortoise buses. I'll let driver Steve Spahr, a gentle bear of a man, tell you in his own words—the very words he bellowed to the riders on my first Green Tortoise trek: "There are no bathrooms. So we have a pee scale, from one to ten. Ten means your neighbors are scooting away from you as fast as they can. You gotta let me know when you hit five, okay?" If you communicate with the driver, you and your bladder should have no problem.

It's really easy to make buddies on the Green Tortoise. And with a dog in hand, you'll find folks even more friendly than usual. People traveling with dogs are on standby status until the bus driver makes sure your dog is clean, friendly, and fairly mellow and that no one on the bus has allergies or a big problem with pooches. Dogs pay full fare, and only one dog per bus is allowed. At night, your dog gets to sleep beside you, if he so desires and your neighbors don't mind. The bus stops pretty frequently, so be sure to take your dog out often so he can stretch his legs and get relief. After all, he can't tell the bus driver what number he's hitting on the "pee scale."

San Francisco is the main base for Green Tortoise, although you can go all the way from Los Angeles to Seattle with a dog. The ride from San Francisco to Seattle costs $59 one way and takes about 25 hours. From San Francisco to Los Angeles (a much less scenic, often less mellow ride), it's $35 one way and takes about 12 hours. A one-way ride from Los Angeles to Seattle costs $79. For more information, write the Green Tortoise at 494 Broadway, San Francisco, CA 94113, or phone (800) TORTOISE (that's 800-867-8647 for those of you who can't stand punching in letters on your phone) or (415) 956-7500.

Get it at Wilkes': Wilkes Bashford Co., one of the more upscale apparel and home stores on Union Square, is a joy for dogs who like shopping. Pooches of any size are welcome to peruse the store's beautiful merchandise (it's to drool for) as long as they're clean and don't do nasty things like leg lifts.

Wilkes Bashford, who happens to own Wilkes Bashford Co., adores dogs. He's been bringing his dogs to the store since 1968. Freddie, a longhaired dachshund given to Bashford by San Francisco mayor Willie Brown, goes to work with Bashford just about every day. And even when Bashford is out of town on business, Freddie makes his rounds at the store. Bashford's driver takes him there in the morning and drives him home in the afternoon.

"I'm a nut about dogs," says Bashford. "Dogs are a vital part of life." Bashford says people "are so surprised" when he invites them to come inside with a dog. "Sometimes they can't believe it. But there's never been a problem with a dog here. They've all been very well behaved."

Wilkes Bashford Co. is located at 375 Sutter Street. Phone (415) 986-4380 for store hours. And while you're at the store, be sure to check out the wonderful little pet section on the lower floor. A few of the items are truly works of art (look at the price tags).

Go organic: The California Harvest Ranch Market, known for its wide selection of fresh organic produce, has a healthy attitude toward dogs. The owners installed two clamps in the front just for dogs. The idea is to hook your dog's leash to the clamp and go shopping, knowing your dog is safe and secure. As always, though, don't leave him unchecked for long. They're open 9 A.M. to 11 P.M. 2285 Market Street; (415) 626-0805.

Help someone with AIDS: PAWS (Pets Are Wonderful Support) is dedicated to preserving the relationship of people with AIDS and their pets. If you've ever been comforted by your dog while ill, you've caught a glimpse of the importance of the work PAWS does. PAWS needs people to do office work, deliver pet food, and walk and care for pets. And if you have room for another dog in the house, PAWS usually has some special animals for adoption. Write them at 539 Castro Street, San Francisco, CA 94114, or call (415) 241-1460.

Hop on a bus: Dogs are allowed on Muni buses and cable cars anytime they're running. Only one dog is permitted per bus. Dogs must be on a short leash and muzzled, no matter how little or how sweet. Bus driver Tom Brown told us about the creative, but ineffective, ways some people muzzle their dogs. "This one man had a part pit-bull dog, and he put a little rubber band around its mouth," said Brown. "No way that dog was getting on my bus."

Dogs pay the same fare as owners. If the owner is a senior citizen, the dog pays senior citizen rates. Lap-sized dogs can stay on your lap, but all others are consigned to the floor. Keep your dog from getting underfoot and be sure he's well walked before he gets on. Call (415) 673-MUNI for more information.

Hurry to the surrey with the fringe on the top: Really cool dogs don't walk around Golden Gate Park with their people. They ride. And not in a car, but in a surrey. With a little pedal power and some good steering, you can cover plenty of ground in a relatively short time while your dog just sits there and does nothing but smile and sniff at the people you pass. Mike's Bikes & Blades, located at Stow Lake in the park, is happy to rent surreys to people with pets.

Small dogs seem to like riding in the basket in front of the surrey (with a sweater or coat under them so they don't get permanent basket marks on their buns), and medium-sized dogs do well sitting snugly on the seat beside their people. Big dogs might prefer to stick with walking, because even the large surreys aren't exactly gargantuan. Rates are $12 to $23 per hour, depending on the size of the surrey. Mike's Bikes & Blades can be reached at (415) 668-6699.

Nab it at Neiman's: Neiman Marcus, the exclusive, expensive department store with the historic atrium, is a very dog-friendly place. Who'd have guessed? One day as I was waiting outside to meet a friend, I saw two dogs and their people walk out with shopping bags. I thought the women must have been Neiman's aunts, but no. The dogs were not related to the store at all; when I asked the store's publicist, she told me that well-behaved, clean dogs are welcome here. Keep in mind that Neiman's is not for the light of wallet, but if you have a chunk of change you want to drop on some quality items, and you don't want to leave your dog behind when you do it, this is the perfect place to come. 150 Stockton Street; (415) 362-3900.

Ride halfway to the stars: As far as cable cars are concerned, opinions vary widely about whether dogs should ride inside or outside. Some drivers feel the outside is better because the cable noise isn't so amplified, and dogs don't get so nervous. Others say the outside is too dangerous—that a dog could panic and jump off.

If you do decide to do the full San Francisco experience and ride outside, have your dog sit on a bench, and hold her securely by the leash and by the body. The standing area is very narrow and precarious. And you never want to go on a crowded cable car with your dog, so stay away from the popular tourist areas during the peak seasons. (For rules, see "Hop on a bus" on page 178.) For more information, call (415) 673-MUNI.

Joe was so terrified when he first boarded a cable car that he got in no trouble at all after barking at the bell. How much mischief could he get into hiding his head under my coat?

But after a while, with the coaxing of our personable California Street cable car drivers Louie and Dave, he started peeking out at the sights. As they regaled us with stories of dogs they'd known, and flea remedies that work, Joe loosened up. He got so relaxed by the middle of our trip that he fell off his seat as the cable car descended the steep hill in Chinatown. Fortunately, we were seated inside.

No one seemed to want to sit next to Joe. In fact, the deeper we rode into the Financial District and the more suits and ties we encountered, the more people avoided even looking at him. Joe got off at the end of the line with his feelings hurt, but his bravery intact.

Saunter across the Golden Gate: Like their people, dogs thrill to a jaunt across San Francisco's most famous landmark. The bridge spans 1.9 miles from the city to Marin County. It's open to pedestrians, both humans and dogs, from 5 A.M. to 9 P.M. daily. There's no fee.

The only thing that the Golden Gate Bridge Authority asks is that you pick up your dog's poop (they've had a problem with this of late) and that your dog wear a leash. You both probably will want to wear sweaters, too—it can be a little nippy when making your way across. But don't let that stop you. The spectacular views at daybreak and sunset make it all worthwhile. Take the last San Francisco exit before the bridge tollway. Free street parking is available on the west side of the bridge, next to the GGBA employee parking lot. For more info, call (415) 921-5858.

Say yippie for hippies: The Flower Power Haight Ashbury Walking Tour is a delight for humans and dogs, and you don't have to be flower children/puppies to enjoy it. This riveting tour guides you through the history of the Haight, from the Victorian era to the Human Be-in, the Digger feeds, the free Grateful Dead concerts, and of course, the Summer of Love. Dogs don't dig the history much, but they revel in the smell of old hippies who sit on the sidewalks.

Humans of all ages and leashed, well-behaved dogs are welcome. The price of the two-hour tour is $15. Dogs are free. For more information, write The Flower Power Haight Ashbury Walking Tour, 520 Shrader Street, #1, San Francisco, CA 94117, or phone (415) 221-8442.

Seize the Bay: Salty sea dogs wag their tails hard and fast when they learn that the Blue & Gold Fleet ferry system permits pooches on all its lines. This is great news, especially since the Blue & Gold Fleet recently took over the Red & White ferry service to Marin, and didn't end its dog-friendly policy. That means well-behaved, leashed dogs can go by ferry from San Francisco to all these destinations: Sausalito, Tiburon, Oakland, Alameda, and Vallejo. And they don't have to pay a dime. Two destinations are forbidden— Angel Island and Alcatraz, both state parks that don't allow dogs.

Most dogs really dig cruising on the bay. Their nostrils flare in ecstasy at the cool, fishy breeze, and they can look positively giddy upon disembarking. Unfortunately, Joe tends to turn a little green at the gills, even on relatively calm days. Craig and I got married on our boat in the bay, with Nisha and Joe at our side. Nisha had the time of her life. Joe looked like the poster boy for Dramamine. He has since put his paw down about riding on any boat, including the ferry.

Fares range from $4 to $7.50 one way for adults, depending on your destination. Joe's favorite trip (when he was still tripping), from San Francisco to Sausalito, is $5.50 one way. Phone (415) 773-1188 for schedules and more information.

Send 'em to the sitter: Once you and your pooch walk through the bright purple door of the San Francisco SPCA's Doggy Daycare Center, you may never want to leave. Ecstatic dogs are everywhere. Water dogs cavort about in the wading pool. Ball dogs sniff through boxes of tennis balls until they select just the right one. Others chase each other around the big 1,400-square-foot room, test out agility equipment, nap on soft beds, and watch doggy videos on the 24-inch color TV. Some even use the "doggy toilet," a big bin of gravel with a real live shiny red fire hydrant.

Most of these dogs belong to owners who feel bad leaving them at home all day while they go to work. "This is a lot like a child day-care center, only I think the dogs have more fun," says Tory Weiser, center coordinator. Some "parents" even leave a bagged lunch in their pooch's very own cubbyhole.

But wait, that's not all! Dogs get two good long walks every day and can be given necessary basic training, too.

Pooches must be a least five months old to spend time here, and they have to have current vaccinations and a friendly demeanor. The cost is $20 daily for three to five days a week. For one or two days per week, the cost is $25 daily. Hours are 7 A.M. to 7 P.M. Monday through Friday. Doggy Daycare Center is located on the side of the SPCA building at 2500 16th Street; (415) 554-3079.

Shop on Beach Street: You can shop for baubles, bangles, and T-shirts with your leashed dog at any of dozens of little stands up and down this Fisherman's Wharf area street. You can even get your dog's caricature done by a local artist. Make sure to take him to nearby Aquatic Park (see page 141) while you're there, especially if he's sat patiently for the artist's rendition. The bulk of the stands on Beach Street are between Hyde and Polk Streets.

Wash that sand right outta her hair: The beauty of taking your dog to Bill's Doggie Bath-O-Mat is that you can bathe your dog without having to clean the tub afterward. (Or, worse yet, having to bathe in the tub yourself afterward!) Bill's is a no-nonsense kind of dog wash, with waist-high tubs and everything you need at your fingertips. The $10 fee includes use of shampoo, combs, brushes, towels, and a doggy blow-dryer. You even get to use a cute doggy apron. Such a deal! Bill, the owner, grooms dogs here, too. He's a nice guy who chats with his customers, gives good grooming advice if needed, and gives great little puppy calendars away in January. Bill's is at 3928 Irving Street; (415) 661-6950.

Wash your socks with your dog: A jug of wine, a loaf of bread, your dirty laundry, your dog, and you. Bring all this and feast at one of four tables outside Star Wash Laundry while your wash is in the rinse cycle. This is a very popular spot among dog owners with dirty clothes, and since the Laundromat owners adore dogs, chances are your pet won't be alone. It's especially enjoyable for your dog after a sprint in nearby Mission Dolores Park (see page 154). Don't forget water for your dog. 392 Dolores Street; (415) 431-2443.

Watch a big-screen flick: Picture this—you, your date, a romantic drive-in movie. The plot thickens, your date takes your hand, the lead characters start to kiss, lips locking. . . . You feel hot breath on your neck and turn in dreamy anticipation. And there, only millimeters from your face, is your dog's big black nose, sniffing away and asking for more popcorn.

Still, taking a dog to a drive-in theater can be fun. At the Geneva Drive-In Theater, a resident cat prowls around cars looking for a handout or a dog to tease. The Geneva is on Carter Street, off Geneva Avenue, next to the Cow Palace; (415) 587-2884.

SAN MATEO COUNTY

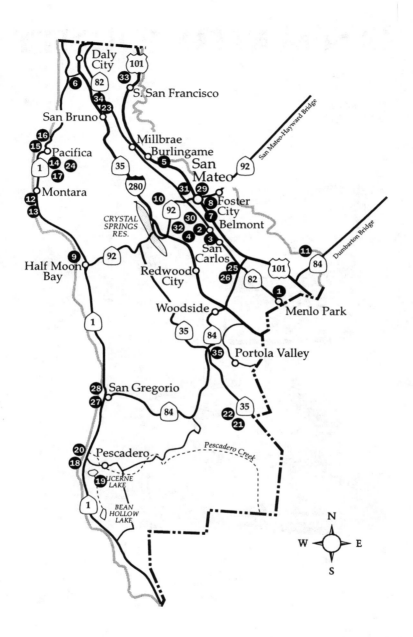

6
SAN MATEO COUNTY

Joe and I were stuck in Redwood City on business all day. After a while, he began to glare at me. His brow wrinkled. His eyes got wide and seemed to float in extra liquid. Then he started groaning like a door in a bad horror movie. It was all too clear. This was a dog urgently in need of a park.

So we got in the car and drove until we found a little city park. I let Joe out and he bounded for a private spot behind a bush. But just as he was getting into position, a woman with a baby stroller bustled up. "No! Bad dog! No dogs allowed. Tell your mother that," she yelled and shot us an angry look.

Joe ran back to the car in a more cowardly manner than I care to admit, tail down, head low. Instead of arguing, we left. Besides, there was a big county park at the other end of Redwood City that looked even better.

Joe was so desperate that by the time we got there he was crossing his legs. But it seemed worth the wait. The park was big and grassy with lots of pine trees and bushes essential for Joe to do his thing. Birds and wildflowers were everywhere. It was one of the more alluring parks we'd ever seen.

But just as we entered, three words on a sign stopped us in our tracks. They were big, bold, and mean: **NO DOGS ALLOWED.** Joe lifted his leg on the sign and we were gone. Thus was our unsavory introduction to San Mateo County.

Once we started exploring San Mateo County in depth, we realized that it wasn't as unfriendly as it first seemed. There are many parks that allow dogs; six even allow them off leash. But some of the biggest and best have an outright ban on canines.

The worst offender is the county Department of Parks and Recreation. There are 15,000 acres of county parklands here, but none of the county's 70,000 licensed dogs may set paw in them. In past editions, I've written about groups that had formed to try to convince the county to open its gates to dogs, but all efforts have failed, and the county shows no signs of allowing dogs in its parks. If you have any friends in high places here, do what you can, but don't be surprised when the answer is NO.

Meanwhile, fortunately, there are some mighty dog-friendly places to visit throughout the county. The Midpeninsula Regional Open Space District has become one of dogs' best friends of late, with the addition in San Mateo County of two more preserves that allow dogs (bringing the total to four), including one that has a 16-acre off-leash area (see Pulgas Ridge, page 209). Be sure to follow extremely good doggy etiquette at all the district's preserves, because there are a lot of anti-doggers out there who would love to get the district to take away our privileges.

The district has unique rules about poop scooping and six-foot leashes. Scooping the poop is appreciated, but because of limited trash disposal sites, if you kick the poop off the trail, that's considered okay. (Helpful hint: Don't wear open-toed sandals.) And retractable leashes are allowed to go beyond the six-foot mark in many instances, which is a rare thing indeed. The exceptions: when you're within 100 feet of parking lots, roads, trailheads, picnic areas, and rest rooms, and when you're within 50 feet of other people or any body of water, including creeks. It's a great policy—one other park districts should follow, says Joe.

The district even offers very cool canine walks in conjunction with the Palo Alto Humane Society. The hikes, called Dog Days Hikes, are about two hours, and they're usually leisurely, although you can end up covering from three to five miles. It's a great way to meet dogs and their people. Pooper-scoopers are provided, but you have to do the scooping. Bring a leash and water for your pooch. For more information, or to make reservations, call the district at (650) 691-1200, or the Palo Alto Humane Society at (650) 327-0631. (The Humane Society also offers easy hikes in other parklands about once a month. Call for a schedule.)

So hats off to the open space district. If the county park system would follow its lead, San Mateo could become a very doggone decent county.

A terrific group called Peninsula Access for Dogs (PAD) is trying to improve the park life of dogs all over the peninsula. For information, write to PAD at 809-B Cuesta Drive, Box 196, Mountain View, CA 94094, or check out PAD's Web site: www.rahul.net/pruski/pads.

ATHERTON

PARKS, BEACHES, AND RECREATION AREAS

• **Holbrook-Palmer Park** 🐾🐾
   See ❶ on page 186.

Roses. Gazebos. Bathrooms that look like saunas. Trellises. Jasmine plots. Tennis courts. Buildings that belong in a country club. People in white linen love it here; dogs are often just plain intimidated. Joe didn't lift his leg once last time we visited.

"Don't put it in your book that we allow dogs," a woman with the Atherton Parks and Recreation Department told us. "We have too many weddings and banquets going on here, and the people don't want to be disturbed."

Don't forget a leash.

Holbrook-Palmer Park is located on Watkins Avenue, between El Camino Real and Middlefield Road. Leave your car at one of several lots in the park. (650) 688-6534.

BELMONT

PARKS, BEACHES, AND RECREATION AREAS

• **Cipriani Park Dog Exercise Area** 🐾🐾🐾🐾 🐕
   See ❷ on page 186.

You want off leash? You want social? Then you want to come here. The folks at this two-acre, fenced-in dog run are so friendly that on your first visit you'll feel as though you've been a regular for many years. Of course, that would be impossible, because the dog run, the newest in the county, opened in 1993. But you get the idea.

People who come here love to celebrate dog birthdays with their park friends. And just about every Friday after work, they gather with refreshments and have a sort of happy hour. Or two. Or three. "You won't find cliques here. We're all in this dog world together, and we enjoy enjoying ourselves and watching our dogs have a great time," says Larry Miller, who heads the Belmont Bowser Club, the group that got this park going and maintains it with volunteer labor.

Dogs adore this grass- and wood-chip-carpeted park. A fire hydrant is the centerpiece and the totem for the boy dogs who come here. Tall pines provide shade, but dogs can frequently be found lounging under the two picnic tables. There are two water spigots for thirsty dogs and pooper-scoopers galore.

The park is located at 2525 Buena Vista Avenue, behind the Cipriani School. It's a little hard to find. From El Camino Real, go west on Ralston Avenue. In about 1.5 miles, you'll pass Alameda de las Pulgas. Drive about another three-quarters of a mile, and be on the lookout for Cipriani Boulevard. It's a small street you can easily miss. Turn right on Cipriani and follow it a few blocks to Buena Vista. Turn left on Buena Vista and park near the school. You won't see the dog run from the street, but if you walk west and enter through the main park entrance, you'll soon see it. Whatever you do, don't take your dog through the school's playground when kids are present. The school really frowns on this. (650) 595-7441.

•**Twin Pines Park** 🐾 🐾 🐾 *See* ❸ *on page 186.*
This park is a hidden treasure, nestled among eucalyptus trees just outside the business district of Belmont. You'd never guess the dog wonders that await within. Your dog may hardly notice she's leashed.

The main trail is paved and winds through sweet-smelling trees and brush. A clear stream runs below. In dry seasons, it's only about two feet deep, but in good years it swells to several feet. Dogs love to go down to the stream and wet their whistles. Past the picnic area are numerous small, quiet dirt trails that can take you up the woodsy hill or alongside the stream.

It's located at 1225 Ralston Avenue, behind the police department. (650) 595-7441.

•**Water Dog Lake Park** 🐾 🐾 🐾 *See* ❹ *on page 186.*
Dogs and their people seem magically drawn to this large, wooded park with a little lake in the middle. Maybe it's the way the moss drips off the trees at the bottom of this mountainous area, or the way the lake seems to create a refreshing breeze on the hottest days.

Or maybe it's got something to do with the name. We asked several dog owners how the park came to be called Water Dog Lake Park.

"I think the lake is kind of shaped like a dog. Actually, it's more like a kangaroo, isn't it?" said the proud owner of a beagle/terrier mix.

"It would be a good place to water your dog, if that were allowed," said a woman with a black Lab.

"When dogs and people were allowed to swim here, you couldn't get the Labs and all those water dogs out of this lake," explained a man with an Irish setter.

We hate to burst the romantic fantasy that a park as alluring as this one is named after man's best friend. But after some searching through historical records, we discovered the biting truth: Water Dog Lake Park was named after salamanders. A colloquial name for a salamander is "water dog," and apparently the little critters used to wriggle all over the place around here. We still think the park is great. Too bad dogs have to be leashed.

One other thing that we discovered about this park: If people would follow their dogs, perhaps a lot fewer would stumble onto the wrong trail. The one that goes up to the top of the park never comes near the lake and leads you more than a mile away from where you started. Joe tried tugging in the other direction, but I ignored him. We got a ride back to the entrance from a teenage boy who felt sorry for us.

Upon entering the park from the Lake Road entrance, take the wide path that goes straight in front of you. It will lead you down to the lake. Neither you nor your dog can go in the water, but you can have a great picnic there, or even go fishing off the little wooden pier.

If you start off taking the smaller trail that veers to the right, you'll get good exercise and a great view of the bay, but we don't recommend it, unless you enjoy getting lost and suffering heat fatigue in the summer. A final word of warning: Watch out for bikers. They're fast here.

Enter on Lake Road, just off Carlmont Drive. Try to come back to the same place. (650) 595-7441.

BURLINGAME

PARKS, BEACHES, AND RECREATION AREAS

At last check, Burlingame's movers and shakers were discussing the possibility of having a dog park somewhere in the city.

Nothing was final, but at press time, it looked promising. If it happens, the sound of clapping paws should be resounding. Call (650) 696-7245 for an update.

•**Washington Park** 🐾 🐾 *See ❺ on page 186.*

This relatively small park has the look of an old college campus. Its trees are big and old and mostly deciduous, making autumn a particularly brilliant time. Bring a lunch and eat it on the thick, knotty old redwood picnic tables. They're something out of the Enchanted Forest. Joe is intrigued by the abundance of squirrels, but he doesn't get too far with his pursuits, since leashes are the law and the police station is around the corner.

The park is at 850 Burlingame Avenue below Carolan Avenue. (650) 696-7245.

RESTAURANTS

Cafe La Scala: The outdoor area at this exquisite Italian restaurant has dozens of tables, but it's still very romantic, with beautiful flowers, soft music, and pastoral murals. It's all very Florentine. Dogs need to sit at the edge of the patio area. In cooler months, the area is warmed by heat lamps. 1219 Burlingame Avenue; (650) 347-3035.

Caprice Restaurant and Cafe: The California cuisine here is very tasty, and the brunches are popular with dog owners. Dine at a half dozen shaded tables out front. 347 Primrose Road; (650) 375-8618.

PLACES TO STAY

San Francisco Airport Marriott: If you need to stay near the airport, and your dog appreciates good views of the San Francisco Bay and is under 30 pounds, you couldn't ask for a better hotel. Rates are $130 to $245. 1860 Old Bayshore Highway, Burlingame, CA 94010; (650) 692-9100.

Vagabond Inn: With prices like this, it's a wonder they still call it Vagabond Inn: Rates are $87 to $97. Dogs are $5 extra. 1640 Bayshore Highway, Burlingame, CA 94010; (650) 692-4040.

DOGGY DAYS

Turn your dog into a cat: Or try a rat. Or maybe even a ballerina. Your dog can be just about anything he doggone well pleases at the Peninsula Pet Masquerade. The daylong event is the toast of the Halloween season for pets (yes, that means cats, too) and their people. All participants, human or otherwise, should come in costume. Those registered for the costume contest will receive a fun trick-or-treat bag.

Admission is free to onlookers. Contestants pay $10 per entry ($25 for groups of three or more people or pets). All proceeds go to support the Peninsula Humane Society. The event is held on a Saturday near Halloween. In the past, it's been at the Hyatt Regency at 1333 Bayshore Highway. Call the Peninsula Humane Society for this year's date and location. (650) 340-7022.

DIVERSIONS

Ask your dog for a date to a movie: It's greasy. It's kitschy. It's unique. (Witness the domed snack bar topped with very pink turrets.) But going to the Burlingame 4 Drive-In Theater is a great way to catch a movie and spare yourself the guilt of leaving your dog home alone. And it's cheap. Dogs are free—unless, like Joe, they have a hankering for popcorn. We saw a real classic here: *Don't Tell Mom the Babysitter's Dead.* Joe loved it. He couldn't take his eyes off the screen, except to lick the sound box.

(Oh, by the way, the theater is also for sale. Catch a flick while there are still flicks to catch.) Tickets are $5.75 for adults. Kids under 11 are free. So are dogs, old or young. 350 Beach Road; (650) 343-2213.

DALY CITY

We called the Daly City parks department to find out what its rule is regarding leashes. A helpful woman read the city ordinance: Animals must be "under control of owner by being saddled, harnessed, haltered, or leashed by a substantial chain, lead rope, or leash, which chain, lead rope, or leash shall be continuously held by some competent person capable of controlling such an animal."

So Joe wore a leash during our Daly City visits. But he put his paw down when it came to donning the saddle and halter.

PARKS, BEACHES, AND RECREATION AREAS

Here's one of the better Daly City parks where pooches are permitted. Many parks in Daly City don't allow dogs. If you're anywhere near the ocean, your best bet is to head to just the other side of the Daly City–San Francisco border and visit magnificent Fort Funston (see page 145).

• **Gellert Park** 🐾 🐾 *See ❻ on page 186.*

The best feature of this flat, square park is that it's right behind the Serramonte Library. It's also conveniently located if you are going to pay homage to someone at the Chinese Cemetery, right across the street. The park is made up of a few sports fields—watch out for flying baseballs, soccer balls, and softballs. The park's trees, which surround two sides, aren't even accessible—they're on top of a very steep little ridge. Your dog may become frustrated, especially since he must wear a leash through all this.

The park is on Wembley Drive at Gellert Boulevard. (650) 991-8006.

FOSTER CITY

John Oliver, former mayor of Foster City, isn't the sort to beat around the bush. When he describes the older women who set out to improve the town by getting recreational vehicles off the streets and enforcing the leash law, he's not kind.

"They are the forces of darkness," he says. "They're a couple of little old ladies right from central casting for their nit-picking roles."

Oliver's feathers are ruffled for good reason. In 1988—a year after he stopped being mayor, and shortly after the "forces of darkness" started crusading for more dog patrols—a cop cited him for walking his little dog, Topper, off leash. The ticket was only $25. It was the principle that distressed him—not to mention the newspaper story. "Topper was an angel of a dog and in a totally empty park. Come on, let's get sensible here," he says.

This is the dog who used to break out of Oliver's truck and run into City Council chambers to find him during meetings. She's the same 20-pound mutt who stayed by Oliver's side during a recent bout of bad luck that forced them into homelessness. "She made life a lot easier when we were living in that truck," he says.

Oliver has always voted for leash laws, but he believes the real issue is control. "If you can control your dog in a safe area, and there's no one around to disturb, why not let her loose for a few minutes?" he asks. "It's a shame it has to cost you if you're caught."

Fortunately, two Foster City parks permit pooches off leash, far from Oliver's "forces of darkness."

PARKS, BEACHES, AND RECREATION AREAS

• **Boothbay Park** 🐾🐾🐾 🐕 *See* **7** *on page 186.*

It's off with the leash once you find the right section of this park, which is the grassy area behind the tennis courts. It's surrounded on two sides by a tall wooden fence and is comfortably far from the road. This little corner of the park is nothing fancy, but it does allow dogs some freedom.

The park is at Boothbay Avenue and Edgewater Lane. (650) 345-5731.

• **Foster City Dog Exercise Area** 🐾🐾½ 🐕 *See* **8** *on page 186.*

This fenced dog run has great potential, but it's a disappointment. Dogs are allowed off leash here, but as soon as they get down to having fun with each other, they kick up clouds of dust. The ground is pretty much packed dirt, with little bits of grass trying to push through.

The view isn't any more attractive, with power lines overhead, the back of City Hall in the foreground, and rows of look-alike town houses in the distance. What this place needs is a few good trees—and some water for the dogs.

There are two good points, though: The fences are very high, so if you have an escape artist for a dog, this place is about the safest around. And there are plenty of large trash cans—six, to be exact—and no shortage of pooper-scoopers.

It's at 600 Foster City Boulevard. Park in the lot behind City Hall. (650) 345-5731.

RESTAURANTS

Dogs dig dining at Foster City's lagoon-side restaurants. Here are a couple that welcome dogs:

O'Donegan's: Eat hearty burgers and other sandwiches with your pooch at any of 10 umbrella-shaded tables on O'Donegan's large wood deck. It overlooks the Foster City Lagoon, so if your dog is a water dog, she'll feel at home here. 929A Edgewater Boulevard; (650) 570-6099.

Papa's Cucina: Don't let the name fool you into thinking you're going to be rolling in meatballs and other Italian cuisine here. Papa's offers a few Italian dishes, but this is primarily a deli. It's a good one, too. Joe Dog recommends the Boston Philly cheese-steak sandwich. He once sniffed out a man eating one, and I doubt he's ever forgotten it. (Neither has the man, but that's another story.) Good dogs can dine with you on the attractive wood-planked deck. 929C Edgewater Boulevard; (650) 572-8268.

HALF MOON BAY

PARKS, BEACHES, AND RECREATION AREAS

• **Half Moon Bay State Beach** 🐾 🐾 🐾 ½ *See* ❾ *on page 186.*

This is the beach air-conditioned by the god of woolly sheep-dogs. No matter how steaming hot it is elsewhere, you can almost always count on brisk weather here. It's cool and foggy in the summer, wet and windy in the winter, and moderate in the fall and spring.

The three-mile crescent of beach is actually made up of four beaches. From north to south, along Highway 1, they are Roosevelt Beach, Dunes Beach, Venice Beach, and Francis Beach. Leashed dogs are permitted on all four beaches (until mid-1994, they were banned from Francis Beach, but that ban has gone bye-bye!).

This isn't the place to come for a 15-minute romp: If you park in the park, it costs $5 per car and $1 per dog. The beaches are all clean and each is almost identical to the next, so your choice of beach should depend on which entry is most convenient. Rangers roam year-round. If you're thinking of breaking the leash law, this is a bad place to try it.

If you can ignore all the RVs and crowds of tents, the area above Francis Beach is a stunning camping spot. Perched on ice plant-covered dunes above the Pacific, it's one of the most accessible beach camping areas in the Bay Area. All of the 53 campsites are available on a first-come, first-served basis. Sites are $12 to $14. Dogs are $1 extra.

From Highway 1, follow the brown and white signs to the appropriate beach. (415) 330-6300.

RESTAURANTS

Cameron's Restaurant: Rich and creamy fountain treats are the specialty here, but burgers, pizza, and healthful salads are big sellers, too. Joe is particularly fond of smelling the aroma of fish-and-chips wafting off tables. Dine with your pooch at the big outdoor patio. 1410 South Cabrillo Highway; (650) 726-5705.

Moonside Bakery: All the delicious treats here are baked daily, except for the soup, which generally isn't baked. (But it's still made fresh daily.) This is truly an exceptional bakery, featuring all kinds of crusty breads and delectable sweets, but specializing in German baked goods. Dine with dog at the many attractive, wooden, umbrella-topped tables outside. 604 Main Street; (650) 726-9070.

Pasta Moon: This restaurant offers several sidewalk tables and every type of pasta imaginable. A *San Francisco Chronicle* food critic calls the house-made pastas here "addictive." Joe Dog suggests ordering the tagliatelle bathed in cream and surrounded by sliced sausage and prosciutto. It's a big plateful that you probably can't finish yourself, so your baleful-eyed canine might get lucky. 315 Main Street; (650) 726-5125.

PLACES TO STAY

Half Moon Bay State Beach: See Half Moon Bay State Beach on page 196 for camping information.

Holiday Inn Express: Just five blocks from Half Moon Bay State Beach, and a few blocks from downtown, this dog-friendly hotel is conveniently located for adventure-seeking pooches and their people. Rates are $79 to $139. Dogs are $10 extra. 230 Cabrillo Highway, Half Moon Bay, CA 94019; (650) 726-3400.

Ramada Limited: Rates are $60 to $115. Dogs are $10 extra. 3020 Highway 1, Half Moon Bay, CA 94019; (650) 726-9700.

The Zaballa House: This 1859 country Victorian is the oldest standing house in Half Moon Bay. Some of the nine quaint bedrooms have fireplaces and Jacuzzis. Breakfasts are fresh and out of this world. If you have any tendencies toward being a psychic, ask to stay in room 6. Many guests say they've felt a "presence" here, and the inn's owners are interested in just what that could be. It's not a bad presence, say those who have felt it, so don't let it spook you out of checking out this room.

The inn is not only dog-accepting, but dog-welcoming. There's the occasional pooch treat, and even a book with photos of all the pets who have been guests here. Dogs love to paw through it on foggy mornings. Be sure the folks here take your dog's picture, so other dogs and their humans can check him out.

Cats are occasionally guests, too, so if your dog likes cats for lunch, you may want to inquire as to their presence when you make your reservation.

Rates are $95 to $170. Dogs are $10 extra. They ask that you bring only one dog per room. 324 Main Street, Half Moon Bay, CA 94019; (650) 726-9123.

HILLSBOROUGH

• **Vista Park** 🐾 *See* ❿ *on page 186.*

You can visit this park only if you live here, unless you choose to walk miles to get to it—there's no street parking for blocks, and no parking lot. And chances are that if you live in this town, your backyard is bigger anyway. There's a little section in the back with several tall eucalyptus trees that leashed neighborhood dogs call their own. It's good for sniffs when you can't get to a better park.

The park is at Vista and Culebra Roads. (650) 579-3800.

MENLO PARK

PARKS, BEACHES, AND RECREATION AREAS

• **Bayfront Park** 🐾🐾🐾 *See* ⓫ *on page 186.*

This place used to be a dump—literally. It was the regional landfill site until it reached capacity in 1984. Then the city sealed the huge mounds of garbage under a two-foot clay barrier and covered it with four feet of soil, planted grass and trees, and *voilà*—instant 160-acre park!

Now it's a land of rolling hills with a distinctly Native American flavor. The packed dirt trails take you up to majestic views of the bay and surrounding marshes. There's no sign of garbage anywhere, unless you look down from the top of a hill and spot the methane extraction plant. Fortunately, very few vista points include that.

Our favorite part of the park is a trail studded with large, dark rocks arranged to form symbols, which in series make up a poem. The concept was inspired by Native American pictographs—a visual language system for recording daily events. At the trailhead, you'll find a sign quoting part of the poem and giving a map of the trail, showing the meaning of each rock arrangement as it corresponds to the poem.

Although leashes are required, dogs seem really fond of this park, sniffing everywhere, their tails wagging constantly. Perhaps they can sense the park's less picturesque days deep underground. Or they may be touched by the Native American magic that imbues these hills.

The park starts at the end of Marsh Road, just on the other side of the Bayfront Expressway. To get to the beginning of the rock poem trail, continue past the entrance on Marsh Road to the second parking lot on the right. (650) 858-3470.

RESTAURANTS

Garden Grill: This restaurant is among the finest dog-friendly restaurants in the state. It's so elegant you can eat like a king—an English king, to be precise. Dine in an old English garden under the canopy of an enormous 400-year-old oak tree. While Garden Grill specializes in traditional English dishes and a charming afternoon tea, it's especially proud of its medieval cuisine. Try the fourteenth-century soup, one of King Richard II's favorites. And your dog will salivate when your server brings you elk, venison, or squab with a hearty fruit and wine sauce. Unlike medieval tourist traps, Garden Grill encourages the use of fork and knife (Joe hasn't mastered this skill yet, but it's recommended for humans). There are 18 tables outside this English cottage restaurant. 1026 Alma Street; (650) 325-8981.

DIVERSIONS

Sniff out a good book: Your dog doesn't have to be Mr. Peabody to appreciate fine books. In fact, even if your dog doesn't know his assonance from his alliteration, he could have fun accompanying you to Kepler's Books. Kepler's, one of the largest and very best independent bookstores around, permits clean, leashed, well-behaved dogs to cruise the aisles with you. Common sense and good manners apply. Please, no leg lifts on the merchandise; Kepler's frowns on yellow journalism. And dogs who lean toward the literary are welcome. Those who jump on the literature are not. 1010 El Camino Real; (650) 324-4321.

MILLBRAE

Now that dogs aren't allowed on trails surrounding Crystal Springs Reservoir, they are howling. But they can still grab a bite and spend the night.

RESTAURANTS

Leonardo's Delicatessen: This truly Italian deli has plenty of outdoor tables, all comfortably far from sidewalk traffic. 540 Broadway Avenue; (650) 697-9779.

PLACES TO STAY

Clarion Hotel: Rates are $89 to $189. Dogs pay a $20 fee per visit. 401 East Millbrae Avenue, Millbrae, CA 94030; (650) 692-6363.

The Westin San Francisco Airport: If you're traveling by air, this is about the most convenient and luxurious place you and your dog can stay: It's only two minutes from the airport. Each of the 390 rooms is tastefully furnished and has two phones, a refreshment center, a coffeemaker, and voice mail. There's even a data port in every room, should your dog need to do some downloading. For humans, there's a fitness center and a yummy Mediterranean-style bistro. Rates are $120 to $310. 1 Old Bayshore Highway, Millbrae, CA 94030; (650) 692-3500 or (800) 228-3000.

MONTARA

PARKS, BEACHES, AND RECREATION AREAS

•**McNee Ranch State Park** 🐾 🐾 🐾 1/2 *See* ⑫ *on page 186.*

State parks usually ban dogs completely, or at least from all but paved roadways. But McNee is a refreshing exception to the rule. At McNee, you can hike at the same level as the soaring gulls and watch the gem-blue ocean below. The higher you go up Montara Mountain, the more magnificent the view. Hardly a soul knows about this park, so if it's peace you want, it's peace you'll get.

And if it's a workout you want, you'll get that, too. Just strap on a day pack and bring lots of water for you and your dog. If you do the full hike, you'll ascend from sea level to 1,898 feet in a couple of hours. As you hike up and away from the ocean and the road, you lose all sounds of civilization, and Highway 1 fades into a thin ribbon and disappears below.

As soon as you go through the gate at the bottom of the park, follow the narrow trails to the left up the hills. You may be tempted to take the wide and winding paved road from the start, but to avoid any bikers, take the little trails. Besides, they lead to much better vistas.

Eventually, you'll come to a point where you have a choice of going left or right on a wider part of the trail. It's a choice between paradise and heaven. Left will lead you to a stunning view of the Golden Gate Bridge and the Farallon Islands. Right will bring you to the top of the ridge, where you see Mount Diablo and the rest of the San Francisco Bay.

This would be Joe's favorite park, but dogs are supposed to be leashed. Still, he always manages to slide down several steep grassy hills on his back, wriggling and moaning in ecstasy all the way.

It's easy to miss this park since there aren't any signs and there's no official parking lot. From Highway 1 in Montara, park at the far northern end of the Montara State Beach parking lot and walk across the road. Be careful as you walk along Highway 1, because there's hardly any room on the shoulder. You'll see a gate on a dirt road just north of you and a small state property sign. That's where you go in. A few cars can also park next to the gate on the sides of the dirt road. But don't block the gate or your car probably won't be there when you get back. (415) 330-6300.

• **Montara State Beach** 🐾 🐾 🐾 ½ *See* ⓯ *on page 186.*

This long, wide beach has more nooks and crannies than your dog will be able to investigate. Around mid-beach, you'll find several little inlets carved into the mini-cliffs. Take your dog back there at low tide and you'll find all sorts of water, grass, mud, and beach flotsam. It's a good place for her to get her paws wet, while obeying the leash law.

The water at the inlets is as calm as pond water. This is where Joe first dared to walk in water. It was only a centimeter deep, but he licked his paws in triumph all the way home.

Off Highway 1, park in the little lot behind the Chart House restaurant. There's also a parking area on the north side of the beach, off Highway 1. (415) 330-6300.

PLACES TO STAY

Farallone Bed & Breakfast Inn: Each of the nine rooms in this homey Victorian inn has a private balcony and a small Jacuzzi. Some rooms have ocean views. A basic breakfast comes with your room. This place used to offer a really relaxing atmosphere with special treatment like afternoon tea and evening wine service, but under new management, it's back to the basics. Well, at least the room prices have dropped.

Rooms are $75 to $110. Dogs require a $25 deposit and are charged a $25 fee for the length of their stay. 1410 Main Street, Montara, CA 94037; (650) 728-8200 or (800) 350-9777.

MOSS BEACH

RESTAURANTS

Pony Espresso: Gallop on over, poochies! They give dogs treats here. So if the veggie pizza and the cozy coffees aren't enough to beckon your human, remind him about the treats and then pull hard on the leash. It's worth a try. Dine at the four outdoor tables in front and in back. 2350 Carlos Street; (650) 728-3540.

PACIFICA

PARKS, BEACHES, AND RECREATION AREAS

• **Milagra Ridge** 🐾 🐾 🐾 1/2 *See* ⓮ *on page 186.*

Follow the trail up to the top of the tallest hill and you'll end up with both an incredible view of the Pacific and a perfect plateau for a picnic. There are hillsides covered with ice plant and even a few Monterey pines along the way. Visit in the spring if you want to be wowed by wildflowers.

Despite the leash law, dogs really seem to enjoy this park. Make sure to keep them on the trail, as the environment here is fragile. And keep your eyes peeled for the Mission Blue butterfly. This park is one of its last habitats.

Milagra Ridge is especially magical at night. You've never seen the full moon until you've seen it from here.

Enter on Sharp Park Road in Pacifica, between Highway 1 and Skyline Boulevard. (415) 556-8371.

• **Pacifica State Beach** 🐾 🐾 *See* ⓯ *on page 186.*

This surfer's paradise has mixed messages for canines. First the bad news: Dogs must be leashed, picnickers abound, and the temptation to sneak a chicken leg can be too much for even the best dog. The beach isn't very wide, leaving little room for exploration.

Now the good news: The setting alone warrants a visit. With green rolling hills in the distance behind you and the pounding sea before you, you and your dog won't regret stopping here. On Highway 1, park between Crespi Drive and Linda Mar Boulevard. The beach is open sunrise to sunset. (415) 330-6300.

• **Sharp Park Beach** 🐾 🐾 1/2 *See* ⓰ *on page 186.*

Don't make the mistake several people have told us they've made—get up at an ungodly hour, gather your fishing gear, and march out to the pier with your dog to catch your supper. Dogs aren't allowed on the pier, perhaps because they tend to eat the bait and the catch of the day. But you may take them to the beach 30 feet below, as long as they're leashed. It's a narrow beach, though, so make sure you go when the tide is out.

Enter at San Jose and Beach Boulevards, or Beach Boulevard at Clarendon Road. (650) 738-7380.

• **Sweeney Ridge** 🐾🐾🐾 *See* **17** *on page 186.*
See page 208 under San Bruno.

RESTAURANTS

Beach Cafe: After a walk on the chilly beach, there's nothing like a hot espresso and homemade croissant at the outdoor tables here. The owners have two Samoyeds, so it's a very dog-friendly place. It's so dog-friendly, in fact, that dogs who visit get a treat or two. Highway 1 at Rockaway Beach Avenue, next to Kentucky Fried Chicken; (650) 355-4532.

Sam's Deli: Sam's is a refreshing spot to hit after an afternoon at Pacifica State Beach. It has good sandwiches at low prices and two outdoor tables. It's at the Linda Mar Shopping Center, just behind the beach, on the same side as Denny's and the shoe stores, about halfway down the row of shops. 1261 Linda Mar Shopping Center; (650) 359-5330.

PESCADERO

PARKS, BEACHES, AND RECREATION AREAS

• **Bean Hollow State Beach** 🐾🐾🐾½ *See* **18** *on page 186.*
The rocky intertidal zone here is terrific for tidepooling, but only if you and your dog are surefooted. To get to the best tidepools, you must perform an amazing feat of team coordination—climbing down 70-million-year-old rock formations while attached to each other by leash. It's not that steep, just awkward. The pitted rocks can be slippery. This maneuver is not recommended for dogs who go deaf and senseless when the alluring ocean beckons them to swim. Besides, the surf can be treacherous in this area.

If you reach the tidepools, you're in for a real treat. But make sure your canine companion doesn't go fishing—we've seen a dog stick his entire head in a tidepool to capture a little crab. Fur and fangs aren't natural in the delicate balance of this wet habitat, so please keep dogs out of the tidepools. The mussels will thank you.

If you decide to play it safe and stay on flat land, you can still see the harbor seal rookery on the rocks below the coastal bluffs. Bring binoculars and you can really get a view of them up close and personal.

The beach is off Highway 1 at Bean Hollow Road. (415) 330-6300.

•Butano State Park 🐾 🐾 🐾 ½ *See ⑲ on page 186.*

Dogs are beside themselves when they learn that much of this 3,800-acre state park is open to them. State parks generally ban pooches from everything but paved roads and campgrounds. But Butano happens to have 11 miles of doggone good dirt fire roads, and leashed dogs are more than welcome to explore. (They're banned from hiking trails, though.) You may meet up with mountain bikers on the fire roads, so keep your eyes peeled and stay out of their path.

This park, nestled in the Santa Cruz Mountains, is resplendent with coastal scrub and redwoods. The ocean views from higher spots are breathtaking.

Dogs can even camp at the 39 sites here. Sites are $12 to $16. Dogs are $1 extra. The day-use fee is $5 if you park inside the park. Dogs are $1 extra. Butano is located five miles south of Pescadero, on Cloverdale Road, and off Highway 1 from Gazos Creek Road. (650) 879-2040 or 879-2044.

•Pescadero State Beach 🐾 🐾 🐾 ½ *See ⑳ on page 186.*

There are three entrances to this two-mile beach, and each one leads to a unique setting on the Pacific. The prime attractions at the southernmost entrance, on Highway 1 at Pescadero Road, are the small cliffs that hang over the crashing ocean. There are even a few picnic tables on the edges of the mini-cliffs for those who like lunch with a built-in thrill. Hold on to your leash!

The middle entrance, reached from the small parking lot, will lead you to a secluded and untamed rocky area. Take one of the less steep trails down and you'll find yourself in the middle of lots of rocks, rotting kelp, driftwood, and a few small tidepools. This is an eerie place to come on a very foggy day. Joe loves it here during pea-soupers.

Perch atop the vista point at this central entrance and you'll get a great view of the Pescadero Marsh Natural Preserve, just across Highway 1. You can't explore the preserve with your dog, a rule the birds and other critters who live there don't mind one bit.

The north entrance is the only one that charges a fee for use—$5 per car and $1 per dog. But many people park beside the road and walk over the sandy dunes to escape the cover charge. This is the most civilized—and mundane—entrance, with a wide beach and lots of kite fliers. Dogs must wear leashes on all parts of the beach.

The south entrance is at Pescadero Road and Highway 1. Follow the signs to the north for the other entrances. (415) 330-6300.

RESTAURANTS

Arcangeli Grocery Company: There's always fresh-baked bread here—still hot—waiting for you after a cold day at the beach. We like to buy a loaf of steaming herb-garlic bread and eat it at the picnic tables on the lawn in the back of the store. 287 Stage Road; (650) 879-0147.

PLACES TO STAY

Butano State Park: See Butano State Park on page 204 for camping information.

McKenzie House: The magnificent site of a single seaside cottage is about to become the magnificent site of several seaside cottages. They'll be New England in style (airy, spacious, and antique-filled) with fenced-in yards for your dog. The plan is for them to be staggered so guests will have privacy. At press time, the McKenzie House, which has long been a heavenly place to take a dog, had just received permits for the additional cottages. Even the original McKenzie house will be torn down to make way for these beauties. To get your name on a mailing list so you'll know when they're opening, call (408) 469-8300.

PORTOLA VALLEY

PARKS, BEACHES, AND RECREATION AREAS

• **Coal Creek Open Space Preserve** 🐾 🐾 🐾 ½
  See ㉑ on page 186.

Joe loves visiting this 493-acre preserve in the winter months because of the little waterfalls that gurgle along a couple of creeks. In fact, year-round, this is one of the best of the Midpeninsula

Regional Open Space District preserves for dogs, because it's generally cooler than most. The dense oak and madrone forests offer a real respite from the hot summer weather.

Banana slugs like this climate as much as dogs, so don't be surprised to see a few lurking on the trails. When Joe Dog happened upon a banana slug here, at first he looked disgusted. Then he barked at it a couple of times, and sat down and moaned at it when it didn't respond. I tugged hard on his leash to get him away, because I knew his next move would be to make a banana slug appetizer out of it.

If rolling meadows are more your dog's style, this preserve has those, too. The five miles of trails will take you through all kinds of landscapes. Let your dog choose his favorite, but make sure he's leashed.

The preserve has two entry points along Skyline Boulevard (Highway 35) in the southernmost part of the county (south of Portola Valley). One is about 1.2 miles north of Page Mill Road, at the Caltrans vista point, on the east side of the road. The other is at Skyline and Crazy Pete's Road, about two miles north of Page Mill Road, also on the east side of Skyline. This one has the closest access to the preserve, but there's only room for about three cars, and you'll need to walk down a fairly steep residential road to get to the trails. (650) 691-1200.

•Windy Hill Open Space Preserve 🐾 🐾 🐾
See ㉒ on page 186.

You can look out from the top of the first big hill you come to and see for miles all around—and though you're on the edge of the suburbs, you'll see hardly a house. This 1,130-acre preserve of the Midpeninsula Regional Open Space District has as many different terrains as it has views, including grassland ridges and lush wooded ravines with serene creeks and drippy redwoods.

There are more than three miles of trails that allow you and your leashed canine companion. But watch out for foxtails. The park is so dry that foxtails seem to proliferate all year.

Start at the Anniversary Trail, to the left of the entrance. The hike is a vigorous three-quarters of a mile uphill, and that may be enough, especially when it's baking. But you can continue down the other side of the hill and loop right, onto the Spring Ridge Trail. Near the end of this 2.5-mile path, you'll come to a wooded area with a small, very refreshing creek. This is a good place to sit a spell before heading back. These two trails are the only ones that permit pooches, so don't try your paw at any others.

Park at the lot on Highway 35 (Skyline Boulevard), 2.3 miles south of Highway 84 and five miles north of Alpine Road. You'll see the big sign for the preserve and three picnic tables. (650) 691-1200.

REDWOOD CITY

Dogs are not allowed in any of Redwood City's parks.

PLACES TO STAY

Good Nite Inn: If you and your small dog are on the road and just plain sick and tired of restaurant food, go to a grocery store, come here, and rev up your microwave. When you're done, put your leftovers in your mini-fridge. Then you can nuke them again for lunch tomorrow. Mmmm good. Not all the rooms come with these mini-kitchens, so if you want one, request it when you make your reservation. For some reason, you can stay only two nights here. Maybe they don't want to give the impression it's a doggy residential hotel. Rates are $43 to $60. 485 Veterans Boulevard, Redwood City, CA 94063; (650) 365-5500.

SAN BRUNO

PARKS, BEACHES, AND RECREATION AREAS

• **San Bruno Dog Exercise Area/Sandberg Field**
🐾🐾🐾🐾 🐕 *See ㉓ on page 186.*
This is a gem of a fenced-in park, where dogs can run their tails off—without a leash. The grass always seems to be green. There's plenty of water, pooper-scoopers galore, and benches for two-legged beasts. As an extra bonus, it has a great view of the bay. And for those who can't get enough of it while driving north on U.S. 101, there's an unparalleled view of that strange sign: "SOUTH SAN FRANCISCO—THE INDUSTRIAL CITY."

The park opened in 1989 after local dog trainer Mal Lightfoot was fined for walking his notoriously obedient dogs off leash. "I spend all my life training dogs to be good citizens, and I was treated like a criminal," says Lightfoot, who runs the San Bruno Dog Training School. "It was the last straw." It took him and dozens of other frustrated dog owners nearly two years of working with—and against—city officials to get the park of their dreams.

Some detailed directions are necessary for finding this out-of-the-way park, even for locals. From El Camino Real, take Sneath Lane west. Just past Interstate 280, turn right on Rollingwood Drive. Go right again at the first possible right, Crestwood Drive. Go left on Valleywood Drive and take a sharp right at Evergreen Drive. The park is in a few blocks, at Maywood and Evergreen Drives in back of the old Carl Sandburg School. Once at the school driveway, take the first road to the right and drive until you see the dog park. (650) 877-8868.

•**Sweeney Ridge** 🐾🐾🐾½ *See* ㉔ *on page 186.*

If your dog appreciates breathtaking vistas of the Bay Area, with a rainbow assortment of wildflowers in the foreground, this 1,000-acre park is a rare treat. But if your canine is like most, he can take or leave such a magnificent panorama.

Still, if you like stunning views and a vigorous uphill climb, take the Sneath Lane entrance. It may be toasty when you start, but bring a couple of thick wool sweaters if you plan to hike along the ridge—it's cold and often foggy up there. The furrier your dog, the more she'll take to the invigorating conditions.

The Skyline College entrance is ideal if you want a more moderate grade, but both trailheads will take you to the same place. The leash law here can come in handy if your dog is of the pulling mentality. Just say "mush" on those steep slopes.

From different parts of the ridge, you'll be able to see the ocean (and the Farallon Islands, on a good day), as well as Mount Tamalpais in Marin, Mount Diablo to the east, and Montara Mountain to the south. Judging by all the canines with flaring nostrils, the scents from all four directions must be as enticing as the views.

For the Sneath Lane entrance, take San Bruno's Sneath Lane all the way to the end. There's usually plenty of parking. The Skyline College entrance, off College Drive, is in the southeast corner of campus, near Lot 2. (415) 556-8371.

SAN CARLOS

PARKS, BEACHES, AND RECREATION AREAS

•**Heather Park** 🐾🐾🐾½ 🐕 *See* ㉕ *on page 186.*

This is one of the few fenced-in dog parks we've ever seen that comes complete with rolling hills, wildflowers, old gnarled trees, and singing birds. Your dog will have the time of his life here, bounding up and down hills or trotting down the winding paved path to the bottom of the park—sans leash. You may be tempted to take some of the tiny dirt trails up the steep hills, but they tend to end abruptly, leaving you and your dog teetering precariously. The only thing the park lacks is water, usually a given at dog parks.

If you have a dog who likes to wander, watch out: There are a couple of potential escape routes near the two gates at the far ends of the park. Apparently, some dog people have not been scooping the poop as they should be, and the city of San Carlos is trying to get them to clean up their act. The city is publicizing the problem to increase public awareness, and is also increasing enforcement. They sent us a fax with the poop on scooping. Please, folks, it's not a fun job, but you've gotta do it.

The park is at Melendy and Portofino Drives. (650) 593-8011.

• **Pulgas Ridge Open Space Preserve** 🐾🐾🐾🐾 🐕
See **26** on page 186.

Dogs were happy when the Midpeninsula Regional Open Space District opened this 293-acre preserve to leashed pooches a few years back. But now that 16 acres in the middle of the preserve has been designated okay for leash-free dogs, dogs are downright delirious. In fact, Joe did a somersault when we checked out the leash-free area, but I think that was actually because he tripped on my foot.

The off-leash area is only for dogs under excellent voice control. That's always the case in off-leash, unenclosed areas, but it's particularly important here because of wildlife—and because of some vociferous folks who would love nothing better than to see leashes be mandatory here again. You know, *those* kind of people. The off-leash area is oak woodland and grassland, so dogs can explore a variety of landscapes. It's located in the middle of the preserve, and accessible via the Blue Oak Trail or the Cordilleras Trail.

Leashed dogs can explore the rest of this fairly flat, oak-chaparral area via three miles of trails that wind throughout. The best time to visit is in the spring, when the wildflowers come to life everywhere.

During your hike, you might see what you think looks like remnants of buildings. You'd be right. The preserve is on land that was once the site of the Hassler Health Home, a tuberculosis sanatorium owned by San Francisco. In the 1980s, the district bought the land and demolished the sanatorium, but you can still see rock retaining walls and steps here and there. Humans like this kind of trivia. Dogs could give a bark.

Exit Interstate 280 at Edgewood Road and drive east almost a mile. Turn left at Crestview Drive and make an immediate left onto Edmonds Road. You'll see signs for the preserve. There's limited roadside parking here, but it's usually enough. (650) 691-1200.

RESTAURANTS

Cafe La Tosca: Dogs sing the praises of this lovely Italian cafe. Dine on tasty pastas and a sumptuous risotto at the two outdoor tables. 777 Laurel Street; (650) 592-7749.

Coffee Club Two: Lots of dogs come here with their owners for a sip of coffee and a pastry on weekend mornings, sitting in any of several chairs outdoors. There's heavy socializing among dog people. 749 Laurel Street; (650) 592-9888.

SAN GREGORIO

PARKS, BEACHES, AND RECREATION AREAS

•**Pomponio State Beach** 🐾🐾 *See ㉗ on page 186.*

This 1.5-mile beach is fine for sunbathing, but you can also go surf fishing for striped bass, search for driftwood, or walk to the south end of the beach and watch nesting ravens along the craggy bluffs. Dogs must be leashed, but they seem to feel right at home here. One of Joe's favorite pastimes is picking up long pieces of driftwood and "accidentally" tripping whoever is walking him as he trots merrily along. There's a $5 fee per car. Dogs are $1 extra.

The beach is on Highway 1, just south of San Gregorio State Beach. (415) 330-6464.

•**San Gregorio State Beach** 🐾🐾 *See ㉘ on page 186.*

This place is usually a little too crowded with families for a comfortable dog walk—even a leashed one, which is the rule. It's sometimes just too difficult to negotiate through all the barbecuers, sunbathers, children, and sand castles. The beach is so popular in part because of a lagoon that often forms at the mouth of San Gregorio Creek. The still water is an ideal depth for children, but dogs tend to enjoy wading through, too. Watch out for crumbling cliffs above. And don't forget that if you park in the lot, there's a $5 entry fee, plus $1 per dog.

It's on Highway 1 just south of Highway 84. (415) 330-6464.

SAN MATEO

PARKS, BEACHES, AND RECREATION AREAS

• **Bayside-Joinville Park** 🐾 🐾 *See ㉙ on page 186.*

Human olfactory senses may be mildly offended by the scents in this park, but dogs seem to thrive on them. Depending on which way the wind is blowing, the odor is bound to hit you at some point. It's a stale smell, like a dishrag that's still in the sink a week after Thanksgiving. Sometimes it's even worse. The alleged culprit is an old compost site across the street, where Shoreline Park will be built in the future. When it's potent, Joe stands nose to the wind, tail trembling, glued in homage.

But the park has some notable qualities. It's just across the street from San Francisco Bay, it's on the Marina Lagoon (sorry, no swimming allowed), and it's well maintained.

The park has two sections. If you're the type who likes the bad news first, start at the Anchor Road entrance and take the path along the lagoon, over a guano-covered footbridge, past the big gray pump station, and onto a little dirt path on the edge of the lagoon. Then go left and take the second, cleaner footbridge over to the better half of the park. It's got a decent-sized field, young trees, and tennis courts. Or you can enter at Kehoe Avenue and Roberta Drive and reverse the path. (650) 377-4640.

• **Beresford Park** 🐾 🐾 *See ㉚ on page 186.*

The bulk of this park is made up of sports fields. But venture behind the garden center and you and your pooch can enjoy a pleasant little leashed romp on a large grassy field. A dozen or so adolescent pine trees are trying to grow despite dozens of daily assaults from male dogs. Several picnic tables and a children's play area near the field make this an adequate spot for a weekend afternoon with the family. People are friendly here—we were twice offered soda and beer by locals, who wanted Joe to "hang" with them.

The park is on Parkside Way at Alameda de las Pulgas. (650) 377-4640.

• **Central Park** 🐾🐾🐾 See ③① *on page 186.*

Bring plenty of quarters if you want to fully experience this strange park on the edge of downtown. It costs a quarter to park in the underground lot; a quarter to put your finger in the pulse machine; a quarter to watch the chicken lay a plastic prize egg; a quarter for the Pen Vendorama; it even costs a quarter for a cup of water at the refreshment stand, although smart shoppers know there's a water fountain within 20 feet.

As you enter the park from the Fifth Avenue side, you immediately encounter the concession stand and surrounding dispensers that rival any at state fairs. The stand has good ice cream and tolerable pizza.

The rest of the park is a lush, green, miniature version of Golden Gate Park. There's a Japanese garden, and although no dogs are allowed inside, the Japanese ambience spills outside. The days we've visited, there was always something going on at the outdoor stage in back of the recreation center. A couple of large meadows are bordered by big shady redwoods. There's even a pint-sized railroad that takes up part of a small field. Someone told us that dogs have been known to chase the cars as they chug along the track. Leashes are a must, a rule you'd be well advised to follow: The fine for loose dogs is not a quarter.

The park is on East Fifth Avenue at El Camino Real. (650) 377-4640.

• **Laurelwood Park** 🐾🐾🐾 See ③② *on page 186.*

A small, clear stream winds the length of this rural park in the suburbs. Joe won't have anything to do with the water and jumps from one side to the other without getting a toenail damp. But normal dogs delight in its fresh scents and enticing sounds. Follow the bike trail—heeding the leash law, as this is a popular spot for bikers—along the stream, and enjoy tree-covered hillsides in a virtually suburb-free environment. Only a few blocks from the Laurelwood Shopping Center, this park is an ideal getaway after a quick shopping trip. The kids can use the playground at the foot of the bike trail.

The park is at Glendora and Cedarwood Drives. (650) 377-4640.

RESTAURANTS

Borel's Deli: You have your choice of deli food or hot food here. "Order the baked, hot turkey. Get extra gravy. Then drop it so your dog can eat it," advises Joe. Dine with your pooch outside at two tables. 99 Bovet Road; (650) 573-7710.

Max's Bakery & Kitchen: You and your pooch can dine on good sweets and soups at several outdoor tables. 111 Fourth Avenue; (650) 344-1997.

The Patio Cafe: Many people bring their pooches here and eat at the outdoor area. They serve tasty hot meals, as well as many kinds of sandwiches. There's also a decent salad bar. 1 Lagoon Drive; (650) 595-0700.

PLACES TO STAY

Residence Inn by Marriott: There's a walking path not far from here, so it's a good place to stay with your pooch. Besides, it's a comfy lodging—not quite home, but it tries to come close. Rates are $159 to $179. Dogs are $10 extra, plus a $75 fee per visit. 2000 Winward Way, San Mateo, CA 94404; (650) 574-4700.

Villa Quality Hotel: Rates are $89 to $99. Dogs require a $50 deposit. 4000 South El Camino Real, San Mateo, CA 94403; (650) 341-0966.

DOGGY DAYS

Get Spooky: Every Halloween, a few dozen dogs (and cats, the party poopers) get dressed up in their favorite costumes and head for the costume contest at the pet supply store Togs for Dogs and Cats Too! The contest brings the usual jokers, princesses, and ghosts, but sometimes it attracts particularly creative dogs. One recent popular participant was a wolf-husky mix dressed in a sheep costume and a wool scarf. Get it? He was a wolf in sheep's clothing. Most dogs didn't understand the literary reference, but the humans got a kick out of it.

Any dog who shows up in costume gets a free bag of treats. The winner gets dog food for a year (unless the winner is a cat, but we don't like to think about those things).

The contest is usually held the Saturday before Halloween. If you don't happen to have a dog costume, Togs for Dogs stocks quite a supply. 24 West 41st Avenue; (650) 574-5364.

SOUTH SAN FRANCISCO

PARKS, BEACHES, AND RECREATION AREAS

• **Orange Memorial Park** 😊 🐾 *See* ㉝ *on page 186.*

Hidden behind the park's large baseball field is a big square of land surrounded on all sides by tall trees. It's good for a quick on-leash romp. There seem to be all kinds of sniffs around the large weeping willow tree in the middle of the field.

It's on Orange Avenue at Tennis Drive. (650) 877-8560.

• **Westborough Park** 🐾 🐾 *See* ❸❹ *on page 186.*

This is a hilly little park with many picnic tables, a tennis court, and a children's playground. Your best bet is to take the narrow, paved path along the back of the park. It's lined with trees and far from the madding baseball field below. Leashes are required.

It's on Westborough Avenue at Galway Drive, just west of Interstate 280. (650) 877-8560.

PLACES TO STAY

La Quinta Motor Inn: Rates are $85 to $109. 20 Airport Boulevard, South San Francisco, CA 94080; (650) 583-2223.

Ramada Inn San Francisco International: Rates at this attractive hotel are $89 to $189. Dogs have to be under 40 pounds to stay here, and they require a $100 deposit. 245 South Airport Boulevard, South San Francisco, CA 94080; (650) 589-7200.

WOODSIDE

PARKS, BEACHES, AND RECREATION AREAS

• **Thornewood Open Space Preserve** 🐾 🐾 🐾
See ❸❺ *on page 186.*

This 141-acre preserve is a former estate, and the views of the valley from parts of this land are magnificent. Dogs can peruse the preserve on leash. Thornewood is the smallest of the Midpeninsula Regional Open Space District's preserves, but dogs dig the one-mile trail that runs through the oak woodland, chaparral, and redwoods here.

Dogs have to stay away from Schilling Pond because swans call it home, and dogs and swans don't mix. In fact, although the pond is almost entirely surrounded by dense vegetation, rangers have spotted dogs swimming after these beautiful birds. If this happens very much, the entire preserve could be off-limits to all dogs, so let's be careful out there.

From Interstate 280, exit at Highway 84/Woodside Road and drive west into the hills, about five miles. The road will make several sharp turns, but keep following Highway 84. Go left at the narrow, signed driveway. It winds through the woods for a third of a mile before reaching the small parking lot on the west side of the driveway. (650) 691-1200.

RESTAURANTS

Alice's Restaurant: You can get almost anything you want at this restaurant, including a table for you and your dog on the large porch. Weekends here are packed with bikers, especially for Alice's colossal breakfasts. If your dog rides in your motorcycle sidecar, this is the place for you. It's at 17288 Skyline Boulevard, on the corner of Highways 35 and 84, just two miles north of Portola Valley's Windy Hill Open Space Preserve; (650) 851-0303.

King's Mountain Country Store: This store has everything from candles and books to dog food, crafts, and camping items. There's even a deli. Classical music plays almost all the time. You and your dog can grab a sandwich and sit at an outside table. 13100 Skyline Boulevard, adjacent to Purisima Creek Open Space Preserve (where no dogs are allowed); (650) 851-3852.

SANTA CLARA COUNTY

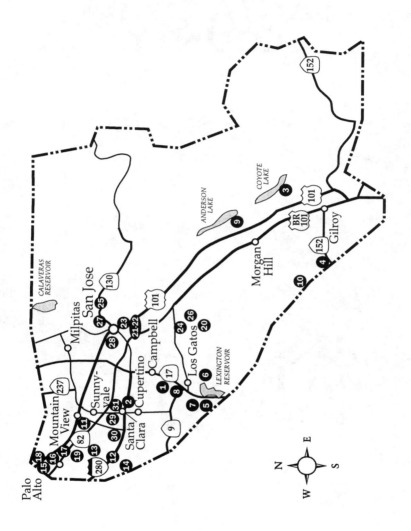

CALAVERAS
RESERVOIR

ANDERSON
LAKE

COYOTE
LAKE

San Jose

Milpitas

Mountain
View

Sunny-
vale

Santa
Clara

Cupertino

Campbell

Los Gatos

LEXINGTON
RESERVOIR

Morgan
Hill

Gilroy

Palo
Alto

152

3

101

BR
101

152

4

10

9

130

25

27

28

23

21-22

26

24

20

17

6

1

8

7

5

237

29

31

2

9

82

11

30

19

13

12

14

15

18

16

17

280

101

N
E
S
W

7
SANTA CLARA COUNTY

While some parts of Santa Clara County are quite scenic, dogs have to face the facts: The place still revolves around Silicon Valley, and it's not a pretty sight. Cookie-cutter duplexes and town houses abound. So do suburban-style office buildings, strip shopping centers, and low-lying metal warehouses. Even dogs with questionable taste wince.

But if you get your dog out of the more populated areas and into the quieter county parks, you'll scarcely know you're in the middle of a megabyting, microchipping mecca. Some of the larger, wilder county parks may put your dog back in touch with the wolf inside herself. One dog we met on a trail at Mount Madonna County Park was sitting and howling every few hundred feet. Her person said she was just happy to be there. Joe Dog thought maybe the dog was just saying "get this leash off me!"

Leashes are the law wherever dogs are allowed in county-run parks, with one sparkling new exception: the Shadowbluff Dog Run area at Coyote-Hellyer County Park (see page 237). Dogs are keeping their paws crossed that the county's movers and shakers see the dire need for more of these leash-free havens before the next edition of this book.

A few other off-leash parks keep dogs from going out of their minds. Palo Alto has three, and Sunnyvale and Santa Clara each have one. Mountain View has several that are open to leashless dogs who have special permits.

The Midpeninsula Regional Open Space District has become one of dogs' best friends of late, with the addition in Santa Clara County of one more preserve open to leashed dogs (see Sierra Azul, page 225). That makes three dog-friendly open space preserves in the county. The district has unique rules about poop scooping and six-foot leashes. See the introduction to the San Mateo County chapter on page 187 for more on these rules.

The district even offers very cool canine walks in conjunction with the Palo Alto Humane Society. The hikes, called Dog Days

Walks & Hikes, are about two hours, and they're usually leisurely, although you can end up covering from three to five miles. It's a great way to meet dogs and their people. Pooper-scoopers are provided, but you have to do the scooping. Bring a leash and water for your pooch. For more information, or to make reservations, call the district at (650) 691-1200, or the Palo Alto Humane Society at (650) 327-0631. (The Humane Society also offers easy hikes in other parklands about once a month. Call for a schedule.)

An exceptional group called Peninsula Access for Dogs (PAD) is working to improve park life for dogs here. For information, write to PAD at 809-B Cuesta Drive, Box 196, Mountain View, CA 94094, or check out PAD's Web site: www.rahul.net/pruski/pads. So far they've been very effective in getting dogs into open space preserves here and in San Mateo County.

As if all this doggy good news weren't enough, Joe (aka "I adore manure") Dog wants to let you know that dogs are allowed at a glorious farm in Los Altos Hills (see Diversions, page 224). Joe becomes Old Farm Dog when we visit, especially when we're near the livestock. His whole demeanor, from his ecstatically sniffing schnoz to his competent swagger seems to say "I may be leashed, but at least I'm not fenced in." (The whole time he's thinking this, he's also praying a cow doesn't escape and find him at nearby Sunnyvale's fenced dog run.) Check it out if you and your pooch want to discover your agricultural roots.

CAMPBELL

PARKS, BEACHES, AND RECREATION AREAS

•**Los Gatos Creek County Park** 🐾 🐾½ *See* ❶ *on page 218.*

Here your leashed dog can romp on grass, have a picnic with you in the shade of Los Gatos Creek's medium-sized trees, and watch ducks and geese in the percolation ponds of Los Gatos Creek, which are good for fishing. Dogs like Joe, who would ruffle duck and geese feathers with his barking, should be kept away from these critters. The Los Gatos Creek Trail runs through here, should you care to take a jaunt.

From Highway 17, exit at Camden Avenue; go west on San Tomas Expressway, south on Winchester Boulevard, and left on Hacienda Avenue to the park. A $4 parking fee is charged in summer and on weekends and holidays. (408) 356-2729.

RESTAURANTS

Orchard Valley Coffee: Enjoy coffee, snacks, and pastries, and nighttime live music, at one of five tables right on the sidewalk at this dog-friendly place. 349 East Campbell Avenue; (408) 374-2115.

PLACES TO STAY

Campbell Inn: Rates are $99 to $185. Dogs are $10 extra. 675 East Campbell Avenue, Campbell, CA 95008; (408) 374-4300.

Residence Inn by Marriott: This is a convenient, comfortable place to stay when traveling with a dog. Residence Inns only have suites and apartments, and they all come with kitchens. Rates are $149 to $189. Extended stays get a discounted rate. Dogs have to pay a $75 cleaning fee, plus $10 per night. 2761 South Bascom Avenue, Campbell, CA 95008; (408) 559-1551.

DIVERSIONS

You doity dog: Even if your dog hates a bath more than anything, he'll surely like it a bit better if it's you working him over and not some stranger. Shampoo Chez (pronounced "Shampoochers") is a wash-him-yourself dog grooming establishment with two branches in the Bay Area.

The current owners say they've hosted about a zillion self-service washes since they began. That's a lot of shampoo and fleas down the drain. A shampoo for any size dog is $10 for 30 minutes of wash time and an additional $1 for each five minutes after that. 523 East Campbell Avenue. (408) 379-WASH.

CUPERTINO

PARKS, BEACHES, AND RECREATION AREAS

• **Fremont Older Open Space Preserve** 🐾🐾🐾
  See ❷ *on page 218.*

This 739-acre preserve smells sweet and clean, but that doesn't disappoint dogs. Pooches have enough trees and ground-level odors to keep them happily trotting along on their mandatory leashes.

Once you park in the small lot, you'll walk several hundred feet on a paved roadway, but be sure to turn right at the first sign for hikers. Otherwise you'll find yourself in the middle of a bicycle freeway. The narrow dirt trail to the right takes you on a three-mile loop through cool woodlands and rolling open hills up to Hunters Point via the Seven Springs Loop Trail. The view of Santa Clara Valley from the top of the 900-foot hill is incomparable. More trails may be open soon, so your dog's feet will be able to explore as never before.

Signs at the entrance warn of ticks, so be sure to give your dog (and yourself) a thorough inspection after your hike.

From U.S. 101 or Interstate 280, take Highway 85 (Saratoga-Sunnyvale Road) south to Prospect Road. Turn right and follow the road to the park entrance. (650) 691-1200.

GILROY

PARKS, BEACHES, AND RECREATION AREAS

• **Coyote Lake Park** 🐾🐾🐾 *See* ❸ *on page 218.*

This county park is full of wildlife no matter how high or low the lake. In fact, when we last visited, we saw foxes, wild turkeys, and a grazing deer—and there wasn't a drop of water in the reservoir. The reservoir had been bone dry for so long that it looked like an enormous open field. Brush and a few trees were starting to emerge from the hard, dry ground.

When it's in this drought condition, the lake bed is a favorite stomping ground for leashed canines—who are usually relegated to picnic areas, the campground, and the one-mile trail connecting them.

The campsites are roomy, and several are shaded by large oak trees. Others look out on the lake—or field, depending on the water level. We like to visit the nearby picnic areas after stopping at one of Gilroy's garlic stores for lunch supplies. Joe has a penchant for garlic-flavored pistachios.

There are 74 sites here, and they're $10, plus $1 for a dog. Phone (408) 358-3751 for reservations. The day-use fee is $4. From U.S. 101, exit at Leavesley Road and follow the signs to the park. (408) 842-7800.

• **Mount Madonna County Park** 🐾🐾🐾½
See ❹ *on page 218.*

This magnificent park is midway between Gilroy and Watsonville (in Santa Cruz County). No matter where you're coming from, it's worth the drive. The mountain, covered with mixed conifers, oak, madrone, and bay and sword ferns, is wonderfully quiet and cool—which is especially appreciated by San Jose dwellers, whose parks are almost never far from the roar of freeways. You may hear the screech of jays and little else.

Try driving on Valley View Road (to the right from the ranger station) to the Giant Twins Trail, where you can park in the shady campsite of the same name—at least when no one is camping there. (When we were there on a perfect Indian summer day in late September, the park was deserted.) Two huge old redwoods, green with lichen, give the trail its name. After half a mile, the trail becomes Sprig Lake Trail and continues for another two miles. Sprig Lake, really a pond, is empty in summer, but in spring it's stocked for children's fishing.

This walk isn't much of a strain. If you'd like more exercise, there are plenty of longer and steeper trails—18 miles in all, and as of this writing, your dog may enjoy every one of them. From the Redwood Trail or the Blackhawk Canyon Trail, you'll be rewarded with views of the Santa Clara Valley, the Salinas Valley, and Monterey Bay. For a walk almost completely around the park, try the Merry-Go-Round Trail.

The park's deer are only one of many reasons you should keep your dog securely leashed, tempting as it might be to let her off. "Dogs have instincts," a friendly ranger said.

Your dog might enjoy a camping vacation here. There are 113 large, private campsites available on a first-come, first-served basis. Sites are $10 to $20 per night, plus $1 for each dog. A $4 day-use fee is always charged on weekends and daily from Memorial Day through Labor Day.

From U.S. 101, exit at Highway 152 west to Gilroy. Continue on 152 (Hecker Pass Highway) through part of the park. The entrance is a right (north) turn at Pole Line Road. Call (408) 842-2341 for park and campground information.

PLACES TO STAY

Comfort Inn: Rates are $55 to $69. Pooches are $5 extra and can stay only at the management's discretion. 8292 Murray Avenue, Gilroy, CA 95020; (408) 848-3500.

Coyote Lake Park: See Coyote Lake Park on page 222 for camping information.

Leavesley Inn: Rates are $50 to $73. Dogs are charged a $10 fee per visit. 8430 Murray Avenue, Gilroy, CA 95020; (408) 847-5500.

Mount Madonna County Park: See Mount Madonna County Park on page 222 for camping information.

LOS ALTOS

Los Altos, like Saratoga and Los Gatos, is a clean town with civic pride, great for strolling. The hand-painted benches and spotless lawns look as if no dog has ever passed through, but in fact dogs are here in force. They're just mannerly.

RESTAURANTS

The Cookie Cafe & Bakery: Grab a cookie for each of you while exploring downtown. 133 Main Street; (415) 949-2521.

Italian Delicatessen: Drop by for great salami smells. Better yet, order one of the delicious specialty sandwiches and dine at the outdoor tables with your pooch. If you have a drop of Italian blood in you, The Godfather sandwich, which is loaded with mortadella, prosciutto, provolone, and lots of other great Italian ingredients, will make you drool. (But you can blame the drool on your dog.) 137 Main Street; (415) 948-6745.

Los Altos Bar & Grill: Here's a sports lover's eatery serving grilled meats, fish, pasta, and heavy-duty desserts (chocolate is the magic word) at five tables on the front patio. Last time we visited, two happy dogs were munching on bites of burgers at the feet of their people. 169 Main Street; (415) 948-4332.

DOGGY DAYS

Walk with the animals: Here's a tradition that has lasted for more than 48 years, and you can understand why. Any and all pets are welcome at the Los Altos Pet Parade, sponsored by the Kiwanis Club. Attending, many in costume, are llamas, horses, hamsters, cats, and dogs. One year Little Red Riding Hood came, with her dog as the Big Bad Wolf. "Everyone in town comes downtown early to get a seat," said a local restaurant owner. Held annually in May, the Saturday after Mother's Day. For information, call city hall at (650) 948-1491 for the number for the current Kiwanis contact.

LOS ALTOS HILLS

DIVERSIONS

Make Maggie an aggy: Dogs and farms belong together. Witness all the happy dogs in James Herriott's stories, or in the movie *Babe,* or in countless other works. "But," you say, "MY dog's a city/suburban dog. Alas, no farm life for her." Before you chuck your overalls, check out Hidden Villa Farm, where a dog (on leash) can sniff out all the earthy, cow patty delights of farm life.

This beautiful 1,600-acre organic farm and wilderness preserve is just what the doctor ordered for city-weary dogs and their people. Kids and adults can take part in all kinds of hands-on activities, but pooches have to pretty much stick to perusing the paths around the pastures and barns. They won't get to roll in any of the smells they revel in, but just getting to sniff the air and see the livestock usually makes their day, week, or year. Make sure you keep a good hold of her leash, and don't forget to scoop the poop (your dog's, not the sheep's, cow's, horse's, etc.).

Dogs aren't allowed on the wilderness trails that branch out from the farm center, and, like people, they're not allowed in the animal pens. 26870 Moody Road; (650) 949-8660.

LOS GATOS

Dogs like Los Gatos but think it needs a name change. Joe suggests "Los Perros."

PARKS, BEACHES, AND RECREATION AREAS

•**Lexington Reservoir County Park** 🐾🐾 *See* **5** *on page 218.*

When the reservoir is full, this park is full of life. Birds sing and the foliage is bright green. But in drought years, everything here—trees, grass, brush—is covered with silt. This death mask must frighten birds away to better nesting areas, because it's utterly silent, except for a few cars kicking up dust on a nearby road.

It can really bake during summer months, too. And since there's no swimming allowed, dogs get miserable fast. (To cool himself off here, Joe rolled on the dusty ground until his entire body was coated with ash-colored silt. He looked like some kind of moving statue on a mandatory leash.)

Exit Highway 17 at Montevina Road and drive east a quarter of a mile. You can stop at any of several parking areas along the road. There is no entrance fee, except for the Miller Picnic Site, where you'll pay $4. (408) 358-3741.

•**Sierra Azul Open Space Preserve**
(Kennedy-Limekiln area) 🐾🐾🐾 *See* **6** *on page 218.*

The wildlife at this 5,000-acre preserve has it pretty good. There's so much steep, rugged terrain and dense chaparral that humans and their leashed doggy interlopers are pretty much forced to stay on the trails, out of critters' ways. Unfortunately for dogs and their people, mountain bikes seem to be everywhere on these trails, and they can go really fast. So on weekends especially, keep your eyes and ears peeled and be ready to dodge the traffic.

This is not a park for the fair of paw. A hike to the 2,000-foot ridgetop can make even the most fit dog sweat. But the views from here or from the 1,700-foot Priest Rock are worth a little panting, at least on your part. Take it easy on your dog, though, and don't let him pant too much. It can get very, very hot here in the summer, and there's virtually no decent shade. The folks at the Midpeninsula Regional Open Space District beg you not to take your pooch here on summer afternoons.

Parking here is a real problem. More on that in the next paragraph, but if you visit on a busy day, have a contingency plan in case you don't get one of the coveted spaces. Also note that the two other sections of the Sierra Azul Preserve (Cathedral Oaks and Mount Umunhum) don't permit pooches.

From Highway 85, exit at Los Gatos Boulevard and drive west a little more than two miles. At Kennedy Road, turn left and follow the road about two more miles to the parking spot at the trailhead. There's currently room for only two cars here. This is utterly inadequate, and the district is working to do something about this. In the meantime, there's room for about seven cars across Kennedy, on Top of the Hill Road. Please be considerate of the residents here, and keep noise to a minimum and don't litter. (650) 691-1200.

• **St. Joseph's Hill Open Space Preserve** 🐾 🐾 🐾 ½
See ❼ *on page 218.*

Want a quick escape from urbanity? Visit this scenic, 173-acre preserve with your leashed pooch. Dogs are allowed on all four miles of trails here, but beware, it can get steep. The trails wind through oak woodlands and open grassland, and at the top of the 1,250-foot St. Joseph's Hill, you'll get magnificent views of the surrounding parklands. Joe loves to sit here and let his nostrils flare.

From Highway 17, take the Alma Bridge Road exit and go across the dam. Public parking is available at Lexington Reservoir County

Park. The trail to St. Joseph's Hill starts opposite the boat launching area at the north end of the reservoir. (650) 691-1200.

• **Vasona Lake County Park** 🐾🐾🐾 *See* **8** *on page 218.*

This is a perfectly manicured park, with grass like that of a golf course. Dogs find it tailor-made for rolling, although they tend to get tangled in their leashes—which the county demands they wear here.

Several pathways take you through this 151-acre park and down to the lake's edge. But no swimming is allowed. And dogs aren't allowed to visit the children's playground either. You can picnic in the shade of one of the large willows or lead your dog up to the groves of pines and firs for a relief session.

From Highway 17, take Highway 9 (Saratoga-Los Gatos Road) west to University Avenue. Go right and continue to Blossom Hill Road. The park will be on your left. Enter at Garden Hill Drive. The parking fee is $4. (408) 356-2729.

RESTAURANTS

Classic Burgers of Los Gatos: This dog-friendly eatery has fine burgers. Dogs drool over them at the four tables on the patio. And they don't just serve hamburgers. "We have everything, even peanut butter and jelly," says one staffer. 15737 Los Gatos Boulevard; (408) 356-6910.

Dolce Spazio Gelato: On warm days, this is the place to come. The homemade gelato is creamy and delicious. When there's a chill in the air, try something from the cafe's espresso bar. The good-sized patio has heat lamps, which helps dogs and their people cozy up to a winter visit. 221 North Santa Cruz Avenue; (408) 395-1335.

MILPITAS

PLACES TO STAY

Best Western Brookside Inn: Rates are $79 to $129. Dogs are $10 extra, and it's requested that they not weigh more than 20 pounds. (Instead of putting your paunchy pooch on a crash diet, try Economy Inns.) 400 Valley Way, Milpitas, CA 95035; (408) 263-5566.

Economy Inns of America: Rates are $64 to $99. 270 South Abbott Avenue, Milpitas, CA 95035; (408) 946-8889.

MORGAN HILL
PARKS, BEACHES, AND RECREATION AREAS

• **Anderson Lake County Park** 🐾 🐾 ½ *See* ❾ *on page 218.*

When there's enough water to keep the reservoir open to the public, dogs love to go along on fishing trips. But when it's low, dogs take solace in dipping their paws in the shady, secluded stream that runs between picnic areas. Call the rangers to find out if the reservoir is open, because if it isn't, it may not be worth a trip. You can't get anywhere near the lake if it's too low.

The only trail connects picnic areas, and it isn't even a half-mile long. There are plenty of picnic tables with lots of shade, but dogs tend to get bored unless hunks of hamburger happen to fall from the grills. The picnic areas can be rowdy, with lots of beer and loud music, so if your dog doesn't like rap, take him somewhere else.

From U.S. 101, follow Cochrane Road east to the park. (408) 779-3634.

• **Uvas Canyon County Park** 🐾 🐾 🐾 ½ *See* ❿ *on page 218.*

In the past, there was a lot of confusion about which trails in this park allowed dogs. Happily, the Santa Clara County parks department decided in 1992 to open all the trails to leashed dogs. You can get a map when you drive through the entrance kiosk.

This is a pretty, clean park of oak, madrone, and Douglas fir trees in cool canyons. The Uvas Creek Trail is a favorite trail. Dogs always appreciate a creek on a warm summer day, and this one doesn't dry up in hot weather. You might also try the wide, dirt Alec Canyon Trail, 1.5 miles long, within sight of Alec Creek, or the Nature Trail Loop, about one mile long, beside Swanson Creek. You may see some waterfalls in late winter and early spring.

Dogs are allowed in the campgrounds and picnic areas of Uvas Canyon. The park has 25 campsites, available on a first-come, first-served basis, for $10 a night. Dogs are $1 extra. The campground is open daily from April 15 to October 31, and Fridays and Saturdays from November through March. It's crowded on weekends during late spring and summer, so arrive early or camp during the week.

From U.S. 101, exit at Cochrane Road; go south on Business 101 to Watsonville Road, then right (west) on Watsonville to McKean-Uvas Road. Turn right on Uvas (past Uvas Reservoir) to Croy Road.

Go left on Croy to the park. The last four miles on Croy are fairly tortuous. (408) 779-9232.

PLACES TO STAY

Best Western Country Inn: Rates are $65 to $85. Dogs are allowed in smoking rooms only. 16525 Condit Road, Morgan Hill, CA 95037; (408) 779-0447.

Uvas Canyon County Park: See Uvas Canyon County Park on page 228 for camping information.

MOUNTAIN VIEW

PARKS, BEACHES, AND RECREATION AREAS

At press time, the city was having workshops and public meetings about the possibility of a leash-free park here. (Currently the only way for a dog to be off leash is to get a training permit.) The city's community services department was doing most of the research on how dog parks work, so that's a sign that good things will soon happen here! For updates, call (650) 903-6331.

• **Rengstorff Park** 🐾 🐾 🐕 (with permit) *See* ⓫ *on page 218.*

This park is typically neat, green, and interesting for people, and it has another excellent feature: A sign reads "Dogs must be on leash (except by permit)." This means that you can get a permit from the city that allows you to train a dog off leash, with the understanding that he'll be under control. Be forewarned, though: If you don't bring the permit along with you when training, you will be ticketed.

Rengstorff Park is at Rengstorff Avenue between California Street and Central Expressway. Call for details on getting a permit. (650) 903-6331.

RESTAURANTS

Blue Sky Cafe: This is a popular neighborhood restaurant in a small house with outdoor tables. Ingredients are strictly fresh, with vegetarian dishes a specialty. Dogs are happy to know that meat is served, too. The owners will be glad to seat your dog on the sidewalk just next to the outside tables. 336 Bryant Street; (650) 961-2082.

PLACES TO STAY

Best Western Tropicana Lodge: Rates are $80 to $100. 1720 West El Camino Real, Mountain View, CA 94040; (650) 961-0220.

Residence Inn by Marriott: You and your dog will feel right at home at the suites at this attractive hotel. They have kitchens and lots of other extras you won't find in a regular hotel. But better than that is the very dog-friendly attitude here. "We take all pets, from snakes to rabbits. We see them as part of the family, and try to accommodate the owners' needs," one manager told us. The place even has a little fenced area for exercising dogs, and staff is happy to point you to nearby trails.

There's a $50 to $75 doggy fee per visit, so it's best to stay for a while to get the most bang for your buck. Dogs are $10 extra per night. Rates are $160 to $229. 1854 West El Camino Real, Mountain View, CA 94040; (650) 940-1300.

PALO ALTO

For dogs, this town is the county's garden spot. Here, you'll find lots of other dog lovers and well-behaved dogs, enticing city parks—all of which allow dogs—and no fewer than three leash-free dog runs. At the Baylands, you and your leashed dog can watch birds and get a good workout at the same time. And many student-oriented restaurants with outdoor seating welcome your dog. If you're lucky enough to have a Palo Alto address, or a friend with one, you may bring your dog to the glorious Foothills Park on weekdays.

The Palo Alto Humane Society offers a wonderful way to perambulate with your pooch. Twice a month, you can join dogs and their people for "Dog Days Walks & Hikes." The leashed hikes at some of the area's more scenic parks provide plenty of exercise for everyone, but beyond that, they're great fun. Joe, Nisha, and I met some enchanting dogs and people on a Dog Days Hike we took. Among them was a couple with five greyhounds and borzois. The man and woman met at Cipriani Park in Belmont (see page 189) with all their dogs, fell in love, married, and combined their doggy households to live—and scoop—happily every after.

The hikes are usually held on Saturday afternoons. Reservations are required. A $5 donation is requested, but members go for free. A little bag of doggy goodies, including a bandanna while supplies last, is included in the price. Contact the Humane Society at (650) 327-0631 for a schedule or for more information.

PARKS, BEACHES, AND RECREATION AREAS

• **Arastradero Preserve** 🐾🐾🐾½ *See* **⑫** *on page 218.*

With 613 acres of rolling savanna grassland and broadleaf evergreen forest, Arastradero Preserve is one of the more peaceful and attractive parks in the area. Dogs dig it, but they have to be leashed. It's a good rule, because mountain lions, rattlesnakes, poison oak, and coyotes can be part of the scene here. And so can bikers.

Anglers are right at home in the preserve. A hike to Arastradero Lake takes only about 20 minutes from the main parking lot, and the fishing can be very good. (Sorry, no swimming, boats, or flotation devices.)

There are 6.25 miles of hiking trails. Joe Dog enjoys the hilly 2.8-mile Acorn Trail when he's in the mood to pant. Bring plenty of water; it can get toasty here.

From Interstate 280, exit at Page Mill Road and go south. Turn right (west) on Arastradero Road (Refuge Road on some maps) and drive into the parking lot. (650) 329-2423.

• **Esther Clark Park** 🐾🐾🐾 *See* **⑬** *on page 218.*

This is a beautiful piece of undeveloped land with some dirt paths, right on the border of Los Altos Hills. There are no facilities but plenty of meadow and eucalyptus trees. A creek bed promises water in the wet season.

Where Old Adobe Road bends to the left and makes a cul-de-sac, the park is the undeveloped land on your right. (650) 329-2423.

• **Foothills Park** 🐾🐾🐾½ *See* **⑭** *on page 218.*

To use this park, privately owned by the city of Palo Alto, you must prove you're a resident or be the guest of one. Dogs are allowed only on weekdays (no holidays, though) and must be on leash, but they can go on all the trails.

The park has a large lake surrounded by unspoiled foothills, plus 15 miles of hiking trails of varying difficulty. At sundown, deer are plentiful. It's a beautiful sight, but be sure to keep tight hold of that leash. This park is heaven on Earth for dogs and people alike. If you don't already live in Palo Alto, it could make you consider moving.

To find Foothills Park from Interstate 280, exit at Page Mill Road and drive about 2.5 miles south. As usual, when you're searching for a really good Santa Clara County park, the road will become impossibly narrow and winding, and you'll think you're lost. But you aren't. The entry fee for Palo Alto residents is $2 per car, $1 for hikers and bicyclists. (650) 329-2423.

• **Greer Park** 🐾🐾🐾½ 🐕 *See* **15** *on page 218.*
This is one of Palo Alto's parks with an off-leash dog run, but it isn't the largest (see Mitchell Park, below). The park is green and pleasant, as are all the city's parks, but it's somewhat noisy because of nearby Bayshore Road. Dogs have to be leashed outside the dog run. There are athletic fields, picnic tables, and two playground areas. The dog run, near the Bayshore side, is small and treeless, but it's entirely fenced, if that's what your dog needs. Bring your own scoopers and water.

The park is at Amarillo Street and West Bayshore Road. The parking lot is off Bayshore, conveniently near the dog run. (650) 496-6950.

• **Hoover Park** 🐾🐾🐾 🐕 *See* **16** *on page 218.*
This park may be small, but dogs don't really care. It's home to a little-known dog run that's not as popular as the run at Mitchell Park (see below), but that's part of the charm. Dogs also dig the little stream that runs through the park.

The park is at Cowper Street between Colorado and Loma Verde Avenues. (650) 496-6950.

• **Mitchell Park** 🐾🐾🐾🐾 🐕 *See* **17** *on page 218.*
This generous, green park has some unusual amenities, including two human-sized chessboards and a roller-skating rink. The park is also a standout in the canine book: It has a four-paw dog run that's completely fenced and has a row of pine trees on one side, water dishes on the other, and scrappy tennis balls everywhere. When we last visited, there were a couple of beat-up old office-style chairs just waiting to be sat upon, knocked over, or at least marked by a leg-lifting varmint.

Sadly, there's been some controversy of late about the future of the dog run. It seems the run, which has been around since 1972, is irritating to some parents who feel it shouldn't be anywhere near children. At press time, it looked like the dog run would survive, but longtime users of the park say its future may be on shaky ground (and not because it's located near the San Andreas Fault).

The park itself has plenty of shade to delight a dog. Remember to leash outside the dog run. For kids, the playground area has sculptured bears for climbing and a wading pool (sorry, no dogs). The dog run is a short walk from the parking lot.

The park is on East Meadow Drive just south of Middlefield Road. (650) 496-6950.

• **Palo Alto Baylands** 🐾🐾🐾 *See* ⑱ *on page 218.*

This is the best-developed wetlands park in the Bay Area for adults, children, and dogs. It's laced with paved bike trails and levee trails. Along the pretty levee paths, benches face the mudflats. Don't forget your binoculars on a walk here. A cacophony of mewling gulls, mumbling pigeons, and clucking blackbirds fills the air. Small planes putt into the nearby airport, and your dog will love the fishy smells coming from the marshes. This seems to be a popular spot for dog exercise. Keep your pooch leashed and on the trails.

Dogs shouldn't go near the well-marked waterfowl nesting area, but they're welcome to watch children feed the noisy ducks and Canada geese in the duck pond, as long as they don't think about snacks *à l'orange.*

From U.S. 101, exit at Embarcadero Road East and go all the way to the end. At the entrance, turn left for the trails, ranger station, and duck pond. A right turn takes you to a recycling center. (650) 496-6997.

• **The Stanford Dish** 🐾🐾🐾 *See* ⑲ *on page 218.*

"The Stanford Dish" is not a park but Stanford University property surrounding the satellite dish used by the physics department. Stanford lets dog owners enjoy it, so long as dogs stay on leash and on the trails and their owners pick up after them. The hill is quite popular, with its grasslands reclaimed from cattle pasture and dotted with oaks. A reforestation project is under way, so in the future it will be even nicer. Cattle still graze on the Interstate 280 side, so there's good reason for the leash rule. A ranger patrols to enforce it.

You can park on campus across the street from the Tressider Student Union and walk up a path to Junipero Serra Boulevard. The dish property borders Junipero Serra. Don't park in the nearby residential areas. (650) 723-4311.

RESTAURANTS

Downtown Palo Alto is a walker-friendly and dog-adoring kind of place. It's full of benches and plazas for sitting, and quite a few restaurants will serve both of you out on the sidewalk or patio. Here are a few snout-licking options.

Boudin: Enjoy fine coffee and pastries here. There are about seven sidewalk tables subject to heavy foot traffic, but most of the feet will be of students who miss their dogs and want to stop and make a fuss over yours. 388 University Avenue; (650) 325-9353.

Fratelli Deli: Hungry for a quick salad, pasta, or sandwich? Pop over to Fratelli and grab a bite. Eat with your pooch at the two outdoor tables. 405 University Avenue; (650) 323-0423.

O'Connell's Eire House Restaurant and Bar: Top of the mornin' to you! Would you like a potato? Or how about one of 18 draft beers and a wee bit of Irish music to accompany it? Dogs and their people don't have to be Irish to enjoy the mood and the food at this clean, good-looking establishment (although we hear certain setters and wolfhounds get special treatment). Dine at any of several shaded outdoor tables. The restaurant is located in a pedestrian walkway between University and Hamilton Avenues and Ramona and Bryant Streets; (650) 326-2000.

Rodger's Plaza Ramona: Snack on gourmet sandwiches and coffee. You're welcome at the relatively quiet sidewalk tables with your dog. It's on Ramona Street, off University Avenue; (650) 324-4228.

Taxi's Hamburger: Taxi's burgers are award winning (yes, there apparently are awards for hamburgers), and 100 percent beef. Just passing by makes dog drool. But you don't have to pass by. Dogs are welcome here. Many patrons of this upscale American-style grill order burgers for their dogs. When we ate here, a woman at the next table ordered a veggie sandwich and split it with her dog. Eventually, the dog got wind of what Joe was chowing down and went on a quest for meat. In the end, all she got was a piece of bun (the hamburger's, not Joe's). Dine at the dozen tables in the covered outdoor area. If your dog seems thirsty, they'll supply a bowl of water. 403 University Avenue; (650) 322-8294.

Torrefazione: All the coffees and pastries at this cafe are served in hand-painted Italian china. Dogs with a keen sense of aesthetics (such as Airedales, says Joe) appreciate this. Coffee fans love the whole-bean coffee, but I'm not even sure what that is. Doesn't sound like Taster's Choice to me, though. Sit outside the historic building that houses the cafe and dine with your dog at the two tables. 419 University Avenue; (650) 325-7731.

World Wrapps: The cooks here take anything that's delicious and slightly exotic and put it in wraps. To them, the world is a burrito, just waiting to be enveloped. We had a really good Thai wrap when we visited. Joe Dog wants to know when they're going to have a dog food wrap. The smoothies are tasty, too. Dine with doggy at the nine outdoor tables, some of which are shaded by trees. 201 University Avenue; (650) 327-9777.

PLACES TO STAY

Cardinal Hotel: Stay here and you're in the heart of downtown Palo Alto. Rates are $62 to $170. 235 Hamilton Avenue, Palo Alto, CA 94301; (650) 323-5101.

Holiday Inn—Palo Alto: Rates are $159 to $179. Dogs require a $50 deposit, and must be under 20 pounds. (That puts the itsy in itsy-bitsy.) 625 El Camino Real, Palo Alto, CA 94301; (650) 328-2800.

DOGGY DAYS

Jog that dog: The city of Palo Alto stages an annual Dog's Best Friend Run at the Palo Alto Baylands. The five-kilometer (3.1-mile) course, which you may run or walk with your leashed dog, begins and ends at the athletic center. Rules are as follows: You must have your dog on a regular six-foot leash, not a retractable one; you can't carry the dog; and she must cross the finish line before you do. (The idea of this last rule is to restrain hot-dog owners who drag their poor dogs across the finish line.) The record will show your dog's racing time, not yours. Nearly 600 dogs show up every year, yet the organizer, recreation supervisor Dave Brees, says he's never seen a dogfight in all the years he's hosted the race.

For your entry fee of $15, you get a T-shirt and the dog gets a bandanna and plenty of treats. Winners receive plaques and photos. The run takes place at the Palo Alto Baylands (see page 233) around the third week of April. Call (650) 329-2986 for this year's date.

DIVERSIONS

Shop with your best friend: You and your dog can drool over dresses and pant over pantsuits as you saunter down the corridors of the upscale Stanford Shopping Center. The huge open-air mall allows leashed, well-mannered dogs to window-shop with you and to join you for a snack at the outdoor tables here. But better yet, dogs are welcome in many of the mall's stores. We know of several that permit pooches, but since it's up to the store managers, and since managers move around a bit, we'll let you and your dog sniff out the dog-friendly places yourselves. Just poke your head in and ask a sales clerk if it's okay if your pooch comes in with you. Rest assured, this is a question they get all the time, so they won't be shocked.

The mall is on El Camino Real and University Avenue, next to Stanford University. (650) 617-8585.

SAN JOSE

We visited San Jose's downtown center hoping to find plenty of dog-friendly outdoor eateries and shopping malls, but we were disappointed. Only one mall—The Pavilion, next to the Fairmont Hotel, with an inviting array of shops and outdoor tables—looked as if it might allow dogs, but it didn't. The same went for outdoor restaurants. But a dog can drink from a fountain featuring wrought-iron fish in elegant St. James Square Park or gaze at 20 terrific pillars of water shooting from the fountain at Park Plaza. Keep your eye on the area if you have a boulevardier-type dog. Any day now, San Jose may change into his kind of place.

Dogs are welcome in most of the city's parks. Leashes are mandatory in all the parks, and there are no leash-free dog runs.

San Jose residents must enjoy most of their city parks—even the best ones—in the shadow of freeways (some literally) and under the buzz of airplanes landing at the central airport. This listing describes several of the larger, clean, green parks. Many others are undistinguished or full of litter. Call the parks department at (408) 277-4573 for more information.

PARKS, BEACHES, AND RECREATION AREAS

• **Almaden Quicksilver County Park** 🐾🐾🐾½
See ⓴ on page 218.

This rustic, 3,600-acre park allows dogs on about half of its 30 miles of trails. Some of these trails are popular for horseback riding, so watch out; although leashes are the law here, they don't always stop dogs who like to chase hooves.

In the spring, the hills explode with wildlife and wildflowers. Any of the trails will take you through a wonderland of colorful flowers and butterflies who like to tease safely leashed dogs. Speaking of insects, there's a downside to this park: Ticks seem to hang out here. "We got 20 off our dog, then three more when big welts developed," a poor San Jose resident writes. Keep your pooch in the center of trails, and the bloodsucking pests will have to go elsewhere for dinner.

Dogs are allowed on the Guadalupe Trail, the Hacienda Trail, portions of the Mine Hill Trail, the Mockingbird Picnic Area, the No Name Trail, and the Senator Mine Trail. Call the park for more information about the trails and the locations of their trailheads.

You can enter the park at several points. We prefer the main park entrance, where New Almaden Road turns into Alamitos Road, near Almaden Way. (408) 268-3883.

• **Coyote Creek Multiple-Use Trail** 🐾 🐾 🐾
  See ㉑ on page 218.

When this trail is completely paved, it will furnish your dog with 13 miles of trail, if she doesn't mind sharing space with bicycles. Some pooper-scooper dispensers are being installed, too. You may take your dog, leashed, on any portion between the Hellyer County Park end and Parkway Lakes, a private fishing concession at the south end, close to Morgan Hill. (Your only reason to go there would be to pull in some of the club's stocked trout or to enter one of its fishing derbies.)

See the directions to Coyote-Hellyer County Park, below. (408) 255-0225.

• **Coyote-Hellyer County Park/Shadowbluff Dog Run**
  🐾 🐾 🐾 🐾 🐕 *See ㉒ on page 218.*

Dogs everywhere want to shake paws good and strong with the folks who worked to create the first county-run off-leash dog area, located in the east end of this 213-acre park. It took almost three years of public meetings to approve the Shadowbluff Dog Run, but patient pooches are getting their just rewards.

The dog run is one acre, enclosed by a four-foot-high chain-link fence. Dogs who have some steeplechase in them might be able to escape, but most dogs are very content to cavort around sans leash. The enclosure has just about anything a pooch could desire. There's shade from a few trees, water to slurp up, and lots of green grass. For humans, there are benches, pooper-scoopers, and garbage cans. Sounds like dogs get the better end of the deal.

Part of the reason the grass is so green is that the dog run is closed the first seven days of every month and each Monday for turf care. At those times, your best bet is to leash up and explore the rest of this park.

It's a generous, rustic park, popular with bicyclists. The best deal for dogs is the El Arroyo del Coyote Nature Trail, which by some miracle allows dogs. Walk to the left at the entrance kiosk and cross under Hellyer Avenue on the bike trail to find the entrance to the nature trail. Cross the creek on a pedestrian bridge to your right; once across, take the dirt path to your left. Bikes aren't allowed, making it all the better for dogs.

Willows and cottonwoods are luxuriant here, and in spring, poppies bloom. Eucalyptus groves provide occasional shade. Watch out for bees and poison oak. Otherwise, this is heavenly territory for your dog.

The park is very easy to access from U.S. 101. Exit U.S. 101 at Hellyer Avenue and follow prominent signs to the park. The dog area is about 100 yards past the entry kiosk. A parking fee of $4 is charged, and that can add up fast, since there's really no good parking nearby. So if you're planning to be a regular, your best bet would be to buy a $50 park pass for the year. It's a small investment to make for your dog's happiness. (408) 255-0225

• **Emma Prusch Park** 🐾 🐾 🐾 *See* ㉓ *on page 218.*

This park, one of San Jose's most attractive working farms, is a museum. Like a symbol of the county, it lies in the shadow of the intersection of three freeways. Yet it's a charming place and, surprisingly, it allows your leashed dog to wander around the farm with you so long as he stays out of the farm-animal areas. A smooth paved path, good for strollers and wheelchairs, winds among a Victorian farmhouse (which serves as the visitors center), a multicultural arts center, farm machinery, a barn, an orchard, and gardens. There are picnic tables on an expanse of lawn with trees.

During the summer and through October, a farmers market is held here every Saturday from 8:30 A.M. to 1 P.M. The city's K-9 Corps of trained police dogs occasionally shows off for children in the park, too. If you think your own dog won't be intimidated by dogs in uniform, call the park to find out when they'll be there.

The entrance is on South King Road, near the intersection of U.S. 101 and Interstate 680/280. (408) 277-4567.

• **Guadalupe Oak Grove Park** 🐾🐾🐾½ *See* ㉔ *on page 218.*

This park is a pleasant exception to most of the others in San Jose—it's undeveloped, beautiful, and doesn't allow bicycles—and sure enough, it may not be open to dogs forever. For years we've been hearing it may "soon" be declared an oak woodlands preserve. It hasn't been, so go and enjoy it.

Dirt trails wind through hills, alternately semi-open and covered with thick groves of oaks. Birds are plentiful and noisy. Be aware of high fire danger in the dry season, and don't even think of letting your dog off leash. The park's ranger loves dogs, but she'll ticket you, and she's heard all the excuses—from "He just slipped out of his collar for a moment . . ." to "I couldn't get my dog through the gate with his leash on . . ."

Guadalupe Oak Grove Park is at Golden Oak Way and Vargas Drive. (408) 277-4661.

• **Joseph D. Grant County Park** 🐾🐾🐾 *See* ㉕ *on page 218.*

Here's another huge, gorgeous, wild park that your dog can barely set foot in. Dogs are limited to the campgrounds, picnic areas, Edwards Field Hill, and the Edwards Trail. But if you don't mind a long, winding drive for one short—albeit satisfying—trail hike, by all means try this park. Stop in at the homey old ranch house that's now the visitors center for directions to the Edwards Trail, which isn't easy to find.

Or try these directions: On Mount Hamilton Road midway between the intersection with Quimby Road and the park border is a white barn on your right as you're heading out of the park. Just past the white barn is an unmarked pedestrian gate on the left, which is the trailhead. This trail is a fine walk through a deciduous forest.

There's a $4 parking fee. The park has 22 campsites, available first come, first served. Sites are $10 and dogs are $1 extra. The campground is open daily from April 1 to October 31 and open weekends in November and in March; it's closed from December to February.

To get to the park from Interstate 680, exit at the Capitol Expressway and drive south to Quimby Road. Turn left (east) on Quimby and wind tortuously to the park entrance. It's a long six miles and the road is often a one-lane cliffhanger. Alternatively, you can get to the park from Interstate 680 via Highway 130 (Mount Hamilton Road). It's similar, but at least it's a two-laner. (408) 274-6121.

• **Los Alamitos-Calero Creek Park Chain** 🐾🐾🐾
See ㉖ on page 218.

Six miles of multiuse trail, both dirt and paved, run along Los Alamitos Creek and Arroyo Calero from the southern end of Almaden Lake Park (which doesn't allow dogs) south to the western entrance of Santa Teresa County Park. San Jose dogs love these trails for their easy creek access and plenty of shade.

Two small adjacent city parks, Graystone Park and Carrabelle Park, have picnic tables and drinking fountains for a break, if you and your dog are making a trek of it. Keep your dog leashed and watch for bicycles and horses sharing the trail with you. You can park on a neighborhood street, but not along Camden Avenue.

From Camden Avenue at Villagewood Way or Queenswood Way, you can pick up a new segment of the Bay Area Ridge Trail that runs all the way to Santa Teresa County Park's western entrance, about 1.3 miles. Where the trail forks, take the westernmost fork—the trail paralleling Camden Avenue—westward across Harry Road and continuing to the county park.

The creek park chain runs parallel to the southern end of the Almaden Expressway. The trails run along the north side of Camden Avenue and along the east side of Queenswood Way. (408) 277-4573.

• **Penitencia Creek County Park** 🐾🐾🐾 *See ㉗ on page 218.*

This county park is largely a four-mile paved streamside trail designed for hikers, bicyclists, and roller skaters. Leashed dogs are welcome, and it usually isn't dangerously crowded. From the western end, at North King Road, you can connect with the Coyote Creek Multiple-Use Trail (see page 237). The Penitencia Creek Trail is paved from end to end, but not designed to go under roads like the better bicycle trails in Walnut Creek, for example. You will have to scramble your way across highways or around fenced portions. Or you'll be confronted with a locked gate protecting water district equipment.

At the Jackson Avenue end, large walnut trees line the creek and shelter some picnic tables. Rest rooms are scattered along the route.

There are parking lots on Penitencia Creek Road and on Jackson Avenue. This is the best portion of the trail for a dog, thanks to a dry lake bed. (408) 358-3741.

- **Shadowbluff Dog Run** 🐾 🐾 🐾 🐾 🐕
See Coyote-Hellyer County Park, page 237.

- **William Street Park** 🐾 🐾 🐾 See **28** on page 218.

This park is a boy dog's dream come true. It's only about 12 acres, but it has 200 trees and 400 shrubs. On a recent visit, I think Joe sniffed out every one of them.

The trees make it a really pleasant, attractive place to visit, even in the armpits of summer. Head for the shade and let your happy, leashed pooch loll and roll in the green grass.

The park is at 16th Street and East William Street. (408) 277-4573.

RESTAURANTS

Bill's Cafe: You and your favorite dog can munch on simple cafe cuisine at this bistro with umbrella-topped tables. 1115 Willow Street; (408) 294-1125.

Grill Master: Frisky Dog and her human, Linda Bagnall, wrote us to rave about this super dog-friendly restaurant. "They treated Frisky like a Queen," they wrote. Well, after checking out the place for ourselves, Joe has news for Frisky. They don't treat all dogs like queens: They treat male dogs like kings. Grill Master not only has delicious kabobs and other grilled (and non-grilled) treats, it has some of the coolest managers and servers around, as far as dogs are concerned. When we visited, doggy Joe got a couple of dog biscuits and a bowl of water before I'd even decided which delectable dish to choose for lunch. Now that's doggone great service. Dine with your dog at the attractive patio tables. They're surrounded by trees, which makes it really inviting in the warmer months. 1408 South DeAnza Boulevard; (408) 725-0334.

PLACES TO STAY

Doubletree Hotel: Rates are $89 to $235. A $50 dog deposit is required. 2050 Gateway Place, San Jose, CA 95110; (408) 453-4000.

Homewood Suites: The suites here are comfy and much more like home than traditional hotels. Rates are $199. 10 West Trimble Road, San Jose, CA 95131; (408) 428-9900.

Joseph D. Grant County Park: See Joseph D. Grant County Park on page 239 for camping information.

Summerfield Suites Hotel: They only have suites here, which makes for a comfy stay. All suites are equipped with a kitchen. It's convenient for people traveling with pooches. Rates are $199 to $229. Dogs have to pay a $75 fee per visit, and they're $10 extra per day. 1602 Crane Court, San Jose, CA 95112; (408) 436-1600.

DOGGY DAYS

Bark in the Park: That's the name of a fun, incredibly popular dog day that takes place at a beautiful park (see William Street Park, page 241) every July. Bark in the park is also what your dog may do because he's so happy to be here. He'll be able to sniff out scads of doggy activities, like musical dog chairs, obstacle courses, and pooch "beauty" contests. There are vendors galore, selling all the things dogs love (including the *California Dog Lover's Companion,* plug, plug), and there's even a misting tent, complete with little wading pools, for dogs who need to cool their paws. The event is sponsored by the Beautification Committee of the Campus Community Association, a nonprofit neighborhood organization. For info about this year's event, call (408) 793-5125.

SANTA CLARA

PARKS, BEACHES, AND RECREATION AREAS

•**Central Park** 🐾 🐾 *See ㉙ on page 218.*

This Santa Clara city park, like most of the others, has a sign that reveals a certain slant: "No Dogs Allowed Except on Leash." If you can get past that, the park is big and has a wide assortment of trees. The creek here is large and deep, but dry in summer. A beautiful round picnic pavilion has tables fully shaded by wisteria vines, the most we've ever seen in one place.

The park is on Kiely Boulevard between Homestead Road and Benton Street. (408) 984-3223.

•**Santa Clara Dog Park** 🐾 🐾 🐾 ½ 🐕 *See ㉚ on page 218.*

It's not much, but this 200-by-200-foot fenced dog run is the only leash-free option in Santa Clara. Located on the grounds of what used to be Curtis Intermediate School, it's a flat stretch of grass bordered by stands of shady trees. Inside, you'll find water, pooper-scoopers, and benches to sit on. The park has been popular with dog owners since it opened in the fall of 1993, with up to 20 dogs using it at a time in the evenings. That's what you get for being the only game in town.

It's at the corner of Pomeroy Avenue and Lochinvar Street, near Lawrence Expressway and Homestead Road. (408) 984-3223.

PLACES TO STAY

Guest House Inn & Suites: Rates are $79 to $129. Dogs are $5 extra. 2930 El Camino Real, Santa Clara, CA 95051; (408) 241-3010.

The Vagabond Inn: Rates are $89 to $99. Dogs are $5 extra. 3580 El Camino Real, Santa Clara, CA 95051; (408) 241-0771.

DIVERSIONS

Go on a pilgrimage: Mission Santa Clara, on the Santa Clara University campus, allows leashed dogs on its grounds. You might make it part of your walk if you're exploring the campus. The building, dating from 1929, is a replica of one version of the old mission, which was first built in 1777 but was destroyed five times by earthquake, flood, and fire. Preserved fragments of the original mission and the old adobe Faculty Club are the oldest college buildings standing in the western United States. The mission is on campus, off El Camino Real. (408) 554-4023.

SARATOGA

RESTAURANTS

Bella Saratoga: The slogan of this Italian date spot is "It's Romantic," and it is, even at the front sidewalk tables next to a short stone wall right on the street. Dogs have to be tied up on the other side of the wall, but they're close enough for your handouts. If it's crowded, dogs aren't allowed, so be sure to visit during "off" times. Sit at one of the three tables by the wall. 14503 Big Basin Way; (408) 741-5115.

International Coffee Exchange: This very dog-friendly cafe serves the best mochas around. They're made with Ghirardelli chocolate and fresh, house-made whipped cream. The cafe also serves pastries and sandwiches, should you want a little nosh with your dog. The cafe's owners recently bought several large bowls for dog food (so you can share your lunch with your pal) and water. The smaller bowls they had before were pilfered one by one. Joe is very ashamed of the humans who did this, and says he's glad he's a dog. Drink and dine with doggy at the outdoor area's six umbrella-topped tables. 14471 Big Basin Way; (408) 741-1185.

Vienna Woods Restaurant and Deli: If you have an appetite for

Austrian food, bring your dog here. You can get bratwurst, potato pancakes, and even apple strudel. The restaurant also serves sandwiches, quiches, lasagna, and other non-Austrian items. Dine with your pooch at the sheltered outdoor tables. 14567 Big Basin Way; (408) 867-2410.

SUNNYVALE

PARKS, BEACHES, AND RECREATION AREAS

• **Las Palmas Park** 🐾🐾🐾🐾 🐕 *See* ⓷ *on page 218.*

With its paved paths, green grass, and beautiful pond, this park used to be the best in town for a walk among rolling hills. Now it's really terrific, because of its recently opened dog run. The two-acre run has everything a dog could possibly desire—shade, water, pooper-scoopers, and even a fire hydrant. It's a kind of fenced-in nirvana. Dogs get deliriously happy when they visit. Some spend so much time rolling in the cool grass that they miss out on hanging with their fellow canines. But do they care? A look at their smiling snouts and flaring nostrils will answer that question.

A quick note about that fire hydrant. Enough dogs have run headlong into it that there was some thought about removing it. So far, it's still here. Doggies, keep your eyes open!

The park is at Danforth and Russet Drives. (408) 730-7350.

PLACES TO STAY

Summerfield Suites: There's supposed to be a 25-pound pooch limit, but so many of the employees here have and/or love dogs that this rule is often bent. The suites are large and very livable, with kitchens and most of the amenities of home. Rates are $94 to $199. There's a $75 pooch fee per visit (they're used to longish-term visitors), and dogs are $10 extra daily. 900 Hamlin Court, Sunnyvale, CA 94089, (408) 745-1515 or (800) 833-4353.

The Vagabond Inn: Rates are $65 to $75. Dogs are $5 extra. 816 Ahwanee Avenue, Sunnyvale, CA 94086; (408) 734-4607.

SOLANO COUNTY

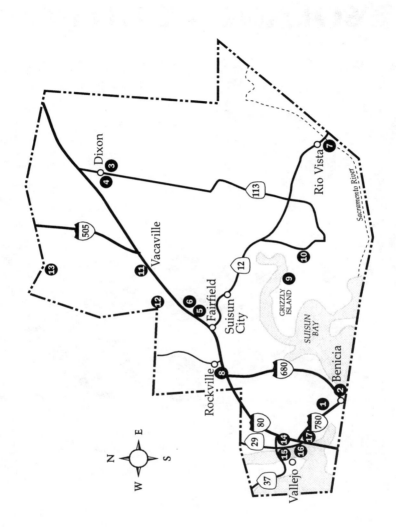

8
SOLANO COUNTY

Solano County is slowly going to the dogs. The Grizzly Island Wildlife Area (see page 253), in the thick of the Suisun Marsh, makes it absolutely worth the trip to Solano County. As long as you visit when dogs can be off leash, your pooch will think she's in heaven. Mud heaven. Bring a towel.

The best doggone news in Solano County is that there's now a dog park in Benicia (see below). It's one of the friendliest pooch parks we've seen. Brava, Benicia!

Two parks in Dixon allow off-leash dogs, but if your dog isn't at perfect heel when you're at either one, leash him fast, or you could find yourself paying a fine old fine.

BENICIA

Until 1997, dogs who lived in Benicia weren't exactly panting with joy. That's because the city's attractive parks, including one that looks like it's something out of Disneyland's Main Street USA, banned dogs. Dogs were pretty much relegated to sidewalks or the Point Benicia fishing pier area (see page 248). But that's all changed now, thanks to the Phenix Dog Park, described below.

PARKS, BEACHES, AND RECREATION AREAS

• **Phenix Dog Park** 🐾🐾🐾🐾 🐕 *See* ❶ *on page 246.*

Dogs here are rejoicing. They finally have a safe, attractive, easy-access park to call their own. Phenix Dog Park, named after a brave retired police dog, has everything a dog could want. It's got a little more than an acre of leash-free running room, and it's fenced, with water, picnic tables (which little dogs love to dodge under during chase games), pooper-scoopers, and small trees that will be big one day. At press time, the ground was dirt, but by the summer of 1998, irrigation should be in and turf should be down. It'll be real purty then.

The folks here are also hoping to install an obstacle course soon. It will be good for training, but also fun for dogs who are chasing each other to use as part of their play,

And here's a first—this pooch park comes with its own barbe-cue grills! And you can use them! Of course, you have to be pre-pared to fend off burger-minded dogs, but if you don't mind, the park people don't mind either. I love this happy, relaxed attitude. Some dog parks I've visited won't even let you bring in a graham cracker for fear you'll be mauled. Those are generally the same parks that ban children. The attitude at Phenix toward children: "You have to allow kids. Kids need to have these friendly interac-tions with dogs," says Gretchen Burgess, who was behind the park's founding. I like this woman's attitude. If you want to help with park fund-raisers or help the park in other ways, you can reach Gretchen and the Benicia Canine Coalition at (707) 746-8405 or (707) 745-4600. The second number is the veterinary clinic where she works.

The park is located in the northwest corner of the 50-acre Benicia Community Park. Enter the parking lot at Rose and Kearny Drives and drive to the far west end. Then just follow the wide asphalt path with the painted paw prints (I love it!) to the dog park. Keep in mind that the rest of the park prohibits dogs, so don't let your dog talk you into visiting anywhere but the pooch park. If you enter the park at another location, the paw prints will still lead to Phenix. (707) 746-4285.

• **Point Benicia Fishing Pier Area** 🐾🐾 *See* ❷ *on page 246.*
Park and fish at this big drive-on pier at the end of First Street that juts into the Carquinez Strait. It's a popular spot among local anglers. If you're not up for fishing, bring a lunch from a nearby restaurant and park yourself on one of the benches near the old train station. You'll be amazed at the numbers of gulls vying for your crusts.

Dogs enjoy the smells of the strait. While the pier itself isn't conducive to dog exercise, there's an area of undeveloped land nearby where they can cut loose as much as their leashes will al-low. There's been some talk of making this area more grassy. I hope this doesn't affect dog access.

This area also happens to be along the Waterfront Trail that winds through the city. The trail is a fun walk for you and your leashed dog, but make sure that when the trail passes through city parks, you and your dog take a detour.

The pier is at the southern end of First Street, just past A Street. (707) 746-4285.

RESTAURANTS

Java Point: You and the dog of your choice are sure to enjoy the soups, sandwiches, bagels, and jammin' good java served here. Dine at the umbrella-topped patio. 366 First Street; (707) 745-1449.

Pacifica Pizza: Choose from a large selection of pizzas to eat at tables shaded by umbrellas. 915 First Street; (707) 746-1790.

PLACES TO STAY

Best Western Heritage Inn: Rates are $65 to $75. Dogs require a $25 deposit. 1955 East Second Street, Benicia, CA 94510; (707) 746-0401.

BETHEL ISLAND

PLACES TO STAY

Sugar Barge RV Park & Marina: Got an RV? Got a dog? Got a boat? Then drive on over to the Sugar Barge and plug 'er in for a few days. Bethel Island, in the heart of the Sacramento–San Joaquin River Delta, is a fine place to visit if you want to sample the delta life with dog. The Sugar Barge has everything from a full-service marina to horseshoe pits. If you send away for a brochure, don't let yourself get too depressed about the photos of the near-empty store with the fluorescent lights or the completely empty, gray dining area with the fluorescent lights. Remember, it's an RV park, not the Ritz.

Rates are $23 to $28. 1440 Sugar Barge Road, Bethel Island, CA 94511; (800) 799-4100.

DIXON

Although it's no more stringent than most, the pooper-scooper law in Dixon has such a formidable name we had to pass it on. It's called the "Canine Defecation Ordinance." Yowza! It doesn't sound like anything *we* want to break.

Here's the good news: If your dog is super obedient and stays really close to you (actually, he'd need to stay at your heel), he can be off leash in the parks here!

PARKS, BEACHES, AND RECREATION AREAS

• **Hall Memorial Park** 🐾 🐾 🐕 *See ❸ on page 246.*

If you have to conduct business with city government and you want your dog to conduct business, too, you couldn't have asked for a better location for a park. It's right behind City Hall.

There's not much in the way of shade here, but on cooler days this park proves a decent stroll for dogs, provided they're leashed or at very firm heel. The park also has a playground, a swimming pool, tennis courts, and picnic areas with barbecues, so it's even better for people.

The park is at Hall Park Drive and East Mayes Street. (707) 678-7000.

• **Northwest Park** 🐾🐾 🐕 *See ❹ on page 246.*

If your dog will stay very close at heel without a leash, she may go leashless at this grassy, 20-acre park. Otherwise, use your leash. With these fairly stringent rules, she probably wouldn't notice her freedom anyway.

The park is on West H and North Lincoln Streets. (707) 678-7000.

PLACES TO STAY

Best Western Inn: This is a convenient place to stay if you have to attend a packed University of California event and no rooms are available in Davis. It's just eight miles away, and a swift drive. They prefer to have small dogs here, but don't demand it. Rates are $60 to $75. Dogs pay a onetime fee of $10. 1345 Commercial Way, Dixon, CA 95620; (707) 678-1400 or (800) 528-1234.

FAIRFIELD

PARKS, BEACHES, AND RECREATION AREAS

• **Dover Park** 🐾🐾 *See ❺ on page 246.*

The atmosphere here is right for relaxing. It's a fairly small park, but it has two ponds with lots of ducks, and big, shady willows, oaks, and firs. It's the place to go if you want to take a stroll with your leashed dog, then sit against a willow tree to read your favorite book.

On the other hand, if your dog doesn't feel like relaxing, this park can be a little too stimulating. Chaseable ducks abound, and the picnic areas are so popular that the smells just beckon dogs. We saw one unleashed mixed-breed fellow swipe a toddler's bag lunch and run away to eat it in peace. He came to the right place.

The park is located at Travis Boulevard and Flamingo Drive. (707) 428-7428.

• **Laurel Creek Park** 🐾🐾 *See ❻ on page 246.*

Remember the kind of park you used to play in as a kid—the

big neighborhood park with a great playground where the ice-cream truck visited several times a day? This is it, only it's better, because there's some room for leashed dogs to roam.

The entire west side of this 40-acre park is open fields and un-developed land. It's the right environment for running around with a dog but the wrong place for keeping cool on hot days since there's no shade.

The park is on Cement Hill Road at Peppertree Drive. (707) 428-7428.

RIO VISTA

Humphrey the humpback whale visited this Delta town, and so should your dog. For now, this is a real, dusty Old West town—not one of those cute villages loaded with boutiques and "shoppes." It's refreshing to find a town with more bait shops than banks. However, in the name of "progress," Rio Vista is soon slated to become home to some major housing developments and all the shopping centers and other unsightly amenities that go with them. Get here now, and take some photos on the old streets with your smiling dog. In a few years, they could be collector's items.

Rio Vista isn't bursting with dog amenities. In fact, it's really appropriate to visit with your dog only if you're on a fishing holiday. Then you and your pooch can slip your boat into the water and take off on the Delta for a few hours. Come back with your catch and eat dinner at the county park as the sun goes down on another Delta day.

PARKS, BEACHES, AND RECREATION AREAS

• **Sandy Beach County Park** 🐾 🐾 1/2 *See* ❼ *on page 246.*

Take your dog to the very back of the park, and he can run around off leash and even do the dog paddle in the Sacramento River! It's not a huge area, but it's all you'll need to show your dog a good time. The closer day-use section is completely off-limits to dogs, so be sure you end up in the right area.

Your dog has another chance of getting wet if he follows you into the showers at the campground. Dogs are allowed at the campground. It's not terribly scenic and can get mighty dry at times, but hey, it's a place to stay on the river. There are 42 sites. Fees are $8 to $15 a night. Dogs are $1 extra. Half the sites are first come, first served. Reservations are recommended during summer.

Take Highway 12 all the way to Rio Vista; follow Main Street to Second Street, and go right. When the street bears left and becomes Beach Drive, the park is within a quarter mile. Bring proof of a rabies vaccination. (707) 374-2097.

RESTAURANTS

Janey's Delta Cafe: They've got every kind of fast food you could ever want here, and several picnic tables for your feast. Try the southern fried chicken, but watch that your leashed dog doesn't dispose of the bones for you. Janey's also has a variety of snout-lickin' good baked treats. 650 Highway 12; (707) 374-2020.

PLACES TO STAY

Sandy Beach County Park: See Sandy Beach County Park on page 251 for camping information.

DIVERSIONS

Roll on the river: Hire a houseboat. There's nothing like cruising around the Delta in your very own house. Your dog can feel right at home, and nothing makes her happier than having you home all the time. Just remember that, as on land, you have to walk your dog—only you have to dock to do it. Call the Rio Vista Chamber of Commerce at (707) 374-2700 for information on houseboat rentals in the Delta.

ROCKVILLE

PARKS, BEACHES, AND RECREATION AREAS

• **Rockville Hills Park** 🐾 🐾 🐾 *See* ❽ *on page 246.*

Hike, fish, and enjoy nature in this 800-acre park filled with trees and trails. The main trail is fairly steep and takes you to the top of the park, where you'll find two small ponds for fishing. After this hike on a summer afternoon, many dogs jump in when they reach the summit. A man told me that a small beagle once disappeared for several seconds and came up with a tiny fish flailing in her mouth. Could this be just another flagrant flailing fish story?

Once you enter the park, you're safe from traffic. But dogs are supposed to be leashed anyway, since the park is officially run by the city of Fairfield, which has a strict leash law. Check out the nature trail that a local Eagle Scout troop has created.

For the most vigorous workout, try the main trail. It's the one that bends slightly to the left and up a steep hill as you enter from the parking lot. The park is often desolate, so use judgment about hiking alone.

It's on Rockville Road, just west of Suisun Valley Road. (707) 428-7428.

SUISUN CITY

PARKS, BEACHES, AND RECREATION AREAS

• **Grizzly Island Wildlife Area** 😊 😊 😊 😊 🐕
See ❾ on page 246.

This is what dogs have been praying for since they started living in cities: 8,600 acres of wide-open land where they can run—leashless—among the sort of wildlife you see only in PBS specials.

This sprawling wetland, in the heart of the Suisun Marsh, is home to an amazing array of fauna, including tule elk, river otters, waterfowl of every type, jackrabbits, white pelicans, and peregrine falcons.

Of course, walking in marshy areas has its pros and cons. But you don't have to get muddy feet here; the landscapes are as varied as the animal life. Dry upland fields are plentiful. You can also canoe down a slough with your steady dog or hike on dozens of dirt trails. Many folks bring dogs here to train them for hunting, which brings us to the unfortunate subject of the park's schedule.

Because of hunting and bird-nesting seasons, Grizzly Island Wildlife Area is open for you and your dog only between mid-January and March 1, between July and early August, and for part of September. (Call for exact dates. These are approximate and are subject to change.)

If your dog helps you hunt for elk, ducks, or pheasant, she's allowed to join you during some of the hunting seasons. Department of Fish and Game staff also occasionally open small sections to people during the off-season, but it's unpredictable from one year to another when and if they'll do it. Even when the park is open, certain sections may be off-limits to dogs. Check with staff when you come in.

To get to the Grizzly Island Wildlife Area, exit Interstate 80 at Highway 12 heading toward Rio Vista. Turn onto Grizzly Island Road at the stoplight for the Sunset Shopping Center. Drive 10 miles, past farms, sloughs, and marshes, until you get to the head-quarters. You'll have to check in here and pay a $2.50 fee. Then continue driving to the parking lot nearest the area that you want to explore (staff can advise you). Don't forget your binoculars. (707) 425-3828.

•**Rush Ranch Open Space** 🐾🐾🐾½ *See* **⑩** *on page 246.*

From freshwater and saltwater marshes to rolling grass-covered hills and meadowlike pastures, this 2,070-acre open-space parcel is home to some wonderfully diverse landscapes.

Dogs are permitted on two of the three trails here. They're not allowed to peruse the Marsh Trail because of the fragile nature of the marsh. But the Suisun Hill Trail is a real hit among canines. That trail takes you into hills with killer views of the Suisun Marsh and the hills and mountains to the north. Rangers tell us that on a clear day, you can see the Sierra Nevada. Dogs are also allowed to amble along the South Pasture Trail, which is longer than the other trails and takes you farther from civilization.

Dogs are supposed to be leashed, partly because some of the land is still a working ranch. You don't want your dog tangling with a cow; they don't always make beautiful "moosic" together.

This is a special place. If you'd like to help support the educational and interpretive activities of the Rush Ranch Educational Council, call (707) 421-1351. From Highway 12, exit at Grizzly Island Road and drive south for a couple of miles.

RESTAURANTS

Valley Cafe: Your dog will have a hard time forgiving you if you're on your way to Lake Berryessa and you don't stop at this cute eatery. That's because the owner loves dogs and makes 'em feel right at home. On the porch is a jar of pooch treats that calls dogs from far and wide. If you cock your head just right, you can almost hear it in the breeze. "Oh doggggggyyyyy! Come eat us!!!! We're really nummmmmyyyyyy!!" Joe heard the cookie jar calling one fine summer afternoon, and he practically jumped into the driver's seat to steer the car into the parking area. Fortunately his foot doesn't reach the clutch.

By the way, humans enjoy the food here. It's tasty, with home-made soup and chili topping our list of favorites. Dine with your dog at the seven umbrella-covered tables outside. 4171 Suisun Valley Road; (707) 864-2507.

VACAVILLE

PARKS, BEACHES, AND RECREATION AREAS

• **Andrews Park** 🐾 🐾 *See ⓫ on page 246.*

If you need a shopping cart, try this park first. For some reason, the creek that cuts through the west end of the park contains more shopping carts than most supermarkets.

The chunk of park to the east of the creek is graced with gentle rolling hills, picnic areas, barbecues, deciduous trees, and a lawn as green and smooth as a golf course. But dogs must be leashed.

The west side of the creek is just a shady trail that officially stops at the first overpass and can get pretty seedy if you continue.

The best parking for the east side is on School Street, near Davis Street. For the west side of the creek, park in a lot at Kendal Street, off Dobbins Street. (707) 449-6276.

• **Lagoon Valley Regional Park** 🐾½ *See ⓬ on page 246.*

The hills you see in the background of this sprawling county park are off-limits to your dog. So are the two reservoirs. In fact, most of the park bans dogs. And you have to bring your dog's license and rabies certificate. All this fun stuff for only $3!

Dogs are allowed to walk by the reservoirs on leash, but that's legally as close as they can go. The section of park that you first enter is the only place dogs are allowed. There are a couple of open grassy areas and a trail that runs along one reservoir. We've seen people fishing with their dogs, which is the most fun you'll have together at this park. But there may be hope for dogs here in the future—the county is considering creating an off-leash area somewhere in the park! This would be a real boon for doggies.

Exit Interstate 80 at Cherry Glen Road and follow the signs to the park. The park is currently closed on Tuesday and Wednesday, but this may change, so call first. (707) 449-6276.

• **Lake Solano County Park** 🐾 🐾 *See ⓭ on page 246.*

It's no picnic here for dog owners. In fact, dogs aren't allowed in the picnic/day-use area at all. The only way to visit this isolated county park with a dog is to use the camping area across the street. It costs $12 per vehicle on weekdays and $15 on weekends during peak season, $10 all week during off-peak season, and $1 per dog—fares higher than the day-use section.

But for dogs who love to swim, it's worth the price of admission. The big freshwater lake is an ideal respite on a hot summer day. Dogs are allowed off leash for swimming—and only for swimming. There are a couple of narrow trails along the shore, but they're very short.

The camping here is typical "pack 'em in" camping. The 90 sites are so close together you can hear your neighbors unzip their sleeping bags. But if you scout it out, you may be able to nab a site that has a little more privacy. There are even a few sites on the lake. Fees range from $8 to $15 a night.

Don't forget to bring proof of a rabies vaccination for your dog. This can be his certificate or just his up-to-date tag. The park is at Highway 128 and Pleasant Valley Road, about five miles west of Interstate 505. For park info or to make camping reservations, call (916) 795-2990 or (707) 421-7925.

PLACES TO STAY

Best Western Heritage Inn: Small to medium dogs are allowed here. Don't try to pass your Saint Bernard off as a lapdog, even if he is your lapdog. Rates are $52 to $57. Pooches require a $10 to $20 deposit. 1420 East Monte Vista Avenue, Vacaville, CA 95688; (707) 448-8453.

Gandydancer RV Park: The office here is made up of old cabooses. It's situated among groves of eucalyptus trees. Sites are $18. Dogs must be leashed. Take Interstate 80 to the Midway exit. 4933 Midway Road, Vacaville, CA 95688; (707) 446-7679.

Lake Solano County Park: See Lake Solano County Park on page 255 for camping information.

Motel 6: If you want to shop at the famous outlet mall in Vacaville and you're traveling with someone who will watch your pooch, this is a convenient place to stay—it's about 1,000 feet from the mall. Shop 'til you drop, then drag yourself back to your dog-friendly Motel 6. One smallish dog per room, please. Rates are $32 for the first adult, $6 for the second. 107 Lawrence Drive, Vacaville, CA 95687; (707) 447-5550.

VALLEJO

PARKS, BEACHES, AND RECREATION AREAS

Only one of Vallejo's city parks, Blue Rock Springs, bans dogs. Here's the best of the rest.

• **Dan Foley Park** 🐾🐾🐾 *See **14** on page 246.*

You won't often see this at Marine World-Africa USA—professional water-skiers practicing their acts over sloping jumps, then landing headfirst in the water when everything doesn't work out perfectly.

But you and your dog will be treated to this unpolished spectacle if you visit this park on the right day. The park is directly across Lake Chabot from Marine World, so you get to witness a good chunk of the goings-on there. Since dogs aren't allowed at Marine World, this is an ideal place to walk them if your kids are spending a few hours with more exotic animals. You still get to hear the sound of jazz bands and the roar of amazed crowds.

Dan Foley Park is so well maintained we initially were afraid it was a golf course. Willows and pines on rolling hills provide cooling shade, and there's usually a breeze from the lake. Leashed dogs are invited everywhere but the water. Even humans aren't supposed to swim in it. Picnic tables are located right across from the water-ski practice area, so if your dog wants entertainment with his sandwich, this is the place.

The park is on Camino Alto North just east of Tuolumne Street. There is a $2 parking fee. (707) 648-4600.

• **River Park** 🐾🐾🐾 *See **15** on page 246.*

With goldenrod as high as an elephant's eye and a preponderance of low brush, this waterfront park looks like a huge abandoned lot. That's actually one of its charms—you don't have to worry about your dog mowing over children in a playground or digging up a plug of green grass. The only parklike features here are a couple of benches along the Mare Island Strait.

A wide dirt path leads you toward the water and far from traffic danger. Unfortunately, the leash law is in effect here, and unless your dog is inclined to wade through several yards of mucky marsh to get to the water, he's not going to go swimming. It's still fun to walk along the water and look at the now-defunct Mare Island Naval Shipyard.

There are two entry points. If you're driving, use the south entrance on Wilson Avenue, just north of Hichborn Street, which has a small parking lot. Otherwise, you can enter at Wilson Avenue just across the street from Sims Avenue. (707) 648-4600.

• **The Wharf** 🐾🐾🐾 *See* **⓰** *on page 246.*

This is the place for hip Vallejo dogs, and it's not even an official park. The paved path along the Mare Island Strait looks toward the old Mare Island Naval Shipyard on the other side of the strait, providing a real nautical atmosphere.

It's also the perfect place to take your dog while you're waiting for your ship to come in, since this is where the Vallejo–San Francisco ferry stops.

There's a substantial strip of grass beside the path where dogs like to take frequent breaks. Here, they can socialize without getting under joggers' sneakers. Leashes are a must.

The wharf area covers almost the entire length of Mare Island Way, starting around the Vallejo Yacht Club. Your best bet is to park at the public parking area of the ferry terminal. (707) 648-4600.

• **Wilson/Lake Dalwigk Park** 🐾🐾½ *See* **⓱** *on page 246.*

What you've got here is a big neighborhood park that's mostly undeveloped, leaving lots of land for trotting around. A concrete walkway takes you by fields, big palm trees, and Lake Dalwigk, a small, fairly dirty body of water that can smell slightly of Porta Potti.

Cross over the lake on a small footbridge and your dog will be in a grassy section surrounded by bushes that shelter her from traffic, in case she happens to slip the leash. Be careful, though— it's so secluded that you may not want to go there alone.

The park is at Fifth and Lemon Streets. (707) 648-4600.

RESTAURANTS

Gumbah's Beef Sandwiches: Here's the beef. If your dog is your lunch partner, Gumbah's (pronounced *Goombah's*) meaty place is where he'll ask to go. Dine at the tables out front. 138 Tennessee Street; (707) 648-1100.

Sardine Can: Get a view of the strait while you eat some of the freshest seafood available. Dogs get great treatment here, including a big bowl of water. Dine at the two outdoor tables. It's at 0 (as in zero) Harbor Way; (707) 553-9492.

PLACES TO STAY

Holiday Inn–Marine World-Africa USA: While the kids are being entertained by dolphins and big cats at the nearby theme park, you and your small dog (the only pooches allowed) can curl up, read a book, and enjoy the peace. Rates are $90 to $175. Dogs are charged a $25 fee per visit. 1000 Fairgrounds Drive, Vallejo, CA 94590; (707) 644-1200.

Motel 6: This one's a mere two blocks from Marine World-Africa USA. Rates are $34 for the first adult, $6 for the second. Kids stay free with parents. This Motel 6, like just about every one, permits one small pooch per room. 458 Fairgrounds Drive, Vallejo, CA 94589; (707) 642-7781.

Quality Inn: Rates are $49 to $59. Depending on your dog's size, you could be charged a fee of $10 to $50 per stay. If you'll be spending only one night and have a Great Dane, consider another lodging. 44 Admiral Callaghan Lane, Vallejo, CA 94591; (707) 643-1061.

Ramada Inn: Rates are $75 to $125. Dogs are charged a $25 fee per visit. 1000 Admiral Callaghan Lane, Vallejo, CA 94591; (707) 643-2700.

DIVERSIONS

Seize the Bay: Lucky dogs! You get to take a ride to San Francisco on the Blue & Gold Fleet ferry. But you're going to have to turn to page 181 to read more about it.

SONOMA COUNTY

Sea Ranch

LAKE SONOMA

32

Cloverdale

3

36

Timber Cove

37

128

Healdsburg

1

6

Guerneville

Windsor

7

116

101

Jenner

8

Occidental

Sebastopol

24-31

Bodega Bay

1

Santa Rosa

12

2

33

Freestone

Rohnert Park

4 5

Glen Ellen

116

23

Cotati

9-22

Sonoma

34-35

12

Petaluma

116

121

N

37

W E

S

9
SONOMA COUNTY

The horticulturist Luther Burbank, who made his home in Santa Rosa and Sebastopol from 1875 to 1926, called Sonoma County "the chosen spot of all the Earth as far as nature is concerned." Practically anything will grow in Sonoma County. It's the Bay Area capital for trees, flowers, and vegetables, as well as goats, sheep, cattle, chickens, pigs, and probably a few farm animals that are just now being invented.

Unfortunately, dogs and farm animals don't mix. Some Sonoma sheep ranchers have been known to impose the ultimate penalty on loose dogs that they see near their livestock: They shoot them. They're not acting under the law of the Wild West, either. It's a county ordinance that dogs harassing livestock in unincorporated areas or on private property may be shot by the property owner.

But fear not. Sonoma County has many enchanting places where the only shot your dog will experience is a shot of adrenaline when he lays eyes on the stunning scenery and some mesmerizing, dog-friendly hangouts. Since the last edition of this book, the number of off-leash doggy areas in Sonoma County has gone up to 20. Oh joy, oh joy! The new leashless wonders are thanks to the towns of Petaluma, Santa Rosa, and Windsor. Most of these parks have very limited off-leash hours, but dogs are thrilled anyway. It's hard to find a Sonoma County dog whose tail isn't wagging a little faster these days.

BODEGA BAY

PARKS, BEACHES, AND RECREATION AREAS

• **Doran Beach Regional Park** 🐾🐾🐾 *See* **❶** *on page 262.*

This Sonoma County regional park offers leashed dogs access to marshland full of egrets, herons, and deer, as well as to the Pinnacle Gulch Trail. The plain but serviceable beach has almost no surf (which is great for dog swims), and there are picnic tables near the beach.

The fee for day use is $3. (It may soon increase.) Campsites are $14 ($12 for Sonoma County residents), plus $1 for each dog. The campground, which has 134 sites, is on a first-come, first-served basis. The park is on Highway 1, one mile south of Bodega Bay. (707) 875-3540.

• **Westside Regional Park** 🐾 🐾 *See* ❷ *on page 262.*

This is an undistinguished but handy park and campground built on landfill right on the water, with picnic tables and barbecues. Spud Point Marina, just to the north, also allows leashed dogs.

The fee for day use is $3. (It may soon increase.) There are 47 campsites, costing $14 ($12 for Sonoma County residents), plus $1 for each dog. It's first come, first served. The park is on Westshore Road, a westward turn off Highway 1 in town. Call (707) 875-3540 for reservations or (707) 527-2041 for park info.

RESTAURANTS

The Boat House: This restaurant in downtown Bodega Bay will allow you to sit with your dog as you eat fish-and-chips, oysters, and calamari at one of the six unshaded tables on their patio. If fish isn't your dog's wish, he can order a burger. 1445 Highway 1; (707) 875-3495.

The Dog House: The name of the restaurant says it all. But if you need more, here are the words of one of the servers: "Dogs are treated better than people here." The Dog House is indeed a very dog-friendly place to dine. The food is unpretentious (hot dogs, burgers, etc.), and the servers love seeing a dog come to the eight outdoor tables. They often offer a bowl of water (and sometimes a snicky snack) before the pooch even gets a chance to peruse the menu. Joe gives it four paws for attitude. 537 Highway 1; (707) 875-2441.

Lucas Wharf: Your dog's nose will flair and drip with excitement as you dine at the outdoor tables here. That's partly because of the tasty seafood specials, but it's mostly because your dog will be getting high on sea smells at this place right on the water. Speaking of water, the folks here love dogs and will provide your pooch with water, should she need to wet her whistle. 595 Highway 1; (707) 875-3522.

PLACES TO STAY

Bodega Bay RV Park: If you have an RV and want to stay in this wonderful area, park 'er here. The managers will point you to some nearby property where you can run your good dog without a leash. Rates are $17 to $25. 2000 Highway 1, Bodega Bay, CA 94923; (707) 875-3701.

Bodega Coast Inn: Rates at this attractive former Holiday Inn are $99 to $298. Dogs are $15 extra. 521 Coast Highway/Highway 1, Bodega Bay, CA 94923; (707) 875-2217.

Doran Beach Regional Park: See Doran Beach Regional Park on page 263 for camping information.

Westside Regional Park: See Westside Regional Park on page 264 for camping information.

CLOVERDALE

PARKS, BEACHES, AND RECREATION AREAS

• **Lake Sonoma Recreation Area** 😊 😊 😊 *See ❸ on page 262.*

This is the only recreation site in the nine counties of the Bay Area run by the U.S. Army Corps of Engineers, and it's too bad. The Corps has a liberal attitude toward dogs, and this park is beautifully developed and managed, not to mention clean. It's also free. You must keep your dog on a six-foot leash, and he's not allowed on the swimming beach at the north end, but rangers told us there's no rule against dogs swimming anywhere else.

If you're the type who doesn't clean up after your dog, here's a warning: Change your act, or stay far from here. Rangers have been known to charge a cleanup fee for owners who ignore the deposits of their dogs.

A large lawn with picnic tables, some shaded, is located at the visitors center. You can rent a boat from the private concession on the lake, which allows leashed dogs on all boats. Follow signs from the visitors center. To reserve a boat, call (707) 433-2200. Waterskiing and camping are also popular here.

For a good dog hike, pick up a map at the visitors center and drive west on Dry Creek Road to the trailheads, which have their own parking lots. There are 40 miles of trails. Here are two of our favorites: There's a bit of shade at the Digger Pine Flat Trailhead. This smooth foot trail goes down to the lake through an unusual forest of digger pines, madrone, manzanita, and blooming desert brush. The buzz of motorboats on the lake blends with the hammering of woodpeckers. You get a good view of the lake fairly quickly. If you'd prefer less of a climb back to the trailhead, take the Little Flat Trail, which starts lower down.

Horses are allowed on these trails, but bikes aren't—a plus for your dog's safety. Unfortunately, it gets bone-dry here in summer, and poison oak is common.

Developed, primitive, and boat-in campsites are available. Liberty Glen Campground has 113 individual campsites. Sites are $8 to $14. To use the primitive sites (no water, but no fee either), you must get a permit from the visitors center. There are 15 secluded sites reachable only by boat. They're $4 to $8. All these sites are first come, first served. Dogs must be leashed or "restrained" in the campgrounds, which in this case means you can put them on a generous rope tether. The idea is to keep them from invading other campsites.

Take U.S. 101 to the Canyon Road exit. Go west to Dry Creek Road and turn right into the entrance. Take a right at the only fork. (707) 433-9483.

PLACES TO STAY

Lake Sonoma Recreation Area: See the Lake Sonoma Recreation Area on page 265 for camping information.

COTATI

Soon there may be a fenced dog park in this quaint town. At press time, it was under consideration by the city council. We think it's a grand idea. Call the city manager's office at (707) 792-4600 for updates.

RESTAURANTS

Johnny's Java: This coffeehouse is home to tasty baked goods. It's a convenient place to stop if you're on your way to or from Camp K-9 (see below). Dine with doggy at the four umbrella-topped tables on the patio. 8492 Gravenstein Highway; (707) 794-0168.

DIVERSIONS

Check out a canine country club: The smell of cow manure from nearby pastures is the first clue that your dog's going to dig Camp K-9. Then there are the chewed-up sneakers, the tipped-over fire hydrant, and the two chunky ducks who waddle by the dogs provocatively—on the other side of the fence.

This day camp for dogs is not exactly Club Med, and that's precisely why dogs enjoy their time here. The camp is set on two acres, with dogs spending most of the time in one of three fenced areas. Dogs can cavort around leashless, try their paws at a somewhat dilapidated agility course, or just spend the day dozing and watching fellow dogs.

Owner Randy Ashton says that while commuters are the biggest users of Camp K-9, people traveling to the nearby wine country find it a mighty pleasant and convenient place to drop off the pooch before hitting the wineries.

The camp is open from 7 A.M. to 7 P.M. Monday through Saturday. You're welcome to stay with your dog and hang out in the largest of the enclosures, or leave him for the day. It's $12 for a full day, $7 for a half day, or $3 an hour.

The address is 6915 Gravenstein Highway (Highway 116). From U.S. 101, take the Highway 116 West exit and travel west for about a mile. The camp will be on your right. (707) 795-5995.

DILLON BEACH

PLACES TO STAY

Lawson's Landing and Resort: When you camp here, you camp in a grassy meadow along the sand dunes. There are no set campsites, just the open meadow. That's great, because sometimes you can have the whole place to yourself. Other times you have to share the meadow with lots of other outdoorsy sorts of folks. Camping is $5 if you arrive before 8 P.M., $13 if you arrive after. Weekly rates are available. Please see Diversions, below, for a truly wonderful experience you and your dog can share while you're in the area. Lawson's Landing is easy to find once you're in Dillon Beach. The address is 137 Marine View Drive, P.O. Box 67, Dillon Beach, CA 94929; (707) 878-2443.

DIVERSIONS

Take a barge to a bivalve: This is one of the very coolest things a dog can do in California, especially if he digs boats and digs clams. You start at Lawson's Landing and Resort in Dillon Beach, where you can buy clamming devices like clam tubes or clam guns, if the ol' shovel and bucket method doesn't appeal to you. Then you and the pooch of your dreams board a barge for a ride out to a place they call Clam Island. During high tides the island disappears, so it's really more of a bar. The ride is great fun for dogs who like to sniff the briny breeze, but the highlight for many dogs is when you disembark on the mudflats of Clam Island. The smells send many a dog into the throes of ecstasy.

Clamming isn't as easy as it may sound. Take whatever help you can get from your dog. Some dogs bark at the small round holes that signify a clam could lurk below. Some even stomp their feet until they get a squirt of water, which definitely means a clam is in residence below. Some, like Joe, enjoy digging for clams, but that's really a no-no where the Department of Fish and Game is concerned. Regulations, regulations. That's okay with me, though, because the thought of eating clams makes me clammy all over. I just go along for the ride.

The best time to go clamming is during very low tides, especially in winter and spring. And that's convenient, because the barge runs only from February to June. You have to take your own boat over to Clam Island other times of year. Folks over 16 need a California fishing license. The fee for the Clam Ride (as it's known here) is $5 for adults, $4 for kids. Dogs go for free, but must be leashed. Lawson's Landing is easy to find once you're in Dillon Beach. The address is 137 Marine View Drive, P.O. Box 67, Dillon Beach, CA 94929; (707) 878-2443.

GLEN ELLEN

PARKS, BEACHES, AND RECREATION AREAS

•**Jack London State Historic Park** 🐾 🐾 🐾 *See* ❹ *on page 262.*
    The extensive backcountry trails here are off-limits to dogs, but the parts of historic interest are not. You're free to take your dog (leashed) the half mile to Wolf House, visiting Jack London's grave en route, and around the stone house containing the museum of Londoniana (open 10 A.M. to 5 P.M., no pets inside). The trail is paved and smooth up to the museum, but then becomes dirt and narrow.

Oaks, pines, laurels, and madrones cast dappled light, and the ups and downs are gentle. Signs warn against poison oak and rattlesnakes. The ruins of the huge stone lodge that was London's dream Wolf House are impressive and sad. A fire of unknown origin destroyed it in 1913. London planned to rebuild it, but he died three years later.

Dogs are also allowed in the picnic areas by the parking lot and the museum. From Highway 12, follow signs to the park. Turn west on Arnold Drive, then west again on London Ranch Road. The fee is $6 for day use, $1 for dogs. (707) 938-5216.

• **Sonoma Valley Regional Park** 🐾🐾🐾 *See* **5** *on page 262.*

This large, welcoming park has a paved, level trail that winds alongside a branch of Sonoma Creek. Better yet for dogs who like to roll, it sports many dirt trails that head off into the oak woodlands above. Varied grasses and wildflowers, madrones, and moss-hung oaks make this a scenic walk. Dogs like to chew some of the grasses, roll on the wildflowers (don't let them do this!), and do leg lifts on the madrones and oaks. They may enjoy it even more than you. If you start at the park entrance off Highway 12 and walk westward across the park to Glen Ellen for about a mile, you'll end up at Sonoma Creek and the old mill, with its huge working waterwheel.

There's some potentially terrific news for the future. The park is considering plans for a leash-free dog park! Private funding is needed to make this a reality. If you've got a few thousand clams burning a hole in your pocket, please give them a call.

The park is just south of Glen Ellen between Arnold Drive and Highway 12. The entrance is off Highway 12. The parking fee is $2. (707) 539-8092.

RESTAURANTS

Jack's Village Cafe: With gourmet/country dishes like local quail with chanterelles or wild mushroom risotto, a meal at Jack's is an exquisite dining experience for anyone. (Joe Dog thinks this sounds as if it were written by a chamber of commerce flunky. . . . He'd prefer to say the food here is snout lickin' good.) But dogs who get to come here feel especially lucky. Not only is the food drool-worthy, but so is the view from the restaurant's large patio. It's surrounded by fruit trees, an herb garden, and flowers, and it overlooks a creek. Joe thinks there's nothing as heavenly as coming here for breakfast on a cool autumn morning and ordering hot oatmeal or country-style French toast—making sure, of course, that you pass a little down to your friend who's giving you "the eye" from under the table.

The restaurant is at Jack London Village, at 14301 Arnold Drive, #23; (707) 939-6111.

PLACES TO STAY

The Big Dog Inn: The logo here is a giant Saint Bernard holding a glass of wine in one hand and resting his elbow on a wine barrel. It's as cute as the inn, and just as dog-friendly. The inn consists of a suite in the main house (where the owners live) and a guest cottage. Dogs are welcome in the cottage. It's an enchanting place, with a cathedral ceiling, country furnishings, a sitting room, a wood-burning stove, air-conditioning, a bath, and an efficiency kitchen.

When you arrive, you'll be greeted with a bottle of local wine, a basket of fresh fruit, and a cheese platter. Your stay also includes a tasty breakfast in the dining room. You and your leashed pooch are free to peruse the inn's six acres. The views of the surrounding Sonoma Valley are quite breathtaking in places. Humans can relax in the inn's swimming pool and spa, but dogs have to stay high and dry. (Never a problem for Joe "I Loathe Water" Dog.)

Dogs really dig it here, but not necessarily because of any of the inn's lovely accoutrements. They seem to know that the owners, Penny and Doug Mahon, are avid dog people. "We love dogs as guests. They're our favorites," says Penny. The Mahons have been breeding and showing the inn's namesakes, Saint Bernards, for more than 30 years. You'll likely find a few Big Dogs around during your visit, as well as one little dog, the resident Jack Russell terrier. He runs the place, of course.

There's one caveat to dogs being allowed here. When the Mahons have a new litter of pups, they have to be careful about pooch visitors. When you call for a brochure or to make a reservation, they'll let you know about the puppy situation. 15244 Arnold Drive, Glen Ellen, CA 95442; (707) 996-4319.

GUERNEVILLE

This wonderful resort community on the Russian River took an economic and aesthetic plunge with the recent floods, but it's recovered so well that it looks better than ever these days.

PARKS, BEACHES, AND RECREATION AREAS

• **Armstrong Redwoods State Reserve** 🐾 🐾
See ❻ on page 262.

As is usual in state parks, you can take a dog only on paved roads and into picnic areas. But here you can give your dog and yourself an exceptional treat. The picnic grounds are a cool, hushed redwood cathedral. You can walk on Armstrong Woods Road, which winds along Fife Creek (usually lush, but dry in the heart of summer) all the way to the top of McCray Mountain, about three miles.

The drive is fairly terrifying, so you may prefer to walk anyway. Hikers, bicycles, and autos all share the road, so be very careful. Your dog must be leashed everywhere in the park. From Guerneville, go about 2.5 miles north on Armstrong Woods Road. The day-use fee is $5. Dogs are $1. (707) 869-2015 or (707) 865-2391.

• **Vacation Beach** 😺 😺 😺 😺 🐾 *See ❼ on page 262.*
Vacation Beach is not really a beach, but an access point where the Russian River is dammed by two roads across it. It's one of several public spots where you and your dog can legally jump into the drink. Here, people picnic, swim, put in canoes, and let their dogs cool their paws. It's free and there are no posted leash rules, but watch out for cars going over the dam roads. No overnight camping is allowed.

From Highway 116 between Guerneville and Monte Rio, turn south at the unmarked road where you see Old Cazadero Road veering north. You can park at the approaches to the dams but not on the crossing itself. (707) 869-9000.

RESTAURANTS

Sweet's River Grill: You have to tie your dog to the other side of the gate bordering the patio, but it's not a problem. Your pooch can still sit right beside you and beg just as effectively. Dine on grilled seafood, steak, chops, you name it. 16251 Main Street; (707) 869-3383.

PLACES TO STAY

Creekside Inn & Resort: Dogs get to stay at two of several cottages and rooms at this fun inn near the Russian River. Bird dogs enjoy lounging in the Quail Cottage, a small, bright cottage with a fireplace. The Deck House, the other poochy haven, is a little larger, with a sunny deck.

The inn is dotted with several large redwoods. The property spans three acres, and dogs are welcome to cruise around on leash. Human guests may hang out in the inn's main dining room and lounge, both of which have fireplaces. Humans can also swim in the pool here. Dogs have to be content to do the dog paddle in the Russian River, not too far away.

Rates are $70 to $80. 16180 Neeley Road, P.O. Box 2185, Guerneville, CA 95446; (707) 869-3623 or (800) 776-6586.

Highlands Resort: If your dog has never been to a bar, ask to stay in the Highland's studio: The large room not only has a cozy fireplace and love seat, but it has its own wet bar. Joe says, "Make mine a mimosa." Teetotaling dogs might prefer the five larger cabins that allow dogs. The cabins have fireplaces, and some have kitchenettes, but no bar.

The Highlands is set on three wooded acres (which dogs can explore on leash), and has the feel of a country retreat. There's a swimming pool and outdoor hot tub—both clothing-optional. In the resort's brochure there's a bird's-eye-view picture of a fellow standing in the hot tub, with just a bit of bun showing. Joe blushed and came back for another look. The owner asked us to mention that people with diverse lifestyles feel right at home here.

Rates are $75 to $125. Dogs are $25 extra for the length of their stay. 14000 Woodland Drive, Guerneville, CA 95446; (707) 869-0333.

River's Retreat: Dogs are so happy when they stay at this little vacation rental just a block from the Russian River that they may refuse to leave. Marcia, the owner of the home, has three dogs, and she's set it up so you and yours feel right at home.

Your pooch gets dog treats when he comes here. And that's just the beginning. This two-bedroom house has a large yard, which is completely fenced. Dogs love to roam around, sniffing all the nooks and crannies. There's some shade back there, and good grass for rolling on. Better yet, there's a little fountain, which humans enjoy sitting around during the summer, and dogs love splashing in year-round.

The house is cozy and peaceful, with a small front porch, a wood stove, a full kitchen (dog-proof, says Marcia), two bedrooms, a living room (with two Labrador retriever pictures), an antique-furnished dining room (with dogsled art), and a large deck with a hot tub and barbecue/picnic area.

During your stay here, you might even get a visit from Hattie, a very friendly dog who lives across the street. Joe thinks she's foxy.

Rates are $150. If you stay for a week, the rate is $800—a significant discount. For privacy and safety sake, the address is given only to those renting the house. For more information or to rent the house, call Marcia at (510) 625-2844. (She lives in the East Bay, thus the different area code.)

Russian River Getaways: If you and your dog want a home away from home while you vacation in the Russian River area, you've hit the jackpot. Russian River Getaways has about 20 beautiful dog-friendly homes for rent on a nightly or weekly basis. The homes are generally quite upscale, but the prices are fairly down to earth.

What we like most about Russian River Getaways is its owner, Camille LeGrand. She loves dogs. Her dogs, Nicholas and Hugo, often come to work with her. "We don't care how beautiful the rental home, we think dogs should be allowed at all of them," she says. (They're not, but that's not Camille's fault.) When you get to her office to pick up the keys for your home, she'll point you in the direction of a couple of hush-hush off-leash spots, and will give your dog a treat or two. Now that's what we call one doggone good person.

Rates for the homes range from $115 to $290 nightly (the $290 home has five bedrooms, a fireplace, a lovely fenced yard with fruit trees, a 10-person hot tub on the deck, and canoes and kayaks for the river, which is one block away). Weekly rates are $650 to $1,740. Russian River Getaways has a very good Web site where you can check out the selection of homes before you decide which you like best; the address is Getaways@wclyx.com. For a brochure describing the homes, write Russian River Getaways at 16201 First Street, P.O. Box 1673, Guerneville, CA 95446, or phone (707) 869-4560 or (800) 433-6673.

Russian River Vacation Homes: Spend your Russian River–area vacation in your own charming private house. This is an ideal way to vacation with your pooch. Russian River Vacation Homes offers more than a dozen beautiful, quaint houses for pets and their people. From a one-bedroom rustic log cabin on the river to a three-bedroom riverside home complete with hot tub, you and your holiday hound will find the home of your dreams.

Joe's favorite is Larissa's House, a sweet one-bedroom home with a flowery, fenced-in yard on the river. Larissa, the owner, lives next door, and adores dogs. In fact, you pretty much have to have a dog to stay here. It's so doggone dog-friendly that the shower is designed so that you and your dog can shower at the same time. Joe is shy, so he doesn't care for this arrangement. If Larissa has time, she'll make sure your pooch has a welcoming bag of treats when she arrives. Dogs fall instantly in love when they meet Larissa, and the love-fest often continues year-round, because she sends them (note: *them,* not *you*) Christmas cards.

Another dog friend, Brandon, asked us to mention his favorite, the Raven House. It's a comfy, fairly quiet place with an Asian-Western style he says the owner improves on year after year. He especially likes all the fun walks he can take from here.

Larissa's House rents for $170 nightly or $600 per week. Rates at other houses range from $150 nightly or $550 per week to $275 per night or $1,400 per week. To see the various houses before you rent one, check out Russian River Vacation Homes' Web site: www.riverhomes.com. (A reader informed us of one potential dud, but that just may have been because of extra high expectations. Either way, it's good to see what you're renting before you rent it.) For a brochure describing all the dog-friendly properties, write Russian River Vacation Homes at 14080 Mill Street, P.O. Box 418, Guerneville, CA 95446, or phone (707) 869-9030, (800) 310-0804 (California only), or (800) 997-3312 (nationwide).

HEALDSBURG

RESTAURANTS

Costeaux French Bakery: Stroll around Healdsburg's good-look-ing town square, with its old buildings and benches for shady rest stops, and then drop in here for dinner or a wonderful pastry snack at an outdoor table. 417 Healdsburg Avenue; (707) 433-1913.

PLACES TO STAY

Best Western Dry Creek Inn: Rates are $69 to $94. Dogs are $10 extra. 198 Dry Creek Road, Healdsburg, CA 95448; (707) 433-0300.

Madrona Manor: So there we were, at a friend's wedding, sur-rounded by the luxurious elegance of this European-style inn. "I'm sure dogs are really welcome *here* . . . not," commented one tipsy wedding guest when he found out about my line of writing. I figured he was right, but decided to check, just in case this spec-tacular Victorian inn permitted pooches.

I came back to Sammy the Sipper with the great news: Dogs *are* allowed. He just about swallowed his martini olive whole. What I didn't tell him is that they're allowed at only one cottage. So your dog can't go with you to the mansion to inspect the handmade Persian carpets, and he can't dine at the inn's high-end restaurant. So what? He's allowed to peruse much of the manor's eight acres (on leash), and he can hang out with you at the enchanting, secluded Garden Cottage. It's the most private of the accommodations here, with its own gardens and sheltered deck. Inside, it's as attractive and unique as outside, with an antique water closet and marble fireplace. It's air conditioned, too, which isn't too common in this kind of place. But it's oh-so-necessary come summertime.

The rate for the cottage is $215, which includes a full breakfast. 1001 Westside Road, P.O. Box 818, Healdsburg, CA 95448; (707) 433-4231 or (800) 258-4003.

JENNER

PARKS, BEACHES, AND RECREATION AREAS

• **Sonoma Coast State Beaches** 🐾🐾🐾½ *See* ❽ *on page 262.*

A string of beautiful, clean beaches runs from Jenner south to Bodega Bay, and you can't go wrong from Goat Rock Beach south to Salmon Creek Beach: Gorgeous bluff views, stretches of brown sand, gnarled rocks, and grassy dunes welcome you. Always keep an eye on the surf and a leash on your dog.

Dogs are not allowed on any of the trails that run on the bluffs above the beaches, on Bodega Head, in the Willow Creek area east of Bridgehaven, or in the seal rookery upriver from Goat Rock Beach. (Watch for the warning sign.) No camping is permitted on any of the beaches, except Bodega Dunes and Wright's Beach, which have campgrounds. These two also charge a $5 day-use fee. Day use of all other beaches is free. For beach info, call (707) 875-3483.

The Bodega Dunes Campground has 98 developed sites, and Wright's Beach Campground has 30 developed sites. Sites at Bodega Dunes are $6 a night and sites at Wright's are $20. There's a $1 fee per dog. Both campgrounds are open year-round. Advance reservations are highly recommended in summer and early fall (you may reserve up to eight weeks in advance). Call Parknet for reservations at (800) 444-PARK. For general beach info, call (707) 875-3483.

RESTAURANTS

Seagull Deli: Don't look up when you eat at the outdoor tables here! Hah. It's an old joke, apparently, based on the deli's name. You and your dog can dine on creamy clam chowder while over-looking the mouth of the Russian River from one of the picnic tables. It's a tasty way to spend part of a crisp autumn afternoon. 10439 North Coast Highway (Highway 1); (707) 865-2594.

PLACES TO STAY

Bridgehaven Campground: Leashed dogs are welcome to visit or stay at this campground in the hamlet of Bridgehaven, where Highway 1 crosses the Russian River south of Jenner. For a day-use fee of $5, you and your dog can swim together. Campsites are $20. Dogs are free. There are 23 sites. The campground is open year-round. P.O. Box 59, Jenner, CA 95450; (707) 865-2473.

Sonoma Coast State Beaches: See Sonoma Coast State Beaches on page 275 for camping information.

OCCIDENTAL

PLACES TO STAY

Negri's Occidental Lodge: There's no official street address here, but it's in the middle of town—you can't miss it. Rates are $44 to $69. Dogs are $8 extra. P.O. Box 84, Occidental, CA 95465; (707) 874-3623.

PETALUMA

Petaluma is a captivating Sunday afternoon stroll, with its tree-lined streets and pocket parks for your dog's pleasure. Victorian buildings, old feed mills, and a riverfront that remains mostly original, but not dilapidated, complete the charming picture. And let's not forget an added canine bonus: Depending on the wind direction, you can often smell fresh cow manure wafting in from the surrounding hills. Dogs thrive on this.

Best of all, dogs get to run leashless during set (if early) hours in a whopping 12 parks! No wonder they call this place PET-aluma.

PARKS, BEACHES, AND RECREATION AREAS

Dogs who live in Petaluma are lucky dogs indeed. A few years back, the enlightened Parks and Recreation Department decided that dogs needed places to run off leash and gave dogs who are under voice control the okay to be leash-free in a dozen parks during certain hours. (Watch your off-leash hours like a hawk: The fine for a first offense is up to $100! Better to invest that money in a good watch.)

Now the city has one-upped itself, and dogs have their very own park, called Rocky Memorial Dog Park. Dogs are singing its praises ("Howlelujah," they're saying). Please see page 280 for more on Rocky Park.

• **Arroyo Park** 🐾🐾🐾 🐕 *See* **9** *on page 262.*

Most of Arroyo Park is very well groomed, with golf course-like green grass and a perfectly paved walking path running through its three acres. However, it seems many dogs prefer the seedier side of the park—the weedier, uncut area on the right as you face the park. We hope that area remains like this for dogs who like to walk a little on the wild side.

Dogs are allowed off leash here from 6 A.M. to 9 A.M. weekdays and 6 A.M. to 8 A.M. weekends. It's just a bone's throw from Wiseman Airport Park (see page 282), though, which is a much safer place to run a dog, since you can get farther from the road. The park is at Garfield and Village East Drives. (707) 778-4380.

• **Bond Park** 🐾🐾🐾 🐕 *See* **10** *on page 262.*

It's green here, so green that Joe couldn't help but run out of the car and throw himself down on the grass and start wriggling and writhing in ecstasy. I thought for sure he'd found something odious to roll in, but underneath him was just clean, green grass. He rolled for about 10 minutes, got up, and heaved himself down in another spot, rolling and groaning and making the children in the playground giggle. The park is pleasant, with some shade from medium-sized trees. With six acres, it's a good size for dogs. And it's set in a quiet area, on Banff way just south of Maria Drive, so traffic is minimal. Off-leash hours are 6 A.M. to 9 A.M. Monday through Friday and 6 A.M. to 8 A.M. weekends. (707) 778-4380.

• **Del Oro Park** 🐾🐾🐾 🐕 *See* **11** *on page 262.*

Del Oro is very suburban. It's got a nice little play area for kids. It's got green grass. It's surrounded by not-too-old suburban homes. It's got soccer goal posts. When we last visited, there were even two Suburban sport utility vehicles parked in front.

Something not terribly suburban, a fire hydrant in one of the grassy areas, is probably the most coveted part of the park—at least for boy dogs. Well-behaved pooches can be off leash here from 6 A.M. to 9 A.M. weekdays and 6 A.M. to 8 A.M. weekends. The park is at Sartori Drive and Del Oro Circle. (707) 778-4380.

•Glenbrook Park 🐾🐾 🐕 *See* **⑫** *on page 262.*
Who'd believe it? When we last visited, a great blue heron landed in this narrow park, which is surrounded by newish homes. This was a wonderful sight, because the land around here looks like it's still in shock from all the recent development.

The park is nearly four acres, and is much longer than it is wide. It's directly across the street from Sunrise Park (see page 281), but it's a little quieter and more attractive, with some medium-sized trees here and there. Its off-leash hours are generous: from 6 A.M. to 9 A.M. and 5 P.M. to 10 P.M. daily. The park is at Maria Drive and Sunrise Parkway. (707) 778-4380.

•Helen Putnam Regional Park 🐾🐾½ *See* **⑬** *on page 262.*
This county regional park is, and will remain, a minimally developed stretch of converted cow pasture with oak trees. A wide paved trail shared by hikers and bicyclists runs between the main entrance and the Victoria housing development (to enter from that end, go to the end of Oxford Court). Dogs must be leashed. There's no shade from the scrub oaks and it can get mighty windy. The paved trail has gentle ups and downs. Some other dirt trails give you steeper hill climbs. About a quarter of a mile in from the main entrance is an old cattle pond good for a dog swim (if the dog stays on a leash—quite a feat).

Parking is $2. Next to the lot is a kids' playground and a picnic gazebo, set by a creek that's only a gully in summer. Drive south on Western Avenue and turn left on Chileno Valley Road. After a half mile, you'll see the turnoff to the park. (707) 527-2041.

•Lucchesi Park 🐾🐾🐾½ 🐕 *See* **⑭** *on page 262.*
This is a well-kept, popular city park with a postmodern community center that impresses people, but doesn't stir dogs much. Dogs prefer strolling through empty sports fields, picnicking at shaded tables, lounging under the weepy willows, watching ducks and the spewing fountain at the large pond, and trotting along the paved paths here. No dog swimming is allowed in the pond, but that's a rule Joe "I Hate H_2O" Dog can live with just fine.

Dogs are allowed off leash here between 6 A.M. and 9 A.M. weekdays and 6 A.M. and 8 A.M. weekends. Be sure to keep dogs away from ducks and geese, who like to lounge beside their pond, because feathers should not fly as a result of the city's kindly offleash allowances. The park is at North McDowell Boulevard and Madison Street. (707) 778-4386.

•McNear Park 🐾🐾🐾 🐕 *See ⑮ on page 262.*

McNear is an attractive seven-acre park, with green, green grass, plenty of shade, picnic tables, and a playground. But the part of the park dogs like best is the enclosed athletic field, where they're allowed to romp off leash from 6 A.M. to 9 A.M. Monday through Friday and from 6 A.M. to 8 A.M. Saturday and Sunday. The field is usually green and almost entirely fenced, but there are a couple of spots where a clever escape artist could slip out, so heads up. It's at F and Ninth Streets. (707) 778-4380.

•Oak Hill Park 🐾🐾🐾🐾 🐕 *See ⑯ on page 262.*

Dogs love running up and down the gently rolling hills on this five-acre park set in the midst of beautiful old Victorian homes near downtown Petaluma. Oak Hill Park is hilly and oaky (surprise!), qualities dogs enjoy. Some good-sized oaks make their home in various parts of the park, and Joe appreciates their shade-giving arms. At last visit, a sign warned of future construction, so some of the rustic nature of this park might be gone by the time you read this.

Dogs are permitted to run off leash in the park's lower section every single day, from 6 A.M. to 10 P.M. These are magnificent hours, matched only at Rocky Memorial Dog Park (see on page 280). The park is at Howard and Oak Streets. (707) 778-4380.

•Petaluma Adobe State Historic Park 🐾🐾
See ⑰ on page 262.

Leashed dogs are welcome here, if they behave well around goats and such, and if you avoid the farm animals' courtyard. From the parking lot, walk across a wooden bridge over a wide, willow-lined creek (dry in summer) to the house, built in 1836 as headquarters for General Mariano Vallejo's 66,600-acre Rancho Petaluma. Clustered around the house are tempting displays of animal hides, saddles, and tallow makings, as well as sheep, chickens, and a donkey. Dogs must use their best manners. If you see them starting to think of lamb chops for dinner, make sure you hang on hard to that leash.

The park is southeast of Petaluma at Adobe Road and Casa Grande Road. From U.S. 101, you'll see an exit sign for the Petaluma Adobe. Admission is $2 for adults, $1 for children. (707) 762-4871.

• Prince Park 🐾🐾🐾🐾 🐕 See ⑱ on page 262.

Dogs are permitted off leash at this attractive 20-acre park during longer hours than they are at most other parks in the city, and they think this is just swell. On a recent visit, a springer-shepherd mix was running around drooling and panting and smiling like a dog in love. His person said when he comes here, he's ecstatic. "Willie loves the grass and the trees. I love the hours for off leash, and I love its safety from traffic," she said. (The park is set back quite far from street traffic.) Off-leash hours are 6 A.M. to 11 A.M. on weekdays and 6 A.M. to 8 A.M. on weekends. The park is across East Washington Street from the airport, just a little north of the airport sign. (707) 778-4380.

• Rocky Memorial Dog Park 🐾🐾🐾🐾 🐕
See ⑲ on page 262.

The scenery isn't great, and the land has nary a tree on it, but Joe couldn't help but give Rocky Memorial Dog Park his four-paw rating. "It's big, it smells good, and we don't need leashes," explains Joe.

This flat, barren nine-acre piece of land is the best thing that's happened to Petaluma's dogs since the park system began allowing them off leash at certain parks during limited hours a few years back. Rocky Park opened in early 1997 and has been drawing a good number of cavorting canines since. Dogs enjoy the smell that can pervade the land; it's beside a marshy area next to the Petaluma River. Fortunately, it's well fenced so dogs can't chase the marsh birds or roll in the marsh muck. The fencing keeps the dogs from escaping to all areas but the parking lot, which leads to the park entrance, which eventually leads a busy road. So if you have a pooch who's prone to running away, be aware the place is safe, but isn't foolproof.

Because it's so barren here, it can really roast on hot days. Be sure to bring water. A sign at the entrance says "No dogs in heat," and I thought it was nice of them to be so concerned about the temperature for dog walking. It took me a few seconds and an eye roll from my husband to realize the sign's true intent.

On our first visit, Joe searched in vain for something to lift a leg on. He found only some garbage cans and a few big weeds, and they were right next to the parking lot. The next visit he just succumbed to the lack of leg-lift targets and took to relieving his bladder like a girl dog. But not, of course, until looking around to make sure no one was watching.

Rocky Park was named after a big-hearted police dog who died at the too-young age of 10 during a narcotics search. It was kidney failure that got him, not the wrong end of a dealer's pistol. Rocky had helped seize a few million dollars of narcotics in his career, but his greatest act came in 1992 when he saved the life of his beloved handler one night. A felon had escaped and the officer chased him to a creek, where the felon got the upper hand and was holding the officer's head underwater. The officer managed to hit a remote control button that opened the windows of the patrol car and released Rocky, who'd seen his friend in trouble. Rocky bolted to the creek and got the upper paw. He saved his friend and helped bag the bad guy. "It was the beginning of the era of Rocky," said Officer Jeff Hasty, a dog handler with the Petaluma Police Department. At press time, a bust of Rocky was set to be mounted in front of the police department.

This is an easy park to visit if you're on U.S. 101 and your pooch is hankering to stretch his gams. Take the Highway 116 east (NOT west)/Lakeville exit and follow the street just over a half mile to Casa Grande Road, where you'll take a sharp right. Drive a few hundred feet past ugly storage bins and trucks and you'll soon hit the entrance to the park. Unlike most of the other city parks with off-leash times, this one has great hours: from 6 A.M. to 10 P.M. (707) 778-4380.

• **Sunrise Park** 🐾 1/2 🐕 *See* ㉔ *on page 262.*

If you're a real estate developer, there's a chance you might enjoy this park. It's very, very narrow, squeezed like an old tube of toothpaste by cookie cutter condos and townhouses. It's too close to traffic. It's not terribly attractive. But in its defense, it does have decent grassy areas and fun (for dogs) weedy patches. Another plus: Dogs are allowed to be off leash here between 6 A.M. and 9 A.M. and 5 P.M. to 10 P.M. every day. Those are some pretty long hours for a pretty slim park. It's at Marina Drive and Sunrise

Parkway. (707) 778-4380.

• **Westridge Open Space** 🐾🐾🐾 🐕 *See ㉑ on page 262.*

Dogs get to peruse the east side of this three-acre park off leash from 6 A.M. to 9 A.M. every day. The park is long and narrow, with plenty of medium-sized trees, which turn a warm red in autumn. When we visited, a fluffy black cat teased Joe from the middle of the road. Joe warns his brethren to watch out for that guy, especially if your pooch is a chaser. The park is located on Westridge Drive, near its intersection with Westridge Place. (707) 778-4380.

• **Wiseman Airport Park** 🐾🐾🐾🐾 🐕 *See ㉒ on page 262.*

Plenty of pooches visit this park, and for good reason. Wiseman is 32 acres of well-kept playing fields, uncut grass, many shade trees, and comfortably wide walking paths. It's also a good place to watch little planes land and take off, because of its proximity to the airport. (They don't call it Airport Park for nothing.) Best of all, it's got a couple of safe areas where you can run your dog off leash during certain hours. From 6 A.M. to 9 A.M. weekdays and 6 A.M. to 8 A.M. weekends, dogs can go leashless from the south soccer field up to and including the north softball field. The best access is at St. Augustine Circle. (707) 778-4380.

RESTAURANTS

Apple Box: A store of antiques and housewares, this charmer also serves good desserts, teas, and coffee. There's a bookshop next door and 10 tables outside, right by the river. Joe's dog buddy Dabney loves the smell of sun on river water, mixed with baking cookies. 224 B Street; (707) 762-5222.

Aram's Cafe: Dine on really good Mediterranean and Armenian food at the five outdoor tables. Aram's is located in downtown Petaluma. 131 Kentucky Street; (707) 765-9775.

Rocket Cafe: On weekends, the dog-loving owners offer barbecue and live music. Other times, enjoy light meals at the outdoor tables. 100 Petaluma Boulevard, #104; (707) 763-2314.

PLACES TO STAY

Motel 6: Rates are $38 for the first adult, $7 for the second. One small pooch per room, please. 1368 North McDowell Boulevard, Petaluma, CA 94954; (707) 765-0333.

Quality Inn: Stay here and get a complimentary continental breakfast. The corporate rooms are on the more deluxe side. Some even have whirlpool baths. (No dog paddling, poochies!) Rates are $69 to $139. Dogs require a $20 deposit. 5100 Montero Way, Petaluma, CA 94954; (707) 664-1155.

DOGGY DAYS

Yikes! What a dog!: If your dog is so ugly that the fleas flee when they see his face, you'll want to know about this one. Petaluma's annual Ugly Dog Contest is a good time for you and your dog, ugly or not. (Beautiful dogs are welcome, so long as they don't mind losing.) It's held on the last day of the Sonoma-Marin Fair and it's open to any dog owner for a $3 entry fee. Water and shade are provided; bring your own pooper-scooper.

A winner is chosen in the Mutt and Pedigreed categories. These winners square off for the Ugly Dog of the Year award. Then there's the Ring of Champions division, in which past winners compete for the title of World's Ugliest Dog. Don't miss it. The event is held at the Sonoma-Marin Fairgrounds, usually on the third Sunday in June. Call (707) 763-0931 for this year's date.

ROHNERT PARK

PARKS, BEACHES, AND RECREATION AREAS

• **Crane Creek Regional Park** 🐾 🐾 *See ㉓ on page 262.*

For years, this 128-acre patch of grazing land in the middle of nowhere has been undeveloped open space for your dog's pleasure. Recent improvements include an upgraded parking lot, the addition of picnic tables, and the widening of 2.6 miles of hiking trails. Unfortunately, the leash law is enforced here, and a sign tells you why: "Dogs Caught in Livestock May Be Shot." Carry water; you may get thirsty just trying to find the place in your car.

From Rohnert Park, drive east on the Rohnert Park Expressway to Petaluma Hill Road. Turn south on Petaluma Hill Road to Roberts Road, and go east for two miles on Roberts Road. You'll find the park shortly after Roberts turns into Pressley Road. A machine is there to collect a $2 parking fee from you. (707) 527-2041.

SANTA ROSA

PARKS, BEACHES, AND RECREATION AREAS

This sprawling city has gone to the dogs in the last few years, and dogs and their people couldn't be happier. It used to be that if you wanted to give your pooch a little off-leash exercise, you'd go out of town or sneak out to a park at night and hope no one was watching. But now the city has two very attractive off-leash dog runs (please see Doyle and Rincon Valley Parks), one in the works (see Northwest Community Park), and four parks that are serving as pilot locations for a trial off-leash program (please see Franklin, Doyle, Youth, and Southwest Parks). That sound you hear is the sound of tails thumping.

The dog parks are wonderful, but if you don't mind getting up early, the parks in the pilot program offer even more room and more doggy heaven scents. Dogs who visit those pilot parks are allowed to run off leash between 6 A.M. and 8 A.M. every day—and the hours are strictly enforced, so be sure to wind your watch. Dogs have to be under voice control, nonaggressive, spayed or neutered, and more than four months old. Of course, as is always the case wherever you go with your dog, you have to scoop the poop. "If our mower people go through and find a pile, we can close down the park to off-leash dogs," said Dan Neff, superintendent of park maintenance. "We don't want to, but that's the way it's got to be." There are stiff fines, from $35 to $500, for being a scofflaw, so be careful out there.

At press time, the experimental phase of this program was set to end in August 1998, but if all goes well, those four parks and more could have a more permanent off-leash setup. Call the parks department at (707) 543-3292 for updates. And be sure to say thanks if they give you good news.

• **Doyle Park** 🐾 🐾 🐾 🐾 🐕 *See* **㉔** *on page 262.*

Doyle Park is a very stately place to take a pooch. A little stone bridge takes you over a stream and into the park's main entry area. The trees here have an elegant, deep-rooted look. The grass is like a cool, plush green carpet. At Doyle, even the squirrels don't look squirrely.

Dogs think it's all grand. But what they think is even better is the fact that they can run around all this splendor without a leash between 6 A.M. and 8 A.M., thanks to an experimental program run by the city's dog-friendly parks department. (If you're reading this after August 1998, please call the number below to make sure the city's experiment was successful and the leash-free hours still apply. See the introduction to this section, above, for more details about the pilot off-leash program.)

Dogs who aren't early birds don't have to sulk because of the hours: Doyle Park is graced with not only the pilot off-leash program, but it has its very own fenced doggy park. It's not as riveting as the rest of the park, but it's got water and some trees, and it's a very safe place to take even an escape artist. Unlike Rincon Park's dog run (see page 286), Doyle's dog run doesn't close during the winter rains. (Joe Dog wants to thank Silke Kuehl and her pooch for writing us and pointing us in the direction of this relative newcomer to the off-leash park world.)

In addition to the rules mentioned in the beginning of this section, there's one that's a little tough if you're a parent of a dog and a youngish child: No children under 10 years old are allowed in the dog run, whether accompanied by a parent or not. The park users devised this rule, which was apparently meant to protect kids from getting mowed over by herds of dogs, and also to protect herds of dogs from lawsuits.

For the main entrance, take Sonoma Avenue to Doyle Park Drive and turn south, driving a few hundred feet over insufferable speed bumps to the parking area. The dog run will be way over to the left. To park closer to the dog run, take Sonoma Avenue to Hoen Avenue and turn south. The parking lot is on the right, and the dog run is on the other side of the ball field. (707) 543-3292.

• **Franklin Park** 🐾🐾🐾 🐕 *See* ㉕ *on page 262.*

Franklin is the smallest of the four parks that allow dogs off leash between 6 A.M. and 8 A.M. (See the introduction to this section, page 283, for details about this wonderful experimental off-leash program. If you're reading this after August 1998, please call the number below to make sure the experiment was successful and the off-leash rule still applies.) It's green and slopey, with enough trees to make any boy dog happy. Be careful, because it's not as safe from traffic as some of the other parks. (But it's not exactly Indy 500 territory around here anyway.)

The park is at Franklin Avenue and Gay Street. (707) 543-3292.

• **Hood Mountain Regional Park** 🐾🐾½ *See* ㉖ *on page 262.*

Dogs and people love the trails in this park, but it's open only on weekends and holidays and closes every summer when fire danger gets high. It usually reopens only in late September. It can also close in winter because of mud slides. Make sure your dog wears a leash. If a sign appears at the Los Alamos Road turnoff saying that the park is closed, believe it.

To get to the only entrance, from Highway 12, turn east on Los Alamos Road (not Adobe Canyon Road, which leads only to Sugarloaf Ridge State Park, where dogs aren't allowed on trails). The road is long, winding, steep, and narrow for the last two miles. It's not for nervous drivers or carsick pooches, but it's a beautiful four-mile drive, with a good close-up of Hood Mountain's bare rock outcropping "hood."

A machine in the parking lot will ask you to pay $2. Call to make sure the park is open before driving here. A final note: Watch out for ticks. They're rampant. (707) 527-2041.

•Northwest Community Park 🐾🐾🐾🐾 🐕
See ㉗ on page 262.

At press time, the area for an off-leash dog park within the park was ready for fencing, awaiting the last few hundred dollars in donations. I'm going to go against my usual rule and describe a dog park before it's actually complete because, as park maintenance superintendent Dan Neff said, "It's definitely a go." By the time you read this, dogs should be tearing around having the time of their lives.

The dog run is a good size, about the size of Rincon's (see below), and will have some shade, water, and benches. If it's anything like Santa Rosa's other two dog parks, dogs are going to be lucky indeed to visit here. The dog area is located just northwest of the park's soccer fields. The park is located on Marlow Road, behind Comstock Junior High School, north of Guerneville Road. If you get a copy of this book hot off the press, you may want to call and make sure the fence is up before you venture over. (707) 543-3770.

•Rincon Valley Community Park 🐾🐾🐾🐾 🐕
See ㉘ on page 262.

The fenced dog park here is one of the most attractive we've ever seen. That's mostly because it has grass. Real grass. Not just a few green sprigs fighting their way through the tough dirt, but good ol' carpety grass. That's not because the dogs here pussy-foot around. In fact, dogs are so happy to be here that they tear around with great gusto. We're not exactly sure why there's so much grass, but we do know that the dog run closes during the rainy winter months, so that could have something to do with it.

A few trees grace the dog run area, and the views of the surrounding hills make it seem like it's in the middle of the countryside. As of this writing, it's actually on the edge of the countryside. By the next edition, it will probably be miles from the countryside, the way development encroaches around here.

The dogs who come to Rincon's dog run are a friendly lot, running to the fence and sniffing all newcomers, tails wagging exuberantly. The people who come here are much the same, except they chat rather than sniff. They're wonderful, outgoing, dog-loving folks—except for one persnickety woman who told me that I must not be in there with my child, who was blissing out on all the dogs. "Didn't you see the rules? No infants or children!" she snipped. "You could sue us if she got hurt." The woman suggested leaving Laura by herself in a stroller outside the gate, since you're not allowed to leave your dog alone in the dog run. Joe wanted to do a leg lift on the woman's ankle, but she left. I expected her to say "And your little dog, too!" and cackle as she flew off, but that's the stuff movies are made of.

Unfortunately it's true: No little kiddies under 10 allowed, even if they're with their parents. A parks department spokesman says the park users made up the rule. So apparently if you've got a kid and a dog, you'll have to hire a sitter in order to bring your dog here. Boo!

The park is on Montecito Boulevard, west of Calistoga Road. Don't forget that it's closed during the rainy months. (707) 524-5116.

• **Southwest Park** 🐾 🐾 🐾 🐾 🐕 *See ㉙ on page 262.*

If your dog doesn't need a park in the hoity-toitiest part of town, this is a mighty convenient and friendly place to take him. First of all, it's relatively close to the freeway, so it's easy to get to if you're on the road. But better than that, it's big and green, with neatly paved paths that meander by cascading willows. It's also far enough from the road that the traffic danger is minimal. Why care about traffic? Because your dog can be off leash here from 6 A.M. to 8 A.M., thanks to an experimental program that's got dogs at its very heart. (If you're reading this after August 1998, please call the number below to make sure the experiment was successful and the off-leash rule still applies. See the introduction to this section, page 283, for more details about the pilot program.)

From U.S. 101, take the Hearn Avenue exit and drive west for nearly a mile. The park is on the left, across from Westland Drive. (707) 543-3292.

- **Spring Lake Regional Park** 🐾 🐾 🐾 *See* ㉚ *on page 262.*

In winter, this county park doesn't offer dogs much more than a leashed trot around the lake. But in summer, it's leafy and full of the sounds of kids yelling and thumping oars. It's more fun here for people than dogs, who must be leashed. This is a good spot for a picnic, roller skating, a parcourse workout, a boat ride, or human swimming (no dogs allowed in the swim area). The path around the lake is paved for skaters, strollers, and bicyclists, and there are short dirt paths off into the open oak and brush woods. You can fish from the banks, where they're cleared of tules and willows.

The parking fee is $3 in winter, $4 in summer; the large lot has some shady spots. Campsites are $14, plus $1 extra for a dog. Ten sites are reservable; 21 are first come, first served. Dogs must have proof of a rabies vaccination. The campground is open daily between May 1 and September 30, weekends and holidays only after September 30.

From Highway 12, on the Farmer's Lane portion in Santa Rosa, turn east on Hoen Avenue. Take Hoen four stoplights to Newanga Avenue. Turn left on Newanga, which goes straight to the entrance. (707) 539-8092.

- **Youth Community Park** 🐾 🐾 🐾 🐾 🐕 *See* ㉛ *on page 262.*

If you like oak trees, come here. Big oaks hang out all over the park. Some really big, really old oaks even have their own fences, so no one can do leg lifts or initial carving on their trunks.

The main attraction for dogs is the big green meadowy lawn area. Pooches love rolling on it and cantering over it. Your dog can be off leash here from 6 A.M. to 8 A.M., thanks to an experimental dog-friendly pilot program. (If you're reading this after August 1998, please call the number below to make sure the experiment was successful and the off-leash rule still applies. See the introduction to this section, page 283, for more details about the pilot program.)

A word of warning: Skateboarders abound here. There's a little skateboard area in front of the park, and kids love skateboarding around the parking lot, too. Joe is fascinated with boarders, but some dogs cringe at the sound.

The park is in the far west reaches of the city, on the west side of Fulton Road, about a quarter of a mile south of Piner Road. (707) 543-3292

RESTAURANTS

Juice Shack: In the summer, come here with your hot pooch and cool off with a creamy smoothie or a fresh organic juice. In cooler months, you can enjoy hot juices here. Hmm. Joe Dog and I would rather go for the hot soup they serve, or the wrap sandwiches. Dine with your dog at the outdoor area under the big pine tree. 1810 Mendocino Avenue; (707) 528-6131.

PLACES TO STAY

Best Western Garden Inn: Dogs can stay in eight rooms here, but only one pooch per room, please. Rates are $65 to $99. Dogs are $10 extra. 1500 Santa Rosa Avenue, Santa Rosa, CA 95404; (707) 546-4031.

Best Western Hillside Inn: Small dogs only, please. Rates are $52 to $61. 2901 Fourth Street, Santa Rosa, CA 95409; (707) 546-9353.

Los Robles Lodge: Rates are $59 to $112. 925 Edwards Avenue, Santa Rosa, CA 95401; (707) 545-6330.

Santa Rosa Travelodge: Rates are $45 to $80. Small pets only, please. 1815 Santa Rosa Avenue, Santa Rosa, CA 95407; (707) 542-3472.

Spring Lake Regional Park: See Spring Lake Regional Park on page 288 for camping information.

SEA RANCH

PARKS, BEACHES, AND RECREATION AREAS

• **Sea Ranch Beach Trails** 😺 😺 1/2 *See* ❸❷ *on page 262.*

Sea Ranch is a private development, but seven public foot trails cross the property leading to the beach, which is also public property. The smooth, wide dirt trails are managed by the Sonoma County Regional Parks, and they offer incomparable solitary walks through unspoiled grassy hills.

All the trails are clearly marked on Highway 1. Each trailhead has rest rooms and a box where you are asked to deposit $3 for parking. No motorcycles, bicycles, or horses are allowed. Keep your dog on leash.

Here are the distances to the beach, listing trails from north to south: Salal Trail, .6 miles; Bluff-Top Trail, 3.5 miles; Walk-On Beach Trail, .4 miles; Shell Beach Trail, .6 miles; Stengel Beach Trail, .2 miles; Pebble Beach Trail, .3 miles; Black Point Trail, .3 miles. Call (707) 785-2377 for more info.

PLACES TO STAY

The Welch House: If you find your dog wandering around this large, exquisite house with a big grin on his snout, do what Dorothy learned to do: Don't look any further than your own backyard for the source of his happiness. The backyard is expansive, the front yard is enclosed and faces the mighty Pacific, and in between is a magnificent, cedar-shingled, two-bedroom, two-bathroom house you can call home. "It's a wonderful place for people and dogs. I couldn't think of coming here and not taking a dog," says a longtime fan of the house.

With a house and area this glorious, it's hard to know where to start a description. In general, the place is top-drawer. "We like to keep it classed up," says dog-loving co-owner Trevor Paulson. "The nicer we make it, the better the dogs get."

The 30-foot-long living room has a huge, slate-faced fireplace and two window beds with views to drool about. The spacious kitchen is stocked with high-quality pots (Circulon, no less), pans, plates, flatware, and even champagne glasses. (You'll probably even find dog biscuits in here, too.) Each bedroom has a separate, completely fenced deck to foil escape pooches and add privacy. A private enclosed spa with an outdoor shower and an extremely comfortably furnished, walled 650-square-foot main/observation deck provides spectacular ocean, meadow, and forest views by day and, as the brochure says, "a celestial panoply of billions of stars" at night. "If it's a new moon, it blows your mind," says Trevor. Tugger and Penney, the sweet dogs owned by Trevor and the house's other co-owner, Dave Welch, helped make The Welch House as dog-friendly as it is. "Even though they're not here when you visit, their spirits are. Consider them your hosts," says Trevor.

From the property, you have access to the beach (with great seal- and whale-watching opportunities) and 10 miles of level hiking trails. The air here is sweet and salty at the same time.

The house is $200 a night and sleeps up to four people. There's a two-night minimum stay. Weekly and off-season specials are available. Dogs are $10 extra per visit. For understandable security reasons, the owners don't give out the address to anyone but guests. For reservations and information, call (707) 884-4235. That's the number for Beach Rentals, the agency the owners use to help them make arrangements for guests.

SEBASTOPOL

PARKS, BEACHES, AND RECREATION AREAS

• **Ragle Ranch Park** 🐾 🐾 🐾 ½ *See* ㉝ *on page 262.*

This Sonoma County regional park, right in the town of Sebastopol, is surprisingly large and wild, once you pass the fields and picnic areas. Unlike most urban parks, it's not very crowded, except during ball games on weekends. Level hiking and equestrian trails wind alongside vineyards and apple orchards, which are in bloom beginning in early April. Waterfowl breed in marshy spots around the creek, so don't yield to the temptation to let your dog off the obligatory leash. The landscape is gently rolling, with reeds and willows lining the creek and oaks with mistletoe on the higher rises. Woo woo, it's kissy stuff.

The park is located at Healdsburg Avenue and Ragle Road. Admission is $2 per car. (707) 527-2041.

PLACES TO STAY

Becky's Guesthouse: This lovely house is tucked away from the road and comes complete with its own 10 acres of woods, yards, and a creek. Very well-behaved dogs may be leash-free when exploring the grounds with their people.

Dog-loving owner Becky Johnson greets guests each morning with dog-shaped toast (for canines) and human-shaped toast (for Homo sapiens). That's just for starters. Humans then sit down to a delicious country-style breakfast, which tastes very appropriate in this restored farmhouse. Becky has so many doggy people stay here that she created a photo album of her canine guests. People love to paw through it. Be sure to bring your camera so you can send her a picture of you and yours.

This is Becky's home, but she devotes the back half of the house to guests. Entrances to the two bedrooms are private, and the rooms have private baths. Dogs and their guests love to relax on the fully fenced-in decks outside their rooms on sunny days.

The room rate is $85. The mailing address is 201 Wagnon Road, Sebastopol, CA 95412; (707) 823-2223.

DIVERSIONS

Sniff out the farm trail: If you're serious about buying home-grown produce and dairy products, or just like farms—and your dog wears a leash at all times and won't do leg lifts on the veg-etables—pick up a Farm Trails map from Sonoma County Farmtrails, (707) 996-2154, or from the Chamber of Commerce, P.O. Box 178, Sebastopol, CA 95473; (707) 823-3032.

SONOMA

Downtown Sonoma is a treat for people, but dogs are banned from all the good spots—the State Historic Park areas of the mis-sion, barracks, etc., and from the Sonoma Plaza, which is full of picnickers wolfing down fine wine and Sonoma Jack. But if you and your dog are there on a fine day, stroll to Depot Park (see below), just northwest of Sonoma Plaza, and follow a paved path in either direction from Depot Park for a mini-farm tour of the town.

PARKS, BEACHES, AND RECREATION AREAS

• **Depot Park** 🐾 🐾 🐾 *See* **34** *on page 262.*

This fine park has a softball diamond, volleyball courts, a bocce court, picnic tables, a parcourse, a small childrens' playground, and fragrant eucalyptus trees for your dog. From here, you can take a paved biking and hiking trail, smooth enough for wheel-chairs, in either direction. You have to leash, but you'll both enjoy the sights and smells.

The trail stretches almost the width of the town, from Fourth Street East westward to Highway 12 and into Maxwell Farms Regional Park (see page 293). Heading east, you can walk about half a mile from Depot Park, passing the Vella Cheese Factory, the Sebastiani Winery, and rows of sunflowers, patches of corn, and grapes in backyard farms. Westward the path stretches about one mile. You'll skirt the Mariano Vallejo Adobe and end up in Max-well Farms park.

Depot Park is northwest of Sonoma Plaza. (707) 938-3681.

• **Maxwell Farms Regional Park** 🐾 🐾 1/2 *See ㉟ on page 262.*

This park offers playing fields, picnic tables, a generous kids' playground, smooth paths, and a large undeveloped area where paths follow Sonoma Creek under huge laurels wound with wild grapevines. The creek is dry in summer, but leashed dogs like to sniff it anyway.

The entrance is off Verano Avenue, west of Highway 12. The day-use fee is $2. (707) 527-2041.

RESTAURANTS

The Coffee Garden: This is a peaceful haven for dogs and their people. The magnificent garden patio has a fountain that fascinates some dogs and makes others look like they need to head to the nearest tree fast. There's actually a big, 160-year-old fig tree in the middle of the patio area, but leg lifts are definitely *not* permitted.

The cafe is housed in the historic Captain Salvador Vallejo Adobe, which was built in the late 1830s. A brochure you can pick up at the cafe explains its history and suggests carefully examining its architecture for various details. Most dogs would rather not have to closely explore the unique adobe brick construction of the walls, as suggested by the brochure, unless there happened to be a little chicken salad splattered on it.

Brandon Dog, pooch extraordinaire of Forest Service spokesman extraordinaire Matt Mathes and his wife (also extraordinaire, says Matt), loves this place. When Brandon visited recently, a guitar player was strumming out some gentle melodies. "Brandon seemed to enjoy the guitar. But he was more interested in the food," says Matt.

The food here is light and very tasty. Try the smoked salmon sandwich or the zesty Chinese chicken sandwich. There's a good espresso menu and a small selection of beers and wines. The Coffee Garden is located on the Sonoma Plaza, at 415–421 First Street West; (707) 996-6645.

PLACES TO STAY

Best Western Sonoma Valley Inn: Rates are $79 to $199. Small dogs only, please, and they're $15 per night. 550 Second Street West, Sonoma, CA 95476; (707) 938-9200.

Sparrow's Nest: This quaint English country-style cottage is a big hit with dogs who like friendly digs. The owner, Kathleen Anderson, loves dogs. In fact, she has what she calls "a herd of pugs" (four, to be exact). When you arrive at the Sparrow's Nest, Kathleen, who lives in the other house on the one-acre property, will greet you with human cookies and greet your pooch with dog cookies. She'll even tell you about a couple of secret dog-walking spots nearby. And there's even a chance that she'll offer to baby-sit for your dog if you want to check out a local winery or two.

The cottage, surrounded by flowers, is as delightful as its owner. It's an airy 500 square feet, with one bedroom (complete with Laura Ashley bedding, so no dirty paws, please!), a living room with a sofa bed, a kitchenette, a bathroom, and a breakfast nook. If you want civilization, there's a phone, cable TV, and a VCR with complimentary videos. Kathleen always provides fresh flowers inside. For breakfast she'll either bring you a delectable continental breakfast of locally made bakery treats (yummm . . . mini quiches, when they're available) or she'll provide you with a certificate for breakfast at a nearby restaurant. Joe suggests eating in so your dog can catch your quiche droppings.

A fenced yard wraps around the cottage, and farther away on the property, ducks, geese, and a few chickens quack around like they own the place. Dogs love all this.

Rates are $85 to $115. The cottage is a mile from Sonoma's town square, at 424 Denmark Street, Sonoma, CA 95476; (707) 996-3750.

Stone Grove Inn: Dogs think they've died and gone to Greece when they stay at this rustic, charming inn. That's because owner Charles Papanteles has a flair for decorating with the old-world Mediterranean flair of his ancestors.

But what really makes Joe say "opa!" is that the inn is surrounded by acres of gorgeous meadows, pastures, and organic veggie gardens. There's plenty of room for walking (on leash). The stone cottage, where dogs are permitted (they aren't allowed in the red barn studio), is really made of stone, and it's small, private, and secluded. It had better be secluded, because it has a detached bathroom and an outdoor shower. We found this kind of fun, but if your bladder is the size of a peanut, this may not be the place for you. Bathrooms aside, the stone cottage, which is more than 100 years old, can be mighty cozy with the potbelly stove blazing.

Rates are $75 to $95. Dogs are $10 extra. The cottage is just a bone's throw from Sonoma's town square, at 240 Second Street, Sonoma, CA 95476; (707) 939-8249.

TIMBER COVE

PARKS, BEACHES, AND RECREATION AREAS

• **Salt Point State Park** 🐾🐾🐾 *See ㊱ on page 262.*

Dogs are allowed only on South Gerstle Cove Beach—south of the rocky tidepool area, which is an underwater reserve—and in the Gerstle Cove, Woodside, and Fisk Mill Cove picnic areas and campsites. Gerstle Cove picnic area is right above the portion of the beach where dogs are allowed, so that's your best bet. The surf is usually gentle here, but if in doubt, you can call for an ocean-conditions recording at (707) 847-3222. As far as walking around, dogs get to do it only on paved roads. They must be leashed everywhere.

The parking fee is $5. Dogs are $1 extra. Dogs are allowed at all campsites here except the walk-in and group sites. The park has about 30 tents in the upland portion of the park. East of Highway 1 are 80 family sites. Sites are $14 to $16 per night. The dog fee is $1. Between March 2 and November 30, reserve through Parknet, (800) 444-PARK. The rest of the year, it's first come, first served.

The park is about five miles north of Timber Cove and six miles south of Stewarts Point, off Highway 1. For park info, call (707) 847-3465.

• **Stillwater Cove Regional Park** 🐾🐾½ *See ㊲ on page 262.*

This is a tiny but delightful beach at the foot of spectacular pine-covered cliffs. Park in the small lot beside Highway 1, leash your dog, and walk down. There is a larger picnic area above the highway, where a $3 day-use fee is charged. From here, you have to cross the highway to get to the cove. Look both ways!

There are 23 campsites, available on a first-come, first-served basis. Sites are $14 per night for up to two vehicles ($12 for Sonoma County residents). Dogs are $1 extra. The turnout is about one mile north of Fort Ross State Park (where dogs are banned). (707) 847-3245.

PLACES TO STAY

Salt Point State Park: See Salt Point State Park above for camping information.

Stillwater Cove Regional Park: See Stillwater Cove Regional Park on page 295 for camping information.

WINDSOR

Until 1992, Windsor wasn't anything but an unincorporated county area. Then it became a town, thanks to the "d" word (development). Then, in 1997, it spawned its very first park, and with that park came a fenced-in dog park. Dogs think Windsor's movers and shakers are very smart people, indeed.

PARKS, BEACHES, AND RECREATION AREAS

• **Pleasant Oak Park** 🐾 🐾 🐕 *See* 🟤 *on page 262.*

You and your dog wouldn't want to travel far to come here—yet. There are plenty of bigger, prettier dog run areas in the county. But the fact is, dogs feel at home running around the park's fenced dog park. Even without trees. Even without water. They don't mind that it's pretty much just a dirt lot with a very high fence and a double gate system (good for escape artists). At least they get to run.

In fact, its relatively barren condition makes obedience a snap. "When I called my dogs, they came right away," said Leslie, the sweet mother of enchanting bassett hounds Annabelle and Max. Annabelle and Max were kind enough to check on the park for us before we had a chance to visit, and while their sojourn there wasn't a howlingly fun time, they did manage to make the best of half a torn-up ball they'd found.

The good news is that the park will be less austere in the future. On the park's wish list are trees, water, and maybe even some grass. Annabelle and Max may soon be able to drag their ears across some fresh turf, which would make them and their ear cleaner mighty happy.

The park is at Old Redwood Highway and Pleasant Avenue. (707) 838-1260.

APPENDICES

10
BEYOND THE BAY

Yes, dogs, there really *is* life beyond the San Francisco Bay Area. And sometimes it can be most spectacular. The following dog-friendly places are excerpted from my book *The California Dog Lover's Companion*, a 800-page scoop on where to take your dog in the Golden State. (The book is available for $20.95 at most bookstores or by calling 1-800-FOGHORN (364-4676), should your dog drool for more. And there's lots, lots more.)

PLACER COUNTY
Lake Tahoe is at home here

RUSTIC COTTAGES

This resort has been dog-friendly since 1925! It recently changed hands (it was formerly Tatami Cottage Resort) and went through a major overhaul. It's now one of the most lovely places we've encountered for a poochy vacation, and with plans for further improvements (new kitchens in all cottages), it's going to be a doggone dynamite place. The new owners are very nice folks, but they did a lot of work on the place and they're a little wary about allowing dogs, so please let your dog inspire them to have confidence in their ilk.

The beds here are one of the biggest draws. One of the resort's new owners handcrafts wrought-iron and brass beds for a living, so his talent was put to use in each of the 18 cottages here. The linens are also first-rate, so the owners ask you not to let your dog on the bed unless you bring your own sheet to cover up the bed first.

The cottages even have new TVs, which get a whopping 30 channels each, not that you want to be a couch tater when you're vacationing in Tahoe. But just in case, each TV has a VCR, so you can bring your own videos or borrow one of the hundred or so the resort loans out to guests. (Reggie Dog, a boxer friend, told us he recently checked out the "Dog Babysitter" video here. He found it a bore, but one of his chauffeurs, Denise Selleck, was mesmerized.) In the morning, you can pick up homemade muffins in the main cottage. (You can nab a homemade cookie there all day.) Joe likes that parenthetical sentence.

Better yet, though, is that the place is on two acres, with a small, semi-enclosed lot where your pooch can run leash-free if you stay with him and have a little faith that he won't escape. The lot isn't anything fancy, but dogs don't mind a little overgrown grass and a tree stump. In fact, most dogs prefer this decor to a perfectly manicured lawn. If you want quaint scenery, just look around the cottages. In the warmer months, fresh flowers adorn most cottage fronts. Lake Tahoe is across the street, but there's no beach access there for dogs. But some Tahoe National Forest land is behind the resort, and it's a four-paw adventure for dogs and their people. Reggie Dog and his people got rather lost on a trail here one day, but they eventually made it back to civilization.

Rates are $59 to $139. Dogs are $10 extra. 7449 North Lake Boulevard, Tahoe Vista, CA 96148; (530) 546-3523 or (888) 778-7842.

MENDOCINO COUNTY
Vacation heaven

THE STANFORD INN BY THE SEA
Do you and your pooch love luxury, rustic surroundings, and the ocean? Have we got a place for you!

The Stanford Inn by the Sea has plenty of all three. There's luxury: The beds are big and comfortable antiques, and the rooms all have fireplaces and French doors leading to private decks. There's rustic scenery: The redwood inn is tucked into a grove of pines, surrounded by 11 acres. There's water: On one side of the property is the Pacific, on the other is the Big River.

What more could you want? Red-carpet treatment for your dog? How's this: Dogs are provided with doggy sheets so they can relax anywhere in your room and not leave it covered with their dogginess. Not enough? Okay, we'll tell all: Dogs get the canine equivalent of a pillow chocolate—dog biscuits wrapped with ribbons. (And humans get the real deal—gourmet chocolates.) There's also a VIP ("very important pet") photo album in the lobby, as well as a collection of dog books. That should get a wag or two out of your pooch.

Humans get the royal treatment at the inn, too. Guests all get to use plush white terry robes, swim in the beautiful greenhouse's heated pool, and partake of wine and tasty snacks at the end of a day of adventuring.

Rates are $190 to $325. Your dog's entire stay will cost him $25.

Additional pooches are $7.50 each. The inn is at Comptche-Ukiah Road and Highway 1. The mailing address is P.O. Box 487, Mendocino, CA 95460; (707) 937-5615 or (800) 331-8884.

SHEEP DUNG ESTATES

People often ask about staying somewhere really dog-friendly. You won't find many better places than the four cottages and one guest house on 320 acres in this rustic haven near Boonville. (The place grew from two cottages and 160 acres since the last edition of this book. Dogs everywhere are applauding.) To attest to this, 80 percent of the visitors here bring dogs!

The place looks much better than its name implies. From the huge windows of the homey, airy cottages, you and your dog can enjoy sweeping vistas of the Anderson Valley and surrounding forests. The secluded cottages each have private roads, wood-burning stoves, down comforters, mini kitchens stocked with breakfast fixings, and covered porches. The newest cottage, the Hill House, actually has its own small guest house, called the Tree Top. It's ideal for couples traveling together.

Owners Anne and Aaron Bennett ask that you bring a sheet if your dog insists on sleeping on the bed with you, because the luxurious bedding can't take the beating dogs give.

Your pooch need not look farther than his own front door for a place to run around and just be a dog. Voice-controlled dogs are free to run and explore the huge property! The Bennetts recently made a 1.5-mile trail that goes to the top of the ridge. "We call it Big Rock Trail," says charming, dog-adoring, and vivacious Anne Bennett. "But guests call it Cardiac Hill." If you and your dog like your walks a little less sweaty, there's a gorgeous 40-acre area with gently rolling hills dotted with firs and oaks. Guests call that one Geriatric Park, but young-at-heart (and body) dogs and people love it. There's even a very large pond where water dogs can practice the dog paddle. Anne says many dogs have learned to swim here because they wanted to be with their swimming humans. Plus, it's nice and safe and quiet, with no jet skis, no waves, none of the stuff that dogs balk at in most areas where they can swim.

There's a two-night minimum stay. Rates for this magnificent chunk of Dog Heaven are $85 to $95 nightly during the week and $125 to $140 per night on weekends and holidays. The Hill House/Tree Top cottages are rented together, and cost $175 on weekdays and $225 per night on weekends. Sheep Dung Estates is about 40 miles southeast of Mendocino, near Highway 128. The Bennetts will give you directions when you make your reservation. (Say, isn't that your dog behind you, handing you the phone?) The mailing address is P.O. Box 49, Yorkville, CA 95494; (707) 894-5322.

MONTEREY COUNTY
Coastal splendor

•Carmel City Beach 🐾🐾🐾🐾 🐕

The fine white sand crunches underfoot as you and your leash-free dog explore this pristine beach. It's the only beach for many, many miles that allows dogs off their leashes, so it's a real gem for dog travelers. Bordered by cypress trees and a walking trail, the beach is also popular among humans, especially on weekends. So if your dog is the type to mark beach blankets and eat things out of other peoples' picnic baskets, you may want to leash him until you find a less crowded part of the beach.

Pooper-scoopers are available at dispensers here, but it's a good idea to bring your own just in case doggy demand is high and they run out. From Highway 1, take the Ocean Avenue exit all the way to the end, where you'll find a large parking area that's not large enough on summer weekends. (At press time, this beach was a wreck because of El Niño storms. But it will probably have returned to its glory by the time you read this.) (408) 624-3543.

CYPRESS INN

Dogs get the royal treatment here, in part because actress and animal activist Doris Day owns this sumptuous hotel. The Mediterranean-style inn is very elegant, with fine oak floors and delicate antiques, but you never feel out of place with your dog. Day's staff makes sure your dog feels especially welcome, right down to offering pet beds and pet food for your four-legged friend. There's no doggy spa yet, but *que sera, sera.*

Rates are from $110 to $285. It's $17 extra for the first pooch and $10 for the second. The inn is located at Lincoln Street and Seventh Avenue. The mailing address is P.O. Box Y, Carmel, CA 93921; (408) 624-3871.

SUNSET HOUSE

It's hard to know where to start a description of this attractive, romantic, extremely dog-and-people-friendly inn.

First, since this is a dog book, let me introduce you to Maggy, a gorgeous husky-wolf mix. "She's part of the team here," says Dennis Pike, who owns the bed-and-breakfast with his wife, Camille. "She is so gentle, so kind. She loves our guests and gets along really well with other dogs. She likes other dogs as much as we do. Maggy gets more pictures taken of her than anyone I've ever seen."

Now let's talk about the Sunset House itself. (Details, details. With the dog-friendly attitude of the Pikes, many people I know would stay here if it looked like Skid Row.) The house was built in the 1960s to be a bed-and-breakfast inn, so all four of the rooms are large (600 square feet), with real brick wood-burning fireplaces and private bathrooms. The rooms are airy, yet cozy, and are furnished beautifully with a mixture of antiques and classic contemporary furniture. You and your dog can see the ocean from three rooms, and the windows you'll see it from are a generous 4-by-12 feet. The inn is located in an attractive residential neighborhood, where it's a very, very quick walk to the leash-free Carmel City Beach and to the quaint shops of Carmel.

The Pikes know how to treat their guests. Every morning, a sumptuous breakfast of eight to 13 types of sliced fruit, warm baked goods, granola, and yogurt is brought to your room. If you prefer, you can dine in the comfy sitting room downstairs, but most guests, especially those with dogs, like the in-room option. The sitting area in front of your fireplace is perfect for sharing breakfast with someone special—and with your human companion, too.

In the evening, Dennis will give you a complimentary bottle of wine, champagne, or port—selected for you from his own collection of 1,300 bottles. "My biggest joy is giving it away," says Dennis. If Dennis gets to know you and your tastes well enough (if you become a regular), he'll even keep his eyes peeled for wines he know you'll love when he's on wine-tasting sojourns. You'll be hard-pressed to find an innkeeper as caring and committed as this man. "This is my calling," he says, and he means it.

Rates are $130 to $190. Dogs are $10 extra. Big, hairy dogs may be charged an extra cleaning fee, so describe your pooch on the phone and you'll know if this applies to her. The Sunset House has a Web site: www.sunset-carmel.com. The inn is located on Camino Real, between Ocean and Seventh Streets. The mailing address is P.O. Box 1925, Carmel, CA 93921; (408) 624-4884.

SANTA BARBARA COUNTY
Where life is rich

• Las Positas Friendship Park 🐾🐾🐾🐾 🐕

In previous editions, I didn't rate this Santa Barbara park very highly. That's because dogs were supposed to be leashed here. But now, this park is a super place to take a dog. What a difference a lack of a leash and an excellent new hiking trail make! The park is home to many ball fields, which, if you visit when they're not being used, are great places to ramble with your dog. (But, as you should always do, clean up after your dog! There's nothing like a little poop on a playing field to foster ill will toward dogs.)

The Sierra Club Trail, built by Sierra Club volunteers, offers a one-mile loop or a 1.5-mile round-trip to Jesuit Hill. (The Jesuit Hill hike is very steep, and not a good hike for most dogs.) The views of the Santa Barbara coast from much of the trail are to drool for.

This hilly, 136-acre park (which is doubling in size soon!) is a fine example of the way parks might go in this era of park defunding; the park is privately operated and funded, yet open to the public. It seems almost everything here is sponsored, from picnic tables to a massive oak tree. (Mercedes-Benz got that one.) But that's okay with dogs, who are glad to have the government's hand out of their piece of Dog Heaven. Anyway, anyone who sponsors a tree is okay by Joe.

From U.S. 101 in Santa Barbara, exit at Las Positas Road and drive south about 1.2 miles to the park's entrance, which will be on your left. (805) 569-5611.

SAN YSIDRO RANCH

A word to the pooches who plan to come here: You lucky dogs!

This top-notch 540-acre resort (where Laurence Olivier and Vivien Leigh wed and Jackie and John F. Kennedy honeymooned) is treat enough. But dogs who stay here get the truly royal treatment, also known as the Privileged Pet Program. The Ranch has been offering the program to pooches for a century. Here's how it goes:

Upon registering at the Pet Register and wolfing down some tasty peanut butter biscuits, the guest dog goes to his cottage and finds his name and his accompanying human's name on a wood-burned sign outside his cottage door. (To him, the sign looks like something to chew on, but it's the thought that counts.) Inside, he'll be greeted by a basketful of VIP goodies, including a personalized bowl filled with squeak toys, rawhides, cookies, and a two-liter bottle of Pawier water. His bed is soft and comfortable and shaped like a steak.

A pet menu offers dining items, including biscuits, canned dog food, and even New York ground sirloin. "Shoes are available at market price," the VIP literature reads, and we're not sure if there's a wink behind that offer or not. We weren't about to find out, since their shoes probably come from I. Magnin, not Payless Shoe Source, which is Joe's usual style.

Dogs must stay in one of the Ranch's 21 freestanding cottages. Rates are $325 to $3,000. Dogs pay $75 per visit. Dog menu items are extra. You must let the staff know ahead of time that you'll be coming with your pooch so appropriate arrangements can be made. 900 San Ysidro Lane, Montecito, CA 93108; (805) 969-5046.

SAN DIEGO COUNTY

A sunny oasis

• Dog Beach 🐾🐾🐾🐾 🐕

"Welcome to Dog Beach!" the sign announces at just about the same place that your dog charges out of the car to meet with all his best buddies. Dogs truly do feel welcome at this San Diego park. They're free to run off leash and to get down to the business of being a dog. As long as they listen when you call and don't get into trouble, they can hang out leashless all day. Many dog people bring a folding chair so they can relax while their dog experiences heaven on Earth.

We've seen several folks visit here because, although they don't have a dog, they get great joy out of watching the footloose creatures tearing around. "They have such innocent happiness when they run about and play so gleefully," said dogless dog lover Maxine Chambers one gray morning. "It makes my day."

There are more dog footprints in the sand than human footprints, and not just because dogs have more feet. People come from many miles around, sometimes bringing their friends' dogs and their neighbors' dogs to participate in the whirlwind of excitement.

Dogs are allowed off leash at the north end of the beach, which is wide enough to be very safe from traffic. It's marked by signs.

If you wander onto the other part of the beach, make sure you do so before 9 A.M. or after 6 P.M., and be sure to leash your dog.

Exit Interstate 5 at Interstate 8. Drive west and follow the signs to Sunset Cliffs Boulevard. After several blocks, bear right at Voltaire Street. Follow Voltaire Street to its end and the entrance to Dog Beach. (619) 221-8901.

DINE IN A DOG (AND CAT AND BUNNY) RESTAURANT

Dogs, sit down. I've got great news for you. There's now a restaurant/bakery dedicated exclusively to pets. You can actually go *inside* this one! The Original Paw Pleasers is a beautiful little restaurant with gorgeous murals of a park scene of happy dogs and cats. It's a cozy, uplifting place, with oak cabinets and even a "tree." (Okay, it's a post disguised as a tree, but it looks enough like a tree that your boy dog might be tempted . . . . Don't let him!) And the food is to die for—if you're a pet. If you're a human, you can use coupons they have in conjunction with eateries nearby and grab yourself a bite to bring here so you can eat beside your dog. Some of the more popular items are "dogolate" chip cookies and "bark-la-va." There's also yogurt with doggy toppings, and a doggy Sunday brunch. Owners Sharon and Loree will even custom-make birthday cakes for your dog.

I rarely mention other animals in this book, but this is too good to ignore. Cats can come here and get a tuna or liver cake with faux cream frosting, or a tuna muffin with a delicious non-dairy whipped topping. Mmm, good! Birds and bunnies can order such yummies as vegetable salads. By the way, if your dog thinks cats and bunnies are part of the menu, make sure there are none inside before you venture in.

The restaurant also sells lots of gift items for pets and their people. It's located in an upscale shopping center in the Hillcrest area of San Diego. This is a must-visit on any dog's list. 1220 Cleveland Avenue; (619) 293-PAWS.

BEYOND THE BAY

11
EMERGENCIES

Chances are your adventuring will go without a hitch, but you should always be prepared to deal with trouble. In this chapter we'll deal first with common hazards—ticks, foxtails, poison oak, and skunk attacks—and then with more serious accidents such as heatstroke, broken bones, and snakebites.

ORDINARY TROUBLE

Ticks are hard to avoid in Northern California. They can carry Lyme disease, so you should always check yourself and your dog all over when you get home from tick country. Don't forget to check ears and between the toes. If you see one, just pull it straight out with tweezers, not your bare hands.

The tiny ticks that carry Lyme disease are difficult to find. Consult your veterinarian if your dog is lethargic for a few days, has a fever, loses her appetite, or becomes lame. These symptoms could indicate Lyme disease. Some vets recommend a new vaccine that is supposed to prevent onset of the disease, but others say it's too early to tell if the vaccine is safe and effective, and advise against it.

Foxtails—those arrow-shaped pieces of dry grass—are the seed cases of wild barley. They're an everyday annoyance, but in certain cases can be lethal—they can stick in your dog's eyes, nose, ears, or mouth and work their way in. Check every nook and cranny of your dog after a walk if you've been near dry grass. Poor Joe once had to have an embedded foxtail removed from his paw by a vet, to the tune of $200. But that was nothing compared to the one that went in through his mouth, and out through his neck.

Poison oak is also a common California menace. Dogs don't generally have reactions to it, but they can easily pass it to people. Advises Charise McHugh, hospital manager at Belmont Pet Hospital: "If you think your dog has trotted through some poison oak, try not to pet him until you get him home and wash him, wearing rubber gloves. If you do pet him, avoid touching your eyes. I've had poison oak in my eye three times, and it's miserable."

If your dog loses a contest with a skunk (and he always will), rinse his eyes first with plain warm water, then bathe him with dog shampoo. Towel him off, then apply tomato juice (canned tomatoes or sauce work just as well) or a mixture of one pint vinegar to one gallon water, or five or six ounces of Massengill douche powder or liquid mixed with one gallon of water.

Prevention of veterinary emergencies is the best cure. When you're in the wilderness with your dog, you should be aware of certain hazards before your dog encounters them. Some vets advise finding out from a ranger if there's a danger of poisonous snakes, and keeping your dog leashed where the ranger suggests. If your dog is sticking her snout down rodent burrows, stop her, because fleas from rodents can carry bubonic plague. The animals themselves may carry rabies.

And if you're a thoroughly cautious dog owner, you may want to follow the advice of some veterinarians and not let your dog drink out of California rivers and streams, often host to the giardia parasite.

SERIOUS TROUBLE

The rest of this chapter describes serious emergency situations that can arise while you're out with your dog. In all these emergencies, get to a veterinarian as soon as possible. Don't rely on the treatments listed here as permanent solutions. These are only stopgap measures so your dog can survive until he gets professional medical attention.

If your dog injures an eye, or starts squinting or blinking, don't wait to take her to the vet. Eye injuries are usually easily treated, but even minor ones should be looked at immediately, since eye infections can progress very fast.

Always speak to a wounded dog in a calm, reassuring voice. Approach an injured animal with caution. It may be necessary to muzzle her if she's snapping in panic, but a word of warning: If a dog is in shock (see "Shock"), use a muzzle only as a last resort. You may have to open the dog's breathing passage, and you don't have time to waste with a muzzle. To improvise a muzzle, wrap a wide piece of adhesive tape around the dog's snout. Don't bind it too tightly. You can also use a strip of cloth, a belt, or a necktie, wrapped snugly around the animal's muzzle and tied off behind the ears.

Unfortunately, courses in first aid for animals are almost exclusively for animal care workers. Karl Peter, D.V.M., a veterinary sciences instructor at Foothill Community College, suggests an alternative: "Any first-aid course for humans is going to give you greater confidence when it comes to dealing with dog emergencies," he says. "While everything may not translate, many techniques do. Those could be the ones that save your dog's life."

Be sure to have a well-stocked first-aid kit close at hand whenever you travel with your dog. It should contain the following:

- Phone numbers of your veterinarian and of a nighttime/weekend vet (probably the single most important item)
- A veterinary first-aid book
- Adhesive tape, one to two inches wide
- Cotton batting
- Large gauze pads
- Gauze roll, three inches wide
- Hydrogen peroxide (3%)
- Petroleum jelly
- Several short, sturdy sticks, such as tongue depressors
- Sterilized knife or razor blade
- Thermometer
- Tweezers or thumb forceps

BLEEDING FROM EXTERNAL WOUNDS

Almost any bleeding (even spurting arterial wounds) can be controlled by the direct pressure method. Tourniquets should be used only as a last resort.

"It can be difficult to be calm when your dog seems to be bleeding profusely," says Cara Paasch, D.V.M., a Bay Area veterinarian. "But the key is not to panic. Sometimes a little blood can look like a lot. Don't rush to make a tourniquet right away."

Get any bleeding dog to a veterinarian immediately. Always check for shock, and treat if necessary (see "Shock"). If the dog is unconscious, elevate his hind end so blood can get to the brain.

If necessary, muzzle the dog. Press gauze, lint-free cloth, or even your hand over the wound and maintain firm pressure. If the bleeding doesn't stop, increase pressure. Check bleeding in five or 10 minutes by releasing pressure. Do not remove the cloth, since this could open the wound. If the wound is still dripping, continue direct pressure. Gravity can also help. If the wound is in the front leg, try to stand the dog on his hind legs while you treat him. This raises the wound above the heart and should slow the bleeding. If you're transporting a dog by yourself and can't maintain pressure by hand, bandage the cloth firmly in place. Get to a veterinarian immediately.

For bleeding from fractures that protrude through the skin, apply pressure between the break and the dog's heart, slightly above the injury. For a compound fracture of the lower leg, for instance, tightly encircle the dog's upper leg with your hands.

Veterinarians advise against tourniquets except in the most dire circumstances. Many say there's rarely a situation when you'll have to use one. If a tourniquet is done improperly, lack of circulation can cause the dog to lose a limb. But if you've tried direct pressure and the arterial bleeding is still profuse, and it looks like a matter of life over limb, you may need to make a tourniquet.

To do so, place a two-inch-wide clean strip of cloth or gauze slightly above the wound, over the bleeding artery. Tightly wrap it twice around the limb, and tie a stick into the wrap. Twist the stick until bleeding is controlled. Secure the stick in place with tape. Cover the dog loosely with a blanket and get to a veterinarian.

BROKEN BONES

If you're within a short drive of a veterinarian, it may be best to carefully transport your dog (see "Transporting a Dog") and let the vet take care of the injury. Some veterinarians say they've seen more harm than good done by improperly applied splints.

But if you're on a long hike, or far from immediate medical care, you may need to make a temporary support for the fracture. Consider muzzling the dog if the injury is painful. Treat only fractures of the lower leg. If you suspect fractures or dislocations elsewhere, carry the dog to a veterinarian as gently as possible (see "Transporting a Dog").

If bones protrude, control the bleeding with direct or encircling pressure (see "Bleeding from External Wounds").

Wrap the leg with cloth or cotton batting. Place rigid sticks, such as tongue depressors, on opposite sides of the break so that they extend past joints at both ends of the break. Wrap with adhesive tape. Be sure not to wrap too tightly, because a lack of circulation might result in loss of the dog's limb. See a veterinarian as soon as possible.

HEATSTROKE

Heatstroke is life threatening, but its prevention is simple. You can avoid most heatstroke by keeping your dog in a cool, shady, well-ventilated area, not exhausting her in hot weather, and providing lots of fresh water.

Never, ever leave your dog in a car on a warm day. Heatstroke generally occurs at temperatures greater than 100 degrees, but it can often happen at much lower temperatures. Although the temperature outside may be tolerable, your car can become an oven, even with the windows partly open—and even in the shade. "The most common problem usually happens when someone parks his car on a hot day to run into a shop for five minutes, and it takes a little longer than he expected," says Rob Erteman, D.V.M., a veterinarian at the Animal Hospital in San Anselmo. "He comes back, and the animal is in big trouble, even if the window is cracked."

Symptoms of heatstroke are rapid panting, bright red gums, high body temperature, and hot limbs. Symptoms can progress to uncontrollable diarrhea, collapse, and coma. Death can occur in severe cases.

Treatment: Normal rectal temperature for a dog is 100 to 102 degrees. If your dog's temperature is above 103 degrees, and she has heatstroke symptoms, treat her immediately and rush to a veterinarian (see "Transporting a Dog"). Rapid treatment is essential, because the dog's condition can deteriorate quickly.

Use any method possible to cool the dog. In mild cases, it is often effective to move the dog to a cool, well-ventilated place and wrap her in a cold, wet towel. But treatment generally calls for bathing the dog in cold water, or even ice. Ice is especially effective when packed around the head. Monitor her temperature every 10 minutes and stop cooling when her body temperature gets down to 103 degrees. Get to a veterinarian as soon as possible.

SHOCK

Shock is insufficient blood flow caused by problems with the heart, or loss of blood volume. It can result from injury or overwhelming infection. If prolonged, it can lead to death.

Symptoms of shock are pale gums; weak, faint pulse; general weakness; shallow, rapid breathing; listlessness or confusion; low body temperature or shivering; semiconsciousness or unconsciousness.

Treatment: Don't muzzle the dog unless snapping becomes a danger to you. Control any bleeding (see "Bleeding from External Wounds"). If the dog is unconscious, keep his airway open by opening his mouth and carefully pulling out his tongue. If the dog is conscious, let him relax and assume the position most comfortable to him. An ideal position is on his side with head extended, but don't force him into it. Cover him lightly with a blanket and transport him immediately to a veterinarian (see "Transporting a Dog").

SNAKEBITES

Although most snakes are not poisonous, California is home to a few types of deadly snakes. Many veterinarians caution that if you know you're in poisonous snake country, you should keep your dog leashed. If your dog is bitten, try to identify the snake, or check the bite marks. Fang marks (two puncture wounds) indicate a poisonous snake. Get your dog to a veterinarian immediately. Depending on where the dog was bitten, and how much venom was injected, serious symptoms can develop rapidly.

Symptoms: At the site of the wound, there may be swelling and severe pain. At first the dog may be restless, panting, and perhaps drooling. These signs can be followed quickly by weakness, difficulty in breathing, diarrhea, collapse, convulsions, and shock. In severe cases, the dog can die.

Many veterinarians advise against treating snakebites yourself before getting your dog proper medical attention. They say people sometimes tie tourniquets too tightly, or cut too deeply and sever an artery. Their advice is to keep the dog as still and calm as possible, since exercise and struggle increase the rate of absorption of the poison. If possible, slide the dog onto a blanket or board and carry him to a veterinarian immediately (see "Transporting a Dog").

But even most veterinarians who counsel against emergency treatment in the field say that if you're hiking and you're miles from any transportation to a vet, you should probably consider treating the wound yourself.

Of two methods for treating snakebites before you get to an animal hospital, vets generally prefer the tourniquet method only slightly to cutting the wound and sucking the venom. Again, keep the dog calm and quiet, muzzling if necessary. Keep the wound below heart level. If the bite is on a leg or the tail, tie a constricting band tightly between the bite and the heart, a few inches above the bite. It should be just tight enough to prevent venomous blood from returning to the heart. Get to a vet as quickly as possible.

If there's no way you feel you can reach a veterinarian in time, you may opt for the cut-and-suction treatment. Tie a constricting band between the bite and the heart, but not too tightly. Sterilize a knife or razor blade over a flame. Carefully make parallel cuts through each fang mark, about half an inch long and no deeper than one-quarter inch. The smaller the dog, and the closer the bone, the shallower the cut. Blood should ooze from the wound. If it doesn't, loosen the band.

Draw the venom from the wound with your mouth, if it's free of cuts and open sores, and spit out the blood. You can also use a suction cup. Continue at five- to 10-minute intervals for 30 minutes, if possible, while in transit to the veterinarian (see "Transporting a Dog"). Watch the dog's symptoms and continue if necessary until you get professional veterinary care.

After your dog has been seen by a veterinarian, remember to keep the wound clean. Snakebites are prone to infection.

TRANSPORTING A DOG

Always use a stretcher to move a dog who can't walk, or greater bodily injury could result. A good makeshift stretcher is a large, sturdy board, but a blanket or even a rug will do.

Carefully slide the dog onto the stretcher, making sure not to bend any part of his body. On a board stretcher, tie the dog gently, but firmly, in place. Speak reassuringly to the dog en route to the veterinarian.

ALL-NIGHT VETERINARY CLINICS

Your dog may need medical attention in the middle of the night, when your own veterinarian is unavailable. Many vets offer on-call emergency service, and there are several all-night clinics in the Bay Area. Be sure to phone first, to be certain hours and location have not changed.

ALAMEDA COUNTY CLINICS

Berkeley

Pet Emergency Treatment Service: Open 6 P.M. to 8 A.M. on weekdays, and from noon Saturday to 8 A.M. Monday. Open 24 hours on holidays. 1048 University Avenue; (510) 548-6684.

Dublin

Tri-Valley Veterinary Emergency Clinic: Open 6 P.M. to 8 A.M. on weekdays, and from 6 P.M. Friday to 8 A.M. Monday. Open 24 hours on holidays. 6743 Dublin Boulevard; (510) 828-0654.

Fremont

Central Veterinarian Hospital and Emergency Services: In the past, this clinic was open 24 hours for emergencies. Currently, a vet is there only until 11 P.M. every night, but animal technicians are there around the clock. The clinic is in the process of restructuring, so it may go back to 24-hour service. 5245 Central Avenue; (510) 797-7387.

San Leandro

Bay Area Veterinary Emergency Clinic (formerly Alameda County Emergency Pet Clinic): The hours may soon change slightly, but at press time the clinic was open 6 P.M. to 8 A.M. weekdays, and from noon Saturday to 8 A.M. Monday. Open 24 hours on holidays. 14790 Washington Avenue; (510) 352-6080.

CONTRA COSTA COUNTY CLINICS

Concord

Contra Costa Veterinary Emergency Clinic: Open 6 P.M. to 8 A.M. weekdays, and 6 P.M. Friday to 8 A.M. Monday. Open 24 hours on holidays. 1410 Monument Boulevard; (510) 798-2900.

MARIN COUNTY CLINICS

San Rafael

Marin County Veterinary Emergency Clinic: Open 5:30 P.M. to 8 A.M. weekdays, and noon Saturday to 8 A.M. Monday. Open 24 hours on holidays. 4240 Redwood Highway; (415) 472-2266.

NAPA COUNTY CLINICS

As of this printing, there are no all-night clinics in Napa County. All animal emergencies are referred to the Solano Pet Emergency Clinic, in Cordelia (see Solano County Clinics, page 315).

SAN FRANCISCO COUNTY CLINICS

San Francisco

All Animals Emergency Hospital: Open 6 P.M. to 8 A.M. weekdays, and 6 P.M. Friday to 8 A.M. Monday. 1333 Ninth Avenue; (415) 566-0531.

Pets Unlimited Veterinary Hospital: Open 24 hours for emergencies. 2343 Fillmore Street; (415) 563-6700.

SAN MATEO COUNTY CLINICS

San Mateo

North Peninsula Veterinary Emergency Clinic: Open 6 P.M. to 8 A.M. weekdays, and 6 P.M. Friday to 8 A.M. Monday. Open 24 hours on holidays. 227 North Amphlett Boulevard; (650) 348-2575.

SANTA CLARA COUNTY CLINICS

Campbell

United Emergency Animal Clinic: Open 6 P.M. to 8 A.M. weekdays, and 6 P.M. Friday to 8 A.M. Monday. Open 24 hours on holidays. 1657 South Bascom Avenue; (408) 371-6252.

Palo Alto

South Peninsula Veterinary Emergency Clinic: Open 6 P.M. to 8 A.M. weekdays, and 6 P.M. Friday to 8 A.M. Monday. Open 24 hours on holidays. 3045 Middlefield Road; (650) 494-1461.

San Jose

Emergency Animal Clinic of South San Jose: Open 6 P.M. to 8 A.M. weekdays, and 6 P.M. Friday to 8 A.M. Monday. Open 24 hours on holidays. 5440 Thornwood Drive (behind the Oakridge Mall); (408) 578-5622.

SOLANO COUNTY CLINICS

Cordelia

Solano Pet Emergency Clinic: Open 6 P.M. to 8 A.M. Monday through Thursday, and from 6 P.M. Friday to 8 A.M. Monday. Open 24 hours on holidays. 4437 Central Place; (707) 864-1444.

SONOMA COUNTY CLINICS

Santa Rosa

Emergency Animal Hospital of Santa Rosa: Open 6 P.M. to 8 A.M. on weekdays, and from 6 P.M. Friday to 8 A.M. Monday. Open 24 hours on holidays. 4019 Sebastopol Road; (707) 544-1647.

Petcare Veterinary Center: Open 24 hours daily for emergencies. 1370 Fulton Road; (707) 573-9503.

ANIMAL SHELTERS

If you don't currently have a dog, or if you'd like to add another pooch to the family, why not adopt one? Dozens of animal welfare organizations in the Bay Area are overflowing with dogs who would love to devote their lives to being your best buddy.

ALAMEDA COUNTY

Alameda City Animal Shelter: (510) 748-4585
Alameda County Animal Shelter (San Leandro): (510) 667-7707
Berkeley Animal Shelter: (510) 644-6755
Berkeley Humane Society: (510) 845-7735
East Bay Animal Referral (Oakland): (510) 841-PAWS
East County Animal Shelter (Dublin): (510) 803-7040
Hayward Animal Services Bureau: (510) 293-7200
Hayward Friends of Animals: (510) 886-7546
Oakland SPCA: (510) 569-0702
Ohlone Humane Society (Fremont): (510) 490-4587
Tri-City Animal Shelter (Fremont): (510) 790-6640

CONTRA COSTA COUNTY

Animal Rescue Foundation: (510) 256-1273
Antioch City Shelter: (510) 779-6989
Contra Costa Humane Society (Lafayette): (510) 284-8449
Contra Costa SPCA (El Sobrante): (510) 223-2272
Martinez Animal Shelter: (510) 646-2995
Pinole Animal Shelter: (510) 374-3966

MARIN COUNTY

Marin Humane Society (Novato): (415) 883-4621
St. Francis Animal Protection Society (Corte Madera): (415) 435-2097

NAPA COUNTY

Napa County Animal Services (Napa): (707) 253-4381
Napa Humane Society (Napa): (707) 255-8118

SAN FRANCISCO COUNTY

San Francisco Animal Care & Control: (415) 554-6364
San Francisco SPCA: (415) 554-3000

SAN MATEO COUNTY
Peninsula Humane Society (San Mateo): (650) 340-8200
Pets in Need (Redwood City): (650) 367-1405

SANTA CLARA COUNTY
NIKE Animal Rescue Foundation (San Jose): (408) 224-6273
Palo Alto Animal Shelter: (650) 329-2671
Palo Alto Humane Society: (650) 327-0631
Santa Clara County Animal Shelter (San Martin): (408) 683-4186
Santa Clara Valley Humane Society (Santa Clara): (408) 727-3383

SOLANO COUNTY
Solano County Animal Shelter (Fairfield): (707) 421-7486
Solano County SPCA (Vacaville): (707) 448-7722

SONOMA COUNTY
Healdsburg Animal Shelter: (707) 431-3386
Petaluma Animal Shelter: (707) 778-4396
Pets Lifeline of Sonoma (Sonoma): (707) 996-4577
Rohnert Park Animal Shelter: (707) 584-1582
Sonoma County Humane Society (Santa Rosa): (707) 542-0882

EMERGENCIES

INDEX

INDEX

B

Marine World-Africa USA 257, 259
Marinwood, CA 101
Market Hall 54
Marsh Trail 77, 254
Marshall, CA **94**
Martha & Bros. Coffee Company **165**
Martinez, CA **70,** 73
Martinez Regional Shoreline 73
Mathes, Matt 293
Matt Davis Trail 96
Max Baer Park 47
Max's Bakery & Kitchen **213**
Maxwell Farms Regional Park 292, **293**
McCray Mountain 271
McKay, Linda 146
McKegney Green 118
McKenzie House **205**
McKinley Square **154**
McLaren Park **154**
McNear Park **279**
McNears Beach County Park 110
McNee Ranch State Park **200**
Meadowlark Country House **125**
Memorial Park Dog Owners Association 107
Memorial Park **107**
Mendocino, CA **300**
Mendocino County **299**
Menlo Park, CA **198**
Merced, Lake **151,** 152
Merritt College 51, 52
Merritt, Lake 49

Merry-Go-Round Trail 223
Midpeninsula Regional Open Space District 188, 205, 206, 209, 214, 219, 226
Mike's Bikes & Blades 179
Milagra Ridge **202**
Mill Valley, CA **94,** 97, 98
Millbrae, CA **199,** 200
Miller, Joaquin, Park **50,** 51
Miller, Larry 189
Miller Picnic Site 225
Miller-Knox Regional Shoreline 74, **75**
Milpitas, CA **227**
Mine Hill Trail 237
Mission Distric 169
Mission Dolores Park **154,** 183
Mission Peak 44, 48
Mission Peak Regional Preserve **43**
Mission Santa Clara 243
Mitchell Park **232**
Miwok Stables 114
Miwuk Indians 101, 109, 111
Miwuk Park **101**
Miwuk Trail 114
Martin Luther King Jr. Regional Shoreline (*see also* San Leandro Bay Regional Shoreline) **52**
Mocca on Maiden Lane **165**
Mockingbird Picnic Area 237
Montara, CA **200,** 201
Montara Mountain 200, **201,** 208
Monte Rio, CA 271
Montecito, CA 304

ABOUT THE AUTHOR

Joe Dog is a native boy, born and bred on Bay Area soil. He's also a dog with a lust for travel. He longs to ride on surreys, trains, and cable cars. He drools to hike the Bay Area's leash-free lands. He quivers at the idea of eating fine food at dog-friendly restaurants and spending the night at some far-flung bed-and-breakfast. Of course, being a dog, he also gets excited about eating horrible things he finds washed up on beaches, but that's another story.

Since Joe is a dog without a driver's license, **Maria Goodavage**, author of *The California Dog Lover's Companion,* and Northern California correspondent for *USA Today* from 1989 until she had a human child in 1996, goes along as chauffeur. "Maria is of invaluable assistance in interpreting my reactions for human consumption," says Joe. "She does a four-paw job."

Joe lives with Maria, her husband, Craig Hanson, and their daughter, Laura Hanson, in a house two blocks from the beach in San Francisco.

ACKNOWLEDGMENTS

Thanks and arf . . .

To my fantastic husband, Craig Hanson, who worked his tail off helping with research for this edition. (He's the one whose ears are still flattened from all the phone calls he made.) He's a doggone great man. I rate him four paws.

To all the readers around the Bay Area who have sent in terrific tips. This book is so much richer because of them.

I would like to give special thanks to Nisha Dog and Bill Dog, who were a tremendous part of this book but have since moved on.

Finally, to friend Lyle York and her dearly departed dog Dabney. They're no longer officially my co-authors, but their work was integral to the success of this book—and in fact, to the success of the entire series of *Dog Lover's Companions*.

Nisha Dog

Bill Dog

CREDITS

Editors	Jean Linsteadt
	Karin Mullen
Production Manager	Kyle Morgan
Production Assistants	Jean-Vi Lenthe
	Jan Shade
	Mark Aver
Research	Craig Hanson
Acquisitions Editor	Judith Pynn
Cover and Interior Illustrations	Phil Frank
Author Photo	Linda Sue Scott

FOGHORN ⚓ OUTDOORS

Founded in 1985, Foghorn Press has quickly become one of the country's premier publishers of outdoor recreation guidebooks. Through its unique Books Building Community program, Foghorn Press supports community environmental issues, such as park, trail, and water ecosystem preservation.

Foghorn Press books are available throughout the United States in bookstores and some outdoor retailers. If you cannot find the title you are looking for, visit Foghorn's Web site at www.foghorn.com or call 1-800-FOGHORN.

The Dog Lover's Series

- *The California Dog Lover's Companion* (800 pp) $20.95—New 3rd edition
- *The Florida Dog Lover's Companion* (602 pp) $20.95—New 2nd edition
- *The Texas Dog Lover's Companion* (602 pp) $20.95—New!
- *The Seattle Dog Lover's Companion* (256 pp) $17.95
- *The Boston Dog Lover's Companion* (416 pp) $17.95
- *The Atlanta Dog Lover's Companion* (288 pp) $17.95
- *The Washington D.C. Dog Lover's Companion* (288 pp) $17.95—New!

The Complete Guide Series

- *California Camping* (768 pp) $20.95—New 10th anniversary edition
- *California Hiking* (688 pp) $20.95
- *California Waterfalls* (408 pp) $17.95
- *California Fishing* (768 pp) $20.95
- *California Golf* (864 pp) $20.95—New 7th edition
- *California Beaches* (640 pp) $19.95
- *California Boating and Water Sports* (608 pp) $19.95
- *Pacific Northwest Camping* (656 pp) $20.95—New 6th edition
- *Pacific Northwest Hiking* (648 pp) $20.95
- *Washington Fishing* (480 pp) $20.95—New 2nd edition
- *Tahoe* (678 pp) $20.95—New 2nd edition
- *New England Hiking* (416 pp) $18.95
- *New England Camping* (520 pp) $19.95
- *Utah and Nevada Camping* (384 pp) $18.95
- *Southwest Camping* (544 pp) $17.95
- *Baja Camping* (288 pp) $14.95—New 2nd edition
- *Florida Camping* (672 pp) $20.95—New!

A book's page length and availability are subject to change.

For more information, call 1-800-FOGHORN,
e-mail: foghorn@well.com, or write to:
Foghorn Press
340 Bodega Avenue
Petaluma, CA 94952

BAY AREA
REFERENCE MAP

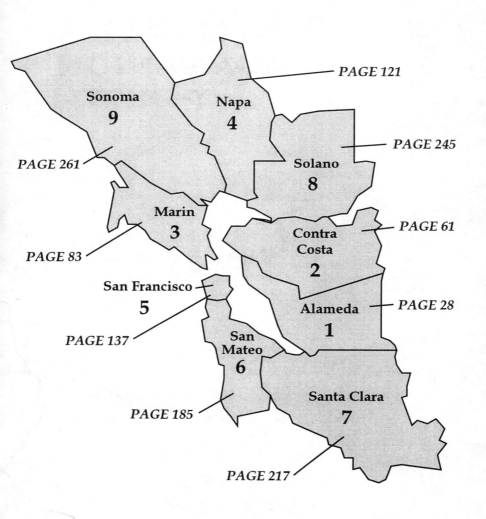

PAGE 121

Sonoma
9

Napa
4

PAGE 245

PAGE 261

Solano
8

Marin
3

PAGE 83

Contra
Costa
2

PAGE 61

San Francisco
5

PAGE 137

Alameda
1

PAGE 28

San
Mateo
6

PAGE 185

Santa Clara
7

PAGE 217